THE ENGLISH WAY

THE ENGLISH WAY

STUDIES IN ENGLISH SANCTITY
from BEDE *to* NEWMAN

EDITED *by* MAISIE WARD

INTRODUCTION *by* BRADLEY J. BIRZER

CLUNY
Providence, Rhode Island

Cluny Media edition, 2016

The English Way: Studies in English Sanctity from Bede to Newman
originally published in 1933 by Sheed & Ward Inc.

This edition includes minor revisions to the original text.
For more information regarding this title
or any other Cluny Media publication,
please write to info@clunymedia.com, or to
Cluny Media, P.O. Box 1664, Providence, RI 02901

ISBN: 9781944418175

Cover design by Clarke & Clarke
Cover image: J. M. W. Turner, *Saint Augustine's Gate, Canterbury*,
circa 1793, watercolor
Courtesy of Wikimedia Commons

CONTENTS

INTRODUCTION

by BRADLEY BIRZER

A FORGOTTEN BOOK IS ALWAYS A TRAGEDY, BUT A FOUND book is equally always and everywhere a treasure. There exist exceptions, of course. A book of dark magic or of fascism is best left forgotten, rotting in the cellar of some humid Florida bookstore. But the books that contain truth, beauty, and goodness—these are the books we should never lose.

One of my favorite current Christian Humanists, Canadian Michael O'Brien, has argued in his own masterful novel, *Sophia House*, that every book that enters the world is akin to the human soul. Some do well, some do ill, and many—simply through the beauty of creation—reflects bits and pieces of divine grace. In essence, when art, a book might very well magnify the Lord.

I have had a book sitting on my shelves for well over a dozen years that I had yet to open. Sadly, I am not alone in treating this book so shabbily and neglecting it so wretchedly. As it turns out, the very copy I own is a 1933 edition that spent most of its life at the Kolbe Memorial Library in Granby, Massachusetts. From what I can tell of the book, no one *ever* checked out this book. And now here it resides, in Hillsdale, Michigan, in perfect condition. It is what booksellers would describe as mint, though it now has my markings and marginalia throughout. No longer mint according to the booksellers, but even more "mint" now that I have made it my own. At least to me.

Needless to write, I finally picked up this book that has so patiently waited for me for over a decade. And, what a pleasure. *The English Way*, edited by one of the most important Christian humanists and publishers of the twentieth century, Maisie Ward, and published by the once glorious exemplar of Christian humanist publishing, Sheed and Ward (named after Maisie's husband and brother), looks at the lives, ideas, and deaths of the great Roman Catholic Anglo-Saxons. Most were saints, but not all. Some who had not yet been recognized as saints soon would be. All, however, served the church with verve. As readily seen in the table of contents, Fathers Gervase Mathew, David Mathew, David Knowles, Bede Jarrett, C. C. Martindale, and Martin D'Arcy, as well as Maisie Ward, Christopher Dawson, E. I. Watkin, Hilaire Belloc, G. K. Chesterton, and Douglas Woodruff each contribute to this work, sometimes twice. Their subjects: Bede; Boniface; Alcuin; Alfred the Great; Wulstan; Aelred; Thomas à Becket; Julian of Norwich; John Fisher; Thomas More; Edmund Campion; Richard Crenshaw; and Cardinal Newman.

In her brief but deep introduction to the book, Ward offers a succinct and satisfying explanation of the Christian humanism behind, above, below, next to, across, and through the work. As Christianity "is universal, it is in every country, but because it is sacramental it is intensely local, found in each country in a special and unique fashion, not a spirit only but a spirit clothed in material form."

The English Way, therefore, is not the same as the French Way or the German Way. And, with the exception of the contribution from Hilaire Belloc, who lauds the Norman invasion as a critical and happy moment for the English and the Celts as a whole, the authors tend to play up the specifically Anglo-Saxon spirit of English Roman Catholicism.

In this vein, the book seems downright Tolkienian, though this great mythmaker makes no appearance here. Still a young man and not having published *The Hobbit*, Tolkien was as yet known only by other British academics. Throughout all of his life and fiction, Tolkien had embraced and promoted the Anglo-Saxon conceptions of law, language, and religion as the highest the world had seen, no matter how ridiculous this idea might seem to twentieth-century Protestant Britons. Whatever the accuracy of Tolkien's assessment, his views permeated the best selling novel of the twentieth century, *The Lord of the Rings*, and continue to influence, no matter how covertly, millions of readers every year.

Taking Christian humanism even further, however, than cultural, linguistic, and religious patriotism, *The English Way* focuses on the contributions of individual human persons, each a unique reflection of the *imago Dei*. Of course, each writer brings his own personality to the study of the subject personalities. In this sense, this is Christian humanism calling upon Christian humanism, a form of grace calling upon grace, the book itself seemingly sacramental.

Yet, while the book might at first glance appear as merely another twentieth-century piece of pious hagiography, this is far from being the case. The writers sympathize with the plight of each of the individuals discussed, but they do so in such a poetic fashion that the reader simply delights in the immersion into deep Catholicism and the meshing of various personalities.

Again, it is hard not to think of that great Anglo-Saxon scholar and myth maker, J. R. R. Tolkien. As he wrote to his great student, W. H. Auden (a convert to Catholicism), each person is an "allegory... each embodying in a particular tale and clothed in the garments of time and place, universal truth and everlasting life."

My own personal bias as a practicing (if not always perfect) Roman Catholic and a patriot of the liberal arts probably comes through pretty clearly in the following part of this introduction, but I believe the best pieces in the book—all of which are excellent—to be those on Alcuin, Alfred, John Fisher, and Thomas More.

In his piece on Alcuin, Douglas Woodruff, always a profound defender of the Western tradition, writes: "Yet there should be a keener sense of filial piety toward the men to whose labours we owe the preservation of Virgil and Cicero, and nearly all the poets and prose writers of ancient Rome." Yet, Woodruff laments, the modern scholar so rarely gives any time or attention to so great a man as Alcuin.

Unquestionably, at least to me, the best piece is the first of the two by G. K. Chesterton. The great twentieth-century man so capably understood the souls of those who came before him. At his best, he notes, King Alfred

> clarified and codified the best laws of the West Saxon tradition; but he became a more important sort of legislator in the moral sphere when he translated Boethius for his people, with very characteristic additions of his own; and so brought into England the full tradition of Europe; the tradition of the Christian creed resting upon the Pagan culture. He had been troubled all his life with a recurrent and rather mysterious disease; and he died at the early age of fifty-two, in the first year of the new century. The night of the barbarian peril was already over, and he died in the dawn.

Alfred, too, gave us the term "Christendom." A saint, a warrior, a skeptic, and a redeemed believer, Alfred is the great Anglo-Saxon Roman Catholic, a model for all leaders who would follow him over the centuries.

> *Out of the mouth of the Mother of God*
> *like a little word come I;*
> *For I go gathering Christian men*
> *from sunken paving and ford and fen,*
> *To die in a battle, God knows when,*
> *By God, but I know why.*

And this is the word of Mary,
The word of the world's desire:
"No more of comfort shall ye get,
Save that the sky grows darker yet
and the sea rises higher."

Then silence sank.

So does Chesterton describe Alfred's mystical encounter with the Virgin in his epic, *The Ballad of the White Horse*. That epic poem inspired so many other Christian humanists, including Tolkien, C. S. Lewis, Christopher Dawson, and Russell Kirk. Dawson went so far as to explain that the poem shaped his entire view of history, while Kirk spent a considerable amount of his life not only pondering the poem, but memorizing it. As Kirk slipped in and out of consciousness during the last hours of his life, he continued to reflect on the poem, finding new meaning in it only moments before passing into eternity.

While he lived three centuries before St. Thomas Aquinas, Alfred was, for all intents and purposes, the perfect Thomistic king as described and hypothesized in his treatise, *On Kingship*.

John Fisher, Father David Mathews argues, carried with him a certain innocence and holy naiveté throughout his life, despite the company he kept of royalty and humanists. "The piety and old-fashioned scholarship, the careful fine calligraphy, the controlled appreciation of good letters, would all seem to have marked out Dr. Fisher for a life of learning and quiet pastoral care; the stole, the doctor's cap; hardly the mitre."

It is, once again, Chesterton who emerges so successfully in this book. In his second contribution to *The English Way*, the grand Christian humanist writes about Thomas More. Chesterton presents More as a man of integrity and honor, a man equally capable of mirth, a "man who died laughing." Whereas scholars divided More into the old and the young, the persecutioner and the persecuted, the writer of

Utopia and the chancellor, Chesterton presents him as the complete man, a man of God. "The difference is that England exists, unlike Utopia; and this somewhat eminent Englishman wanted England to continue to exist; and especially the England that he loved."

The Catholic Church canonized Sts. Thomas More and John Fisher in 1935, only two years after the appearance of *The English Way*.

The beatification of these two saints is not the only thing that makes the timing of this book meaningful. One could make the fine case that the entire Christian humanist revival and, especially, the Catholic literary revival of the twentieth century originated with Sheed and Ward. Certainly, scholars such as Maritain, Dawson, Chesterton, and Belloc had published before Sheed and Ward came into existence as a press. Yet, it was the vision of Frank Sheed and Maisie Ward that harnessed and promoted the movement from the 1920s through the early 1960s. Their business and personal correspondence now residing at the University of Notre Dame reveals not only their profound and unending love for one another, but also for the Roman Catholic Church and its intellectual, literary, and artistic treasures. In 1929, for example, Sheed encouraged his employee, Tom Burns, to work closely with Dawson. Burns and Dawson has already edited four issues of the mischievous Catholic journal, *Order*, when Sheed suggested they might do something in book form. The resultant collaboration, *A Monument to St. Augustine*, brought together the greatest Christian humanists of England and the European continent to celebrate the life and work of St. Augustine on the 1,500th anniversary of his death. With the book an immediate success, Burns and Dawson began the short-lived but immensely influential book series, *Essays in Order*, featuring the works of Maritain, Dawson, Nicholas Berdyaev, François Mauriac, Carl Schmitt, E. I. Watkin, Theodor Haecker, Thomas Gilby, and Herbert Read.

For nearly four decades, as Sheed remembers in his autobiography, *The Church and I*, they believed they were ushering in a new, reformed, purified, and intellectual Catholicism throughout the Western world. "For the twenties on into the sixties, euphoria reigned among Catholics. We were happy in the Church and confident in its future. Converts were pouring in—up to thirteen thousand in one notable year in England, over thirty thousand a year in the United States."

It was near the beginning of this euphoric revival that *The English Way* appeared, immediately after *Essays in Order*, the centerpiece of Sheed and Ward at the time. Certainly, *The English Way* appears confident and just, ready to approach a skeptical English-speaking audience with historical, real, and tangible examples of intellectual as well as spiritually-charged Catholics, most of Anglo-Saxon origins.

Why I spotted and rediscovered *The English Way* just when I did, I have no idea. But I am very glad to have been so blessed. Now, of course, you hold it in your hands. Be thankful—to the subjects, to the authors, to the press, and, of course, to He who makes all such things possible.

Out of the mouth of the Mother of God...go we.

FOREWORD

by MAISIE WARD

"CHRISTIANITY IS THE RELIGION OF THE INCARNATION of Godhead in humanity, of the Absolute in the relative, of Eternity in time." Because it is universal it is in every country, but because it is sacramental it is intensely local, found in each country in a special and unique fashion, not a spirit only but a spirit clothed in material form. St. Gregory, as we know, once counselled St. Augustine not to destroy the temples which had been used for pagan worship but to consecrate them to Christ. So, too, the Englishman was not to be changed *for* but *into* the Christian. The Medievals were wont to paint the Infancy and the Passion of Our Lord in the setting of their own lives, and William Langland "saw Christ walking in the fields in the dress of an English laborer." In Langland, says Christopher Dawson, "Catholic faith and national feeling are fused in a single flame."

This book does not attempt to analyze the English Way of being Catholic, but to present certain characters, certain ideas, from which the reader may make his own analysis and paint his own picture. The various writers have chosen characters who in their opinion are very English and very Catholic.

There have been two sharp breaks in the national life—the first was at the Norman Conquest; the second was at the Reformation, when the national and religious life ceased to flow in the same full stream. But something remained unchanged right through. Phrases from Mr. Chesterton's study of Alfred the Great would find themselves at home in the study of Challoner: "supremely the type that proves to the world what is called a fanatical fixity of faith without fanaticism...in which solitary and supernatural conviction expresses itself in energy but not often in ecstasy": "There is always something about him indescribably humble and handy, like one who unpretentiously hammers away at an inherited task."

"What we call England," says Mr. Belloc, "was made, grew from, began, upon a Sussex hill in 1066. Not that the blood which we call English began then and (God knows) not the landscape nor the deep things which inhabit the native soul. All these are immemorial; the English imagination, the English humor, the English Englishry is from the beginning of recorded time."

Those "deep things which inhabit the native soul" make in each land its own special "Way" of being Catholic.

SAINT BEDE (672–735)

by GERVASE MATHEW, O.P

"I, Bede, a servant of God and a priest of the monastery of the blessed apostles Peter and Paul, which is at Wearmouth and Jarrow, being born in the territory of the same monastery, was given by kinsfolk at seven years of age to be educated by the most reverend Abbot Benedict and afterwards by Ceolfrid; spending all the remainder of my life in that monastery, I wholly applied myself to the study of scripture. Amid the observances of the rule and the daily charge of singing in the church I ever took delight in learning and teaching and writing. In the nineteenth year of my age I received the diaconate and in the thirtieth the priesthood, both of them at the hands of the most reverend Bishop John and at the bidding of Abbot Ceolfrid. From the time of my admission to the priesthood until my fifty-ninth year I have endeavored for my own use and for that of my brethren to make brief notes upon the holy Scriptures, either out of the works of the Venerable Fathers or in conformity with their meaning and their interpretation."[1]

When Bede lay dying in his cell at Jarrow on the vigil of Ascension Day in the year 735 his disciples noted the same serene aloofness which we can still trace in so much that he has written. It was already darkening, and the last of the light barely defined the skin coverlets and the little chest and the worn writing tablets. Small as was his cell, the white walls seemed high against the darkness as he lay stretched on the stone flooring with his two disciples bent above him.

He had lain ill since before Easter, and now he knew that it would soon be time to die, for he had finished with his book of extracts from the Blessed Isidore and his translation of St. John was almost ended. The treasures in his casket—the spice and incense and embroidered linen—had been distributed among the mass priests of his house. As he lay there he murmured ceaselessly—antiphons from the office for *quinquagesima*, uncouth Northumbrian verses on man's destiny and the need for prudence, and aphorisms culled for his pupils' sake. Again and again his mind would wander back to Paulinus's life of Ambrose, and he would repeat the saying of the dying bishop: "I have not so lived that I am ashamed to live among you, yet neither do I fear to die, for we have a loving lord."

For nearly sixty years he had lived in his Northumbrian abbey, years spent in the round of choral duty and in untiring industry for the sake of his disciples. "I would not that my children should learn a lie." We can still trace the course of ceaseless study; that laborious handbook the *De Arte Metrica*, written while he was yet a deacon; the treatises on Orthography and on Tropes; the *De Temporibus* and then those happier years spent "pasturing in the flowery meadows of the fathers." He had written of the nature of the rainbow and of the color of the Red Sea; of clouds and of frost and of the River Nile; of the astrolabe and of bloodletting; of the seven wonders of the world, and of the seven stars that hang between the earth and sky. He had learned so much, he had written so much, he had been interested in so little.

He had taken the habit at a time when the worship of the old gods still lingered in the country places and when many of the wandering leaders of the northern Church followed the Celtic rites. He had

1. *Historia Ecclesiastica Gentis Anglorum*, lib. V, cap. xxiv.

witnessed the return of Roman order, the dioceses of the Roman pattern, the victory of the Benedictine Rule. It was an age in which these changes bred a sudden and unjustified self-confidence in those whose lives were passed within the framework of religious custom. The monastic system whose bare outline seemed so imposing in a society where institutions were still incoherent had not yet been put to proof. Something of the old pagan wonder at the magic runes still stirred the mind of the Northumbrians as their slow thoughts brooded on the holy house. The golden chalices and the worked heavy jewels were but the inmost wonder of such shrines. An element of wizard strength still hung about the fine cut wood of these high new abbeys, the thrones of a priesthood of more subtle power than that which once served their fathers' gods. Yet the wonder which the Christianized herdsmen could but half express would change to a stronger passion as the tale of the rich treasure chests spread eastward. It was an essential limitation of the monastic outlook that the heathen world did not concern them, save as a field for the preaching of Christ's Gospel. How trivial and remote the chaffering of the Norse traders seemed to them—an occasional galley storm-beached, the rapid bargaining talk. In the background of the life of Jarrow and Monkwearmouth, behind the careful chanting and religious custom, there passed unperceived the northern movements. Threatening the whole new system, bringing in time destruction and the sword, there moved the friendless sea.

Again, in so far as the country life was present to them in the runes for fertility and for protection, the monks could not but feel the quick contempt bred of their prized and recent learning. They could understand the herd rearing and appreciate each danger of the fells, but the peasant gatherings roused scorn as the ceorls stood through the warm nights in summer with the linden wood shields upon their shoulders and the scramasax hafts tapping their cross-garters, while they gazed with an innocent and heavy wonder at the kindling of the Midsummer Fire.

But the monks could see with such clear pleasure the tide of the

Anglian Renaissance, the new sculpture on the High Crosses, the fresh illumination—the rood of Bewcastle, the Gospel of Lindisfarne; the coming of the Byzantine art *motifs* to the north, the twisted foliage and the vine and the acanthus leaf, the old gold and the vermilion, the cloisonné and the green of patined bronze.

Through all his life Bede had lived remote in serene appraisement. He had no share in the inverted classicism, half-Greek and half-Latin, of the school of Canterbury or in the growth of the Christ saga in the north. He had had his training in the old rhetorical tradition of the last years of the Empire, and he could appreciate Aldhelm's intricacy or Aethelwald's; the cadencies of their clause rhythm, the allusive obscurity of epithet, the changing color of the simile. He writes of the shining luster of the new style. It had had no influence upon his own. He was still less affected by the literary movement in Northumbria, which was to culminate a lifetime later with the poems of the Vercelli book. He prized such verses, since they witnessed to a talent bestowed by God and used to His glory, and it would seem that he had himself received the gift of facile improvisation. But such a gift, the *dulcis canor* of Richard Rolle, often accompanied the strong affective mysticism of the northern contemplatives, and those of his verses which remain to us harbor no echoes of the new Christian epic in the North. He had learned his quantities from Ausonius and his metaphors from the Cathemerinon, and while the gleemen in the great hall at Bamborough sang to the glory of Christ victorious and of his chosen war band of apostles, godlike heroes, twelve high descended leaders of the hosting, Bede wrote in his laborious hexameters of leaf-laden boughs and of flower-strewn fields and of the Four Last Things.

There was nothing unnatural in such detachment from the interests of his time. The quick play of Bede's imagination was haunted by phantasms of the coming judgment, when the skies should open and the stars fall and each Christian learn his eternal destiny. To him each Catholic was an exile homesick for paradise—*non hic habemus manentem civitatem*. Through all his work the same conceptions, often the same phrases, are recurrent: *Peregrini in huic saeculo, in patria, in via, in itinere huius exilii*, and at last *a carnis ergastulo soluti coeleste regnum intramus. A carnis ergastulo*, a whole philosophy lies implicit. Man's body the slave's prison of his soul.

Though St. Bede's three references to Plato would seem to have been drawn from some *catena aurea* of the sayings of the wise, he was none the less the first of the English Platonists as he studied the shadow world in which he lived preoccupied by the world it shadowed. Such an attitude is nowhere plainer than in his fourteen works in exegesis, for as he "bruised the precious spices of the word of God" he knew that the literal meaning is to the allegorical as water is to wine. His mind rose upward from the sea that typified the world of sense and the spittle that signified man's wisdom to the golden lily of Resurrection and the silver of God's word.

The long years of contemplation, while it enhanced his consciousness of an unseen world around him, yet freed him from that sense of multiplicity which is the nemesis of the Platonist mood. The overwhelming consciousness of the fair harmony of creation, the sacramental concord of created things—*pulchra rerum concordia, mira concordia sacramenti*—which characterized the later years of his labor, was the expression of a mysticism rather than of a philosophy. This is true also of a doctrine of number which led him to see in the world of phenomena a notation of God's music. He came to prize the numeric value of each letter in the Holy Name. The ten which represents the I in *Iesu* was the dearest to him of all the numbers, for it signifies the reward of Heaven, since it is the multiple of five and two, that is, of man's five senses multiplied by the love of his neighbor and of God.

Such vision seems fantastic to us, for it is impossible of attainment, yet it had formed the natural counterpoise to a neo-Platonism derived through those fathers who had learned of the *Enneads* before the quick darkness of the early Middle Ages had settled. For it led him to seek not for absorption, but union—a complete union of intention and will and desire, a following of Christ even to the exact placing of footsteps. His work had been hampered by the ill-equipped scriptorium of his house and by the need of books; he had been sickly from boyhood; he had always had his detractors; even his orthodoxy had been denied, but his serenity was undisturbed, for to him the perfection of the Christian life lay not in renunciation, but in acceptance.

Yet in so far as his mysticism linked him with a great body of solitaries who waited in a silence of the faculties unbroken by study it led to an increasing alienation from that Celtic tradition of learning that was already one of the most vital elements in the Catholic scholarship of his time. There was so vivid a contrast between the quiet years of study at Jarrow—*sequens vestigia magnorum tractatorum* and the eager and glamorous life of the Irish schoolmen among the bandying of dispute. For Bede was content to teach his pupils "out of the works of the venerable fathers or in conformity to their interpretation." He had no zest for new discovery, and he was conscious that he was the heir of a great tradition, a tradition that it was his life-work to perpetuate in the north.

It is true that he held the "Scotti" to be holy men skilled in both learnings, the sacred and profane, and eager to impart them to others. His own master, Trumhere, had been their disciple, and much of the material detail of monastic scholarship had been affected by their influence. But their spirit remained alien to his own as he wrote in delicate half-uncials of the Irish script that Prudence is the mother and the nurse of the virtues.

The increasing contact of his later years can only have emphasized a wide divergence. He must have felt all the Benedictine distaste for gyrovagues[2] as he listened to the wandering scholars in the hospice at Jarrow, long-haired monks with painted eyelids, disputing on the sixteen colors of the four winds of the sky. Yet there is no trace of this in his writings, and such vagaries lie hidden in the wide charity

2. Editor's Note: Wandering and usually dissolute monks of the early Church.

of his reticence. It was left to St. Aldhelm of Sherborne to express the Anglo-Roman attitude to Celtic learning; the Irish, he noted, gave suck from wisdom's udder, but in dispute they snarled their syllogisms like molossian hounds.[3]

Such a judgment was necessarily superficial. The eighth century in the lands of Celtic culture was the seeding-time of a harvest that has not yet been garnered. The hampered thought and clumsy perverted Latin of the Irish scholars foreshadowed the dear glory of Erigena,[4] and in their delight in dialectic as dialectic they were the precursors of those great schoolmen of the thirteenth century who were to see in every syllogism a theophany of the Incarnate Word.

The growing divergence between the traditions of the Celtic and Northumbrian schools was a cardinal misfortune of that age. St. Bede himself has suffered from it, for it led him to spend his life away from the quicker current of Catholic thought, seeking for truth not in the judgment but in the concept. He was never to be freed from a certain scorn for that imperfection of intellect, the reason. To him the one road to the knowledge of God was the road to Calvary, a journey beyond abstract reasoning and judgment, the ripening of a field which in this life was never to be fully garnered.

Though he had taught for many years since it was God's will that he should be master in Jarrow school, his wide patristic knowledge had been chiefly motived by his strong love for the fourfold sense of Scripture—"the fountain of gardens, the well of living waters which run with a strong stream of Libanus."[5] But for the great commentators that might have remained for him a garden enclosed, a fountain sealed up. He had had no will to tread the winepress of God's word alone. It was the Fathers who had led him *in Regis cellaria*, and reading them he pastured among lilies.

3. Editor's Note: Greek mastiffs.

4. Editor's Note: John Scotus Eri[u]gena, Irish theologian, Neoplatonist and poet.

5. Editor's Note: Mount Lebanon.

But if his learning had been inspired by his devotion to God's word, his devotion to God's word resulted from his devotion to the Word made flesh—the devotion that is so apparent in the most self-revealing of his books, the commentary upon the Song of Songs, to the golden blossom Christ and the Church His body. Bede's words as he lay dying: "My soul desires to see Christ my king in His beauty," serve both to summarize and to explain his teaching. For it was his realization of the Incarnation as a present fact that led to his strong loyalty to the Catholic Unity: *indivisa in se, a aliis vero divisa*—in antithesis to the city of hell, the impregnable city of God.

"For we being many are one bread, one body." The Pauline conception of the Church remains apparent throughout the Christocentric trend of all Bede's thought. It is this that explains so much by which his work is differentiated, a sense of the individual significance of each human life and a formal courtesy of style alien to the literary convention of his age. For he knew that the men of whom he wrote were the threads from which Christ's seamless coat was woven, temples of the Holy Spirit and the vine-branches, the Resurrection and the Life. And it was this that brought him when already old to the study of the history of the Church, for to him Church history was the Fifth Evangel. Even "the Ecclesiastical History of the English Nation" may be regarded as yet another essay in exegesis, a somewhat elaborate commentary on a sentence from the Epistles: "Who has called you out of darkness into his marvelous light who in time past were not a people, but are now the people of God."

Such an attitude to history is not without disadvantage, yet it has served to enhance St. Bede's value and repute as an historian, for the methods of his exegesis, the careful naming of authority and the slow weighing of contrary opinion, was to bring him fame as one of the multitudinous fathers of historical criticism. While since the years of contemplation had freed him from the bias of party prejudice, it was a sequel to his detachment that he should write objectively. And this is made more evident by his love of right order; all that he has written is marked by the sober restraint of the Benedictine tradition. Yet though writing in a clean and simple Latin he shows something of that sense of texture which characterizes so much Anglo-Saxon prose, linking it to the *opus anglicanum* of the tapestries. Akin to the limited perspective of such woven shadows the historical horizon of the *Historia* seems also rigid and near, and, when the clearness of his perception is admitted, his figures from the past stand as if tapestried, angular, a little hard and flat.

This same rigidity of terrestrial outlook had led him to view the future unsuspecting the rending of his pictured figures in the burning of the monasteries and the glare of Norse sea raids. The lay magnates in his countryside may not have shared the sense of his security; the years of his religious life had witnessed the fading power of the Northumbrian kingship and the Scandinavian ferment. But pasturing in the meadows of the fathers he had no thought for the Eorlcund-men without the gates and their harsh clamor. He had no concern for the crude apprehensions of "scarlet-clad spear leaders" or Hordaland and Rogir and the wild "hersir" culture. Such matters were not fit subjects for meditation for those who had risen to follow the authority of the monastic elders and the rule of the prudent Father Benedict.

In the spring Bede died, he was still serenely unconscious of ruin impending. There were no longships in sight in that stormy season as he looked out on the green following seas running southward from the coast where the "horse-whales" lay on the cold foreshore. A father had said of the northern region that from thence the waters of the earth pass down. This was a fact worthy of all credence, and in the monastery they kept as ornament the finely-polished bones of horse-whales' teeth. But for the rest he knew little of the Hyperboreans or of the customs of the north.

Living on the far limit of the Roman world, Rome was to him *Caput et Domina Orbis*, the Holy See. An ever-conscious membership of a visible society, united by a common rule and a common worship, a worship that was ordered to God's glory and a rule that was a manifestation of His power, had brought with it a new stability in that world of change. To Bede, living under the protection of the lord abbot of "the monastery of the Holiest Apostle St. Peter in Saxony," the passing kings had signified so little. "The most glorious" King Ceolwulf, and "the ferocious" Egofrid were only shadows half reflected in the repeated epithet of cloistered talk. But his abbots had been the support and protection of the liberty and peace of the spirit, the oracles of God's will. They had fostered his patristic learning and had shared with him his quiet pleasures—the religious anagrams and the rhymed acrostics, the riddles on the sacred mysteries and the tales of holy death. "God has ordained the youth Hwaetbert to the leadership of souls and to a spiritual dukedom," St. Bede writes of a new abbot, "who by love and zeal for the pieties has long won for himself the name Eusebius. The blessing conferred by your ministry, dearest bishop, has confirmed the election of the brethren, so there returns to me the delight of searching carefully and with my whole soul for the wonders of the sacred scriptures. Therefore, aided by your prayers, most beloved of pontiffs, I begin the fourth book of my Allegorical Exposition of Samuel, and I will endeavor to communicate to my readers all that I can of mysteries, if He will but unlock them Who holds the key of David." How well that passage expresses the ordered power of a serene theocracy in its relation to the central duty of St. Bede's study.

Yet there must have been much even within the brotherhood of the twin monasteries of the two apostles from which Bede stayed remote, an imprudent neglect of the midday sleep and the unwise fasting of the over-zealous or the field sports and the crude jesting of some younger monks. He has no share in that preoccupation with the body which marks so much of the asceticism of his time. He had none of the zest for loud color and contrast of the school of St. Aldhelm or their innocent delight in a sophistry. The traditional love for the classics reminded him of the parable of the prodigal son: the Christian scholars had gone into a far country, and the pagan verses they were fain of were the husks the swine did eat. Yet in an age when the literary vocabulary was singularly rich in invective and the studies of his contemporaries seamed by their feuds, we can find no trace in Bede's writings of any personal enmity. The failings of his companions were forgotten in the quiet charity that has made his *Historia* the chronicle of a Golden Age, and no divergence between him and them disturbed his tolerance. He had learned that in his Father's house there were many mansions. And in Britain, as he notes, "there are found many excellent pearls of all colors—red and purple and violet and green and white."

All his life he was to retain this spirit of unchanging tranquility. He knew, for he had read it in St. Isidore, that he was living in the sixth age of the world. He knew, as he wrote to Bishop Egbert, that evil men abounded on the earth. But he seemed to be at the last rebirth of better things. The return of the old civilization to Northumbria had been reflected even in the trivial surroundings of his life of prayer, as he thought of the fine new glazing on the lanterns in the choir he could remember the days of his monastic childhood and the smoke upon the horn. His memory must have been checkered by such contrast, the old arch priest of Coldingham, the rude clumsy gestures with which he unhooked his travelling spear and the present prior speaking with a certain nicety of phrase and prudent diction of the holy abbot in his new sarcophagus beneath the turf. He had no presage of the coming ruin as he dreamt of the final victory of Roman order, of the columns re-erected, and of the broken wall cleared of the moss, and of the endless colonnade.

His life had been spent among the treasures amassed by the great abbots of his house *Religiosi Emptores*—the silk hangings embroidered in the *rotellae* with winged dragons, the silver arm-reliquaries and the cups of onyx. The life in the scattered steadings and in the rush-strewn halls of the chiefs must have seemed very far away. The quiet of the monastery was hardly broken by the coming and going of the poor at the abbey gate, or by the visit of some benefactress upon pilgrirnage, the leathern curtains shrouding her as the great ill-made wheels of the royal cart jolted on the rock-strewn northern way. There would be ale at the hospitium for the nobles of the retinue while her household priest brought tidings of the Royal Curia, the princesses and their praised virginity and the virtue of the queen.

It was not seemly that the horse-thegns of the retinue should discuss such matter on the ale-bench, nor would it be needful for them to hold communion with any of the monkfolk vowed from childhood to God's service. For the ordered security of a life of prayer had been sufficiently safeguarded by the strength of Rome; there was among the precious muniments of the house "a thing by no means to be despised, a letter of privilege from the lord Pope Agatho, by which the abbey was rendered safe and secure forever from any foreign invasion." All in that great community were conscious of the protection of a central power, of the wealth of the abbey treasure, of the high tradition of their learning and of the sacrosanct immunity of their lives.

Yet how remote was such knowledge from the same conceptions mirrored in the imaginings of the thegns, themselves gesithcund-men[6] and "dearly born," they were well aware of the blood-price of each monk and knew there were no stronger rune-binders this side the Wendel sea. They had heard of the red twisted gold in the sacrist's keeping and of the embroidered coverlets from Greek-land of the worth of many hides. They even shared in some memory of Roman strength, for they had heard the gleemen sing of it. "With the Greeks I was, with the Finns and with Caesar, he who had rule over towns and feasting, riches and joys and the realm of Welsh land." But they could remember other echoes from the chanting: "a broken shield of linden and bronze inset," "the tarred oars foam besprinkled and the driving of the wave." And for two years now they had taken note of the omens, they had seen the moon blood-pitted and the sun hanging a dark shield in the sky.

6. Editor's Note: Companions of a king.

But even if Bede had foreseen the end of so much effort, flames from Jarrow and Monkwearmouth and a half-quenched civilization beyond Humber, it is unlikely that it would have influenced his life-work or disturbed the tenor of his years of study. For his life's purpose had been the fulfilment of God's will, and this, implying an overwhelming trust in Providence, involved an entire acceptance of the future. While though he did not conceive of so natural a disaster as the Viking raid, he was not unprepared for sudden cataclysm. For nearly sixty years he had awaited the advent of the Lord. And he could remember the Yellow Death when he was a child in the abbey and the nights after so many burials when he had stood alone with Ceolfrid in the great high-fashioned nave, the old man in the abbot's stall with his lips moving ceaselessly. The light had fallen on the veins of the statues' breakage and the Merovingian ivory.

There had been winged lions on the chancel imposts and writhing basilisks carved upon the frieze, and in the darkness beneath the rafter the rood whose wood seemed almost living. But he had been conscious then of another presence and of the angels chanting in the choir.

There was no one now left in the abbey to share that memory, but it was to stay with him till he died. Years after he was to say to his disciples: "I know that angels visit the canonical hours and the congregations of the brethren. What if they do not find me among them? Will they not say where is Bede? Why comes he not to the prescribed devotions?"

The presence of an unseen world around him and the duty of the prescribed devotions had been the motifs in Bede's life.

SAINT BONIFACE (680–755)

by AELFRIC MANSON, O.P

THE CHARACTERISTICS WHICH DISTINGUISH A NATION are difficult to determine: we tend to hypostatize the virtues in the form of our own nationality, and are surprised when we meet them elsewhere. What is an Englishman? What is that type of mental outlook and behavior which, through the centuries, marks him out? The problem is complicated by the various influences that the dwellers on this island have experienced. It is not just the question of the continuity of a race living for generations on its own soil. The Norman Conquest, for example, meant the coming of a new people into the old stock; and a new consciousness. Will a man before that Conquest manifest the same traits as a man after it? Is each of them the genuine unalterable Englishman? So we may reflect when dealing with this English saint who lived three hundred years before the Normans came. For Boniface impresses us with an almost fantastic resemblance to what would now be considered as typically English greatness. He combined the love of travel and adventure of an Elizabethan with a genius for statesmanship and administration. He was a man, we might say, using an imperial ability for the extension of the Kingdom of God. It would have been of great interest to have known what he looked like. But there is nothing approaching a contemporary portrait: in the eighth century there were no portrait painters, or even cameras. Many of his letters remain, and these are of great importance for the events of his career and the general life of his period. But he was not a great writer; his style is the common style of the age, and although we can draw general observations about him from his letters—his affection for his friends and his fidelity to them, his love of books in general and of the Scriptures in particular, his profound dependence upon intercessory prayer—we miss those personal indications which make us intimate with a man, like Lamb, for instance, who can convey his individuality through words. There is, however, one delightful exception. Boniface himself was, rigidly, a total abstainer; and he imposed the practice in the monasteries he founded. Not that he had a puritanical dislike of wine or beer; it was because he considered drunkenness the most common failing of his countrymen. And far from wishing to impose a universal taboo, he recognized that wine was meant expressly to make joyful the heart of man. In a letter to his friend Egbert, Archbishop of York, after asking him to send Bede's commentaries on the Scriptures, which would be useful for the sermons of the missionaries, and having sought his advice on a disciplinary matter, he concludes: "Lastly, we have sent across to your grace with the bearer of this letter, two measures of wine as a proof of affection, that, at our loving entreaty, you may use it to spend a happy day with your brethren." This provision for an episcopal "happy day" surely reveals a pleasant and humorous aspect of the austere exile who, at that moment, bore the burden of an entire new province of the Church upon his shoulders. But it is a glimpse only; for the most part he remains a hidden figure. He was, in fact, one of those men whose personality is best understood by their achievement, whose character and ideals remain expressed in the work they left behind them. What Boniface created was what Boniface was: in it there lies incarnate all he stood for, his dreams and ambitions, his vision, his very essence.

He lived over eleven hundred years ago. But the interest he provokes is not simply that of a great missionary and a great saint. He was certainly both of these. He is also an exceedingly actual figure, for he was one of the makers of the unity of Europe, that shattered unity which today we are trying to rebuild. Most people would admit that Germany is at the center of this problem: it was her defection at the Reformation that made definite the long-threatened cleavage in the West: it is her renascent nationalism that seems to menace the formation of a new international order. The matter is urgent, and it is of extreme importance to recall that Germany's entrance into Christendom and civilization was made possible by an Englishman for whom his nation's riches were not a hoard for private and exclusive possession, but a divine gift to be shared, to be used for the common good.

Boniface is rightly called the Apostle of Germany, because, as a member of the Body of Christ, he was supremely conscious of his responsibility in building up that Body; his was a self-giving life spent in *aedificationem corporis Christi*. This was the principle that made the unity of Europe possible, a principle that in no way denies the rights and functions of individual nations but, on the contrary, fulfills them by making them contributing members of a great community, incorporated into Christ. It is the divine life which flows into the world through the Risen Christ that alone provides a sufficient force to unify the multitude of minds and wills either of the nations of Europe or of all mankind. Thus it was in the beginning of our civilization: thus it will have to be if our modern attempts are to succeed. In the seventh century, the Roman Empire, which had been for several centuries the mainstay of at least political and legal unity in Western Europe, was no longer a reality. No man living could remember it: the ruins of its cities and its roads alone survived as visible witnesses of past magnificence. The empire had retired to the East, and Constantinople had become and was to remain for generations the outpost and bulwark of civilization. Only in a few cities of Italy did the Imperial authority still strive to uphold its name in the West: in vain, for the latest horde of barbarians, the Lombards, proved irresistible. The barbarians: these were the tribes who had swept down from the north into Gaul, into Spain, into Italy, across the sea to Africa, across the northern sea to England: these were the new people, as yet a chaotic mass, who had broken down the old order, and who constituted the elements from which Western Christendom was to be fashioned. That process had begun; the passing of the empire had not been altogether a loss, for it allowed the chief instrument of the new order to develop in freedom. As the Dark Ages changed into the Middle Ages, the creative role of the Papacy became more and more evident. Already it was the one great missionary force of the West. In 596 St. Gregory the Great had sent forth Augustine and his band of fellow Benedictines to convert the pagan Anglo-Saxons of Britain. That mission had been successful; in a hundred years the Christian Church was flourishing in every part of the island. Its progress inspired and stimulated civilization, and Anglo-Saxon England, the England of Bede, became the center of learning in the West. It was from this mature and vigorous society that Boniface went forth to be the agent of another Gregory in the conquest of further realms for the unity of Christ.

He was born about 680, probably at Crediton in Devonshire, then in the kingdom of Wessex, the last of the Anglo-Saxon kingdoms to receive the Faith. His parents were Christians of noble rank. As a child he seems soon to have shown his desire to become a monk, and he was accepted as an oblate of the abbey of Exeter. There he remained until adolescence, when he was sent to complete his studies at the abbey of Nursling, in the diocese of Winchester. Both his new abbot, Winbrecht, who was also his master, and the bishop, Daniel, were to remain his friends for life. His studies were primarily Scriptural, and it was here that he acquired that profound love and knowledge of the Bible which is so evident in all his letters as a missionary. He must have learned also some at least of the seven liberal arts; verse making, at any rate, he never forgot—it was a favorite Anglo-Saxon elegance, and both his letters and those of his friends often conclude with a few lines of somewhat barbaric elegiacs. He probably owed this literary formation to the renowned teacher St. Aldhelm.

His proficiency was soon noticed and he was made the master of the abbey school. But he was a destined apostle, and we are told that he managed to combine this work with preaching to the people outside. When he was thirty (about 710) he received the priesthood; monasteries were still mainly lay communities, so this may be taken as a sign of the consideration in which he was held. Details of this early period do not abound, nevertheless it is clear that he stood every chance of becoming a distinguished ecclesiastic in his native church. He was even chosen (between 710 and 716) by the synod of Wessex to convey the synodal decrees to Brihtwald, the Archbishop of Canterbury, probably with the intention of linking the Wessex clergy more closely with the primatial see. It was a tribute to his statesmanlike qualities. Everything was pointing to a tranquil, successful career. But Boniface had seen a vision; his talents were to be used in a wider field and for a more adventurous purpose. His career at home came to a sudden close.

It was, as we have seen, a missionary age. Even from a natural point of view the great movement must have appealed to the spirit of youth eager for the conquest of the world. In his own island the subject must have been vivid: there was the story of his people's conversion, not so long ago; missionaries from Ireland; missionaries from Rome. There were the tales of still more recent heroes, the exploits of the men of his own race impatient to hand on the Good News they had received. Willibrord had been working among the pagans in Frisia (Holland) since 692 and, it was said, had done wonders. And there were others. He was caught into the current. He had to go. But where? His thoughts turned to those heathen who were his ancestors, the Saxons remaining in Germany. This was his first ideal, and though he never achieved it, he never lost it. He would take the Gospel to the Saxons. But he was inexperienced. He must learn something about missionary technique. He would therefore make a preliminary survey of Willibrord's work in Holland and thus gain the necessary experience. So, in 716, having wrung permission from his reluctant abbot, he set sail with three companions from the port of London.

Events on his arrival were not encouraging. The local duke, Radbod, was at war with the Franks; Willibrord had had to retire, and his life's work seemed ruined. Boniface, however, made his way to the ducal court at Utrecht and received permission to remain and preach. He did not remain very long; having gained an idea of the life, he returned to England and his abbey. Meanwhile abbot Winbrecht had died, and the monks decided to elect Boniface as his successor. But Boniface had other ideas. He managed to dissuade them, and in 718 set out again, this time for Rome. He carried with him two commendatory letters from Bishop Daniel, one for the spiritual and lay authorities whose dominions he would pass through on his way, the other for the Pope. He did not wish to be a mere spiritual adventurer. He had a sense of order. He wanted the sanction of the highest authority of the Catholic Church. He was going to Rome to offer his services to the Vicar of Christ.

He picked up many companions on the journey—the Anglo-Saxons had a passion for pilgrimages to Rome—and, though the winter was severe, they reached the city safely, and offered their thanks at St. Peter's tomb. Then, a few days later, came the audience with the Pope, St. Gregory II. He was a welcome visitor, for this pope had long had plans for Germany, and had already sent his legate to reform the Church in Bavaria. It was the first of many interviews, and the Pope retained him until May 719. We have no details of those conversations, we only know their result. The historic significance of that result indicates their importance. They represent Boniface's initiation to the Apostolate; the Pope was equipping the young man for his first great test. It was to be a difficult experiment, and he must accordingly be well instructed. The Roman emperors had sent forth their legions to add new territories to the empire by force of arms. The Emperors had gone from Rome; and now Gregory, the servant of the Ruler of the World, was quietly planning for a more enduring kingdom, the pacific conquest of lands the legions never reached.

Boniface went back to Frisia. He was armed with a formal papal letter, authoritatively assigning him as a missionary to the heathen, making him the Pope's collaborator in the spreading of the Word of God. He was to conform to the Roman liturgy in the administration of the Sacraments—and Boniface's work proved to be one of the great influences that secured the general acceptance of that liturgy in the West. He was to refer all difficult cases to the decision of the Holy See—here also his work did much to make effective the appellate jurisdiction of the Roman Court. Finally, to emphasize his special adoption as a missionary of the Pope, Gregory changed his name from Winfrith—the Anglo-Saxon name he had hitherto borne—into that of Boniface. It was as though he was given a new identity as the Pope's man.

He assisted Willibrord for three years, converting the heathen, destroying their idols, and building churches. But he had not come to stay, and when Willibrord, in 722, wished to consecrate him bishop as his successor, he pleaded that his mission was not to a single diocese but to the heathen at large, and that, in any case, he had not reached fifty, the canonical age. He won his point, and departed for central Germany. He began in Hesse and Thuringia, a densely wooded and mountainous territory. Irish missionaries had been there before him, but they had failed to organize their conquests. The Christian faith had not developed, and the people remained half pagan. The priests themselves had degenerated, some of them even shared in the worship and banquets of Thor. So Boniface could expect no help from them. He was alone. His only encouragement came from the letters he received from his friends, especially the nuns, across the sea. He wrote for advice as to how he should proceed to Bishop Daniel at Winchester. Daniel counselled him not to begin by denouncing the errors of the pagans and the genealogies of their gods.

He should first convince them, by discreet and gentle questioning, that the existence of their gods was insufficient to explain either their own origin or that of the world; then show the pointlessness of their sacrifices, compare their myths with Christian doctrines, make them appreciate the imposing *fact* of Christianity, and tell them the story of its triumph in the pagan world. A wise apologetic in the spirit of St. Gregory the Great, Boniface found it successful, and he sent a report of results together with some difficulties for solution, to the Pope. The return letter answered his difficulties and invited him to Rome.

Gregory was satisfied: his experiment had turned out well. The young apostle had had over three years' trial and had proved his genius. He was to be rewarded by receiving a higher command. When Boniface arrived the Pope began by questioning him as to the faith he had been teaching. "Apostolic father," he answered, "as a foreigner I find it hard to understand your speech; give me but time, and I will set forth my faith in writing." The delay was granted and he sent in his profession of faith. Then the Pope gave him another interview in the Lateran which lasted most of the day. At the end he told him that he intended to make him a bishop. This time there could be no refusal: it was the command of Christ's Vicar. He was to be a bishop, but the Bishop of Germany, of all Germany across the Rhine. He was not to be the subject of any metropolitan, but was to be attached directly to Rome. Boniface acquiesced, and his consecration took place on St. Andrew's Day, 30th November, 722. He took the ancient oath used by the bishops of Italy, of fidelity to St. Peter and his successor. Then the Pope gave him a collection of the canons of councils to direct him in his ministry, and letters to Charles Martel, the powerful leader of the Franks, asking for his protection, and to the various peoples he was about to evangelize.

He thus left Rome for the second time with increased prestige as a member of the Catholic hierarchy and a legate of the Roman Pontiff. He was welcomed by Charles Martel, who agreed to afford his mission the protection of his power. Charles was by no means the ideal pious prince. He was still very much of a barbarian and pre-eminently a warrior. But he stood for the preservation of Christianity in the West. The old Merovingian monarchy of the Franks had become senile: Charles reorganized it—just in time to meet the menace of Islam. For the soldiers of Mohammed, having devastated Christian Africa and mastered Spain, were threatening to complete their work by subjugating the lands beyond the Pyrenees. Ten years after his meeting with Boniface, Charles saved our civilization at the great battle of Poitiers (732) and checked their advance forever. Protection by such a man was of the greatest help to Boniface; not that he had any belief in forcible conversions, but because freedom from aggression and a peaceful environment were the essential preliminaries of the work he had to do. He was conscious of his debt; in after years he wrote to Bishop Daniel: "Without the protection of the king of the Franks I can neither rule the people of the Church nor defend the priests and clergy, the monks and nuns of God; nor can I avail to check even the heathen rites and the worship of idols in Germany without his mandate and the fear of him." We are reminded that it was upon no fancy mission that the apostle was engaged; without the awe inspired by the great Frank's name an effective slaughter would have speedily terminated the rising Church of Germany.

All was well when he returned; his converts were flourishing, and his first act was to hold a confirmation. Then he decided upon a bold project. The worship of sacred trees is to be found in many of the "primitive" religions of mankind, and among the Germans the tree was the most impressive symbol of their belief. It seemed to them to possess a living personality, to concentrate within itself the forces that directed the mysterious life of nature. The dark gods possessed it as their presence chamber. On a mountain at Geismar in Hesse there was one of these trees, a venerable and massive oak dedicated to Thor, so ancient that it seemed coeval with time. It stood there, a mighty witness to the reality of the god, a central shrine, a holy place. Season after season it put forth majestic evidence of its vigor, and as long as it remained the confidence of the people in their myths could not be troubled. This Boniface realized, and he determined to cut it down. It was a spectacular occasion. Crowds gathered to see the conflict between the new religion and the old. Surely Thor would not permit this terrible sacrilege. The onlookers waited in silence, waited for a sign. But the Thunderer gave no sign, and the Christian bishop advanced calmly to do his dreadful work. Ringing sounds of the hatchet—persistent—on and on. The people watched petrified. It was unbelievable. Then, as the deadly noise continued undisturbed, fear gripped them. The certainties of their faith were shaken, the convictions of their lives unanchored, chaos in their minds: the gods were impotent. Suddenly an ominous cracking, then a fearful crash; the oak of Thor had fallen.

It was a potent lesson and brought respect for Christianity. Boniface built a chapel on the spot. He found much of the resistance gone, his work prospered and the Christian community grew. At Amoeneburg he dedicated a chapel to St. Michael which was later to become a monastery and a missionary center. The next year he passed on into Thuringia and remained there for seven years (724–731). Here also the Church was only a survival. He at once began energetically to rebuild and organize. He secured the cooperation of some of the nobles, preached everywhere, put up numerous churches for the faithful, and started the monastery of St. Michael at Ohrdruff, near Gotha. To have a monastery was to have a powerhouse: it was not only an imposing house of prayer and worship, it was also the source of the apostolate and of civilization. From the monastery a succession of men went forth to convert and instruct, and by the monastic activity, artistic, literary, agricultural, the barbarians learned the elements of a humane order. But monasteries must have monks, and Boniface's helpers were very few. He turned unhesitatingly to his native land and sent an appeal for more. He had been absent over fifteen years, and it would have been natural enough if he had been almost forgotten. Time dims the closest friendships, and a missionary exiled in an unknown land is not a public figure. It is therefore a most remarkable testimony to the force and attraction of his character, that his appeal was answered at once and abundantly. A veritable monastic exodus began. Wessex gave him all he needed, monks, priests, nuns, schoolmasters, in plenty. He welcomed them; they ensured the permanence of his work, they gave him the means for every development. The chapel at Amoeneburg became a monastery, and another sprang up at Fritzlav near where the oak had been. Ohrdruff received a solid establishment. Three convents of women soon balanced these three foundations for men. The great missionary had reason for legitimate pride; his labors had not been in vain, the harvest he had prepared was being gathered.

His success, however, did not make him forget that he was primarily the servant of the Pope. He kept in close touch with Rome and duly sent his pastoral difficulties for the Pope's decision. A letter from Gregory II, dated November, 726, in answer to one of his, gives us some idea of what those difficulties were. Among people who only recently were pagan the Church's marriage law naturally raised many problems. The Pope tells him that the canonical rules about impediments to marriage are not to be pushed to extremes. It is doubtless best if they are respected by all those who know that they are united by blood relationship, but one must remember that they are barbarians, and it will suffice if marriage is forbidden to the fourth degree inclusively. A passage in this letter has been quoted as sanctioning divorce and remarriage in the case of the husband of a sick wife. Boniface's letter no longer exists and we can only conjecture the precise nature of the case in question. Gregory then goes on to other matters. He uses St. Paul's principles to solve the question of meat consecrated to idols. Lepers may receive communion, but separated from the faithful. A priest who is accused without decisive testimony may be absolved by his oath alone. Oblates once given to God may not return to the world. Sacraments have an objective value which is not diminished by the unworthiness of the minister; hence there can be no re-baptism of those baptized by an unworthy priest, though it may be conferred on children taken from their parents and who cannot remember whether they received it or not. Confirmation may not be administered twice. Religious should not leave their house in time of infectious diseases—as if they could escape from the hand of God. Not two or three but only one chalice is to be placed upon the altar for Mass, as Christ did when he instituted the Eucharist. In spite of the fact that Boniface had sworn in his consecration oath not to communicate with evil priests, he was not to refuse to eat with them—providing they were not formal heretics—but to try to convert them by example and word.

This list of replies well illustrates both the complexities of the missionary's daily life and the prudent moderation of his superior. It was his last letter from the Pope, for Gregory died in February 731. With the new pontificate came a new stage in the construction of the Church in Germany. Gregory III, in answer to Boniface's congratulations on his accession, sent him a letter and the pallium. The letter contained certain decisions which were more rigorous than those of his predecessor—marriage, for example, was excluded to the seventh degree. The pallium made him an archbishop. It meant that Germany, which had hitherto been a diocese, was now to become a province; it would have to be divided into dioceses with bishops instituted by Boniface, who was now the metropolitan. He himself was to have no fixed see, in order to preserve his freedom of general supervision. He was to be careful when selecting bishoprics only to choose cities of sufficient importance to befit the episcopal dignity.

Thus those statesmanlike qualities which we noted in his youth were now given their full chance. And he proved himself worthy; it is magnificent to watch the gradual realization of his plans, the unfolding of that achievement which still lasts. He turned first to Bavaria, a country which then comprised upper Austria, the region round Salzburg, the Tyrol and a part of Styria. It had long been Christian but was failing in vigor from the lack of that corporate expression and discipline which is given by councils; these were not held because there was no metropolitan, a deficiency which also entailed the slackening of the bond with Rome. Boniface spent nine years in the work of organization (732–741), but his main activity began after his return from his third and final visit to Rome in 738.

It was sixteen years since he last left the city, and he had many things to discuss with the Pope. Among other matters he was dissatisfied with the rigor of the Pontiff's decisions mentioned above, for though he was obedient he was never servile. He came with a crowd of disciples, was made very welcome by Gregory, and stayed for the best part of a year. The probable reason for this delay was his desire to attend a council and hear its decrees. When he left Rome—forever—in the spring of 739, he took with him several letters from the Pope. One of them was addressed to the bishops of Bavaria; it presented the legate and reminded them that synods must be held twice every year. Immediately on his return, Boniface proceeded with his work. There were already several diocesan sees in Bavaria—Salzburg, Frising, Ratisbon, and Passau—but they were all vacant except the last, and their respective territories were not delimited. He filled the sees and marked out the territories. Then he had to summon a national council of Bavaria. No documents of this council remain, but that it was assembled cannot be doubted, otherwise the strong movement for ecclesiastical reform which began in Bavaria about this time would have no source of origin. The legate's work was completed by the foundation of many monasteries.

He went on at once to Hesse and Thuringia. His task was more difficult here. Bavaria had been Christian for generations and it had been a part of the Roman civilization. There was a tradition of order; there were cities. Here the people had scarcely emerged from barbarism and there were few towns. How was he to obey the Pope's command not to erect bishoprics in insignificant localities? He did what he could. In Hesse he made Buraberg the episcopal see; it was not an important town but it lay between the two monasteries of Fritzlar and Amoeneburg and was thus central for the rising Christian community.

He appointed as its bishop Wittan, one of the Anglo-Saxons who had answered his appeal from England. In Thuringia, which was naturally divided by a great forest, he created two dioceses: Erfurt near his monastery of Ohrdruff in the north, and Wurzburg on the Mein, a rising town and the ducal residence, in the south. This organization was completed and confirmed by the Pope in 742. Boniface had been a faithful servant; he had made the Church of central Germany in twenty years. He had been laboring now for a quarter of a century. He was getting old. He was worn out. His friends were passing away. Gregory II had long been gone; in October, 741, Charles Martel died; in November Gregory III followed him. It was time for Boniface to retire.

He did not retire: he took upon himself a task equal in magnitude to the former—the reform of the Frankish Church. That church had indeed fallen from its high estate. Boniface's letters bear witness to a terrible decadence. No councils had been held for eighty years, the metropolitan hierarchy had ceased to exist. Some of the episcopal sees had been vacant for years; others were in the hands of laymen or corrupt clerics. Bishops lived in concubinage, hunted, and went to war. The inferior clergy were grossly ignorant and taught strange and superstitious doctrines. And to crown all, bands of Irish priests, admitting no ecclesiastical control, wandered from diocese to diocese, teaching what they liked, living as they pleased and irritating everyone with their peculiar Celtic customs.

Boniface saw that the restoration of synods was the essential remedy. He gained Carloman, Charles Martel's son, to the project, and received encouragement from the new Pope Zachary. Four great councils were held between 742 and 744, and through them Boniface, who presided over them as papal legate, drew the Frankish Church out of chaos. The metropolitan hierarchy was re-established: there were to be archbishops at Reims, Sens and Rouen. A council must be held every year. Rigid prescriptions were laid down for the reform of the clergy. Superstition was to be rooted out from the faithful. All these reforms were confirmed at a great council of the Frankish Empire in

747 with Boniface at its head. The council fathers promised life-long obedience to the Pope, unity with the Roman Church and obedience to the canons. This profession of faith was sent to Rome and placed on the tomb of St. Peter, an expression of the unity between the Churches of France and Germany and the Roman See.

After thirty years Boniface's work was done. This great assembly had given a solemn consecration to his life's program. The organization he had striven for was achieved: the bishop at the head of his diocese gathering his clergy round him each year at the diocesan synod; the metropolitan, with his pallium from the Pope, at the head of his province, gathering his bishops round him each year at the provincial synod, and acting as the link with Rome.

Truly the Popes had been wise in choosing their servant. Boniface sent the decrees of the Council to Cuthbert, the Archbishop of Canterbury, and suggested that he should reform his Church in like manner. The advice was taken. The Council of Cliff inaugurated reforms identical, sometimes even in words, with those of the Frankish Council.

While he had been pursuing his work among the Franks Boniface had founded, through the agency of his disciple Sturmi, a monastery in the forest of Buchenau between Hesse and Bavaria. It was an adventurous affair for Sturmi and his companions, and they had many difficulties in the dense forest before they found a suitable site. Finally they discovered the marvelous locality where the abbey of Fulda was eventually built, a vast circular valley cut across by the River Fulda, protected by the Rhone mountains. They cleared the forest and in 744 began to build. Boniface came himself, bringing a number of helpers, and a stone church dedicated to St. Savior was put up. Gradually the great abbey arose, and whenever he could the archbishop would come to watch its progress. He initiated the monks in the Rule of St. Benedict and in the Scriptures, and he introduced total abstinence.

Then he sent Sturmi to study Benedictine observance in the principal religious centers of Italy, especially in Rome and Monte Cassino.

After a year Sturmi returned and was made abbot, and he raised Fulda to rank among the most famous abbeys of Christendom. In his own lifetime it housed over 400 monks. It became a center of German civilization. Boniface loved it: he meant it to continue his work after his death. That is why he secured its exemption from all other authority save that of the Pope. It was situated, he told Pope Zachary, "in the midst of the nations I have evangelized." He wanted to be buried there when he died.

The reform of the Frankish Church had restored the metropolitan jurisdiction, and yet Germany was without a metropolis. In the early days Boniface had had no fixed see in order that he might have freedom to control the entire country. But now that the episcopal organization was completed, there seemed no reason why it should not receive its final complement. Boniface had thought the matter over, and it had been discussed at the Frankish councils. Cologne was the most obvious situation. It was the largest town in Germany; it was a convenient center for apostolic operations in Frisia and Saxony. Pope Zachary agreed to this. But the moment was unpropitious, for the corrupt group in the Frankish clergy, furious at the reforming decrees, made a violent opposition, and succeeded in preventing his enthronement. Not only this, they also succeeded in temporarily ruining the metropolitan organization in Gaul. The Pope had sent the pallium to the three sees, but the Archbishops of Sens and Reims had disappeared. Only the metropolitan of Rouen remained.

It was a severe blow to Boniface. But he made the best of things and chose Mainz as his see. There he found fresh trials. The Saxons, whom from his youth he had hoped to evangelize, burnt down thirty of his churches and slaughtered the faithful. His work was now confined to his diocese, though as papal legate he consecrated King Pepin at Soissons when that prince, by the Pope's decision, superseded the senile Merovingian dynasty. He was now growing very old and obtained Zachary's reluctant permission to consecrate his faithful disciple Lull to be chorepiscopus[1] and later his successor. Pope Zachary died in March, 752, and was succeeded by Stephen III. Boniface sent a letter of filial devotion in 753. When the Pope crossed the Alps in the winter of 753 to secure the aid of the Franks against the Lombards, Boniface was too feeble to go to greet him, and he took this as a sign of his approaching end. He put his affairs in order, committed his diocese to the protection of Pepin, held his last diocesan council, and bade his dearest friends farewell.

It was a strange farewell. This venerable man of over seventy, with a great life's work behind him, was not preparing for a peaceful death in bed. He was a missionary: that had been the dynamic force in all his life: and he was going to die a missionary. He was saying farewell because he was departing, for the last time, to the mission field. Saxony was impossible, so he would go to Frisia where his work had first begun. He embarked on the Rhine with about fifty followers. They came first to Utrecht, where Eoban, Boniface's friend, was bishop. Then they went on into the marshy land beyond. Here were the pagans, and Boniface began his work. He was successful, and converted many. He arranged to hold a confirmation at Dokkum, near the sea, and waited with his followers for the arrival of the neophytes. But in their place there came a band of heathen bent on slaughter. One or two of Boniface's men were armed, but he restrained them. The end was brief. When they rushed at him the saint raised the book he was reading to protect his head. The sword slashed through both book and head, and that great life was over. His body was taken back in triumph to Fulda, and he lies among the nations he evangelized.

1. Editor's Note: Similar to today's auxiliary bishop.

ALCUIN (735–804)

by DOUGLAS WOODRUFF

To MEN WHO LEARNED IN EARLIEST YOUTH TO KNOW and dread Wackford Squeers, the memory of Alcuin should be particularly dear; for he showed, a thousand years before Charles Dickens wrote, that it is possible to be both a Yorkshire schoolmaster and a holy man. An instinct, implanted in parents for a good end, makes them believe that their children will fare best in the hands of teachers who are also, more or less, in Holy Orders; and the prefix "Rev." has always been a marked asset in an educational career, whether to qualify a man for a headmastership or to enable him to start a select preparatory school on the south coast. Today that large and healthy tribe, the schoolmaster-parsons, no longer enjoy quite the monopoly they used to, but they remain a characteristic feature of the English landscape, and can continue to fortify their self-confidence with the knowledge that their pedigree is one of extreme range and extinction, stretching far beyond Dr. Arnold and Dean Colet, and that it contains no name greater than that of Alcuin or Albinus of York, the only Englishman who has been allowed to educate the whole of Europe.

Yet his name means little in the English educational world, and little pride is taken in the fact that this island supplied, from the cathedral school of York, the man who was the chief of the agents of Charlemagne in the great and vital revival of learning which lives in history as the Carolingian Renaissance. Foreign scholars have collected and edited the many writings, the nearly three hundred letters, the biographies and treatises on educational subjects which enable us to know much more about Alcuin than we know about any of his contemporaries except Charlemagne himself. But the two volumes in Migne's *Latin Patrology*, which are wholly occupied with the works of Alcuin, have remained a well in which few Englishmen have troubled to dip a bucket. The English writing on Alcuin is scanty, and so little has he passed into popular knowledge that his name is a name to stump people with, and he remains cloistered from the world in books of reference.

The reasons for this neglect are primarily religious, for no age is harder for a modern Englishman to understand than the eighth century, with its eager scholars, who yet kept all their scholarship so subordinate to their religion. To Alcuin, as to Alfred the Great, study and the pursuit of knowledge was a part of the Christian life, and the liberal arts were not practiced as ends in themselves but as subserving, in one way or another, the great end of enriching the Christian life and advancing in the understanding of revelation. Of the seven liberal arts which were the basis of education, only geometry lacked a clear and immediate connection with the Church. Grammar, dialectic, rhetoric, all three were the training for the preacher and the apologist. Music was for the better worship of God, and astronomy and arithmetic had no higher use, though they had other uses, than to enable the feasts of the ecclesiastical year to be correctly placed. A liberal education in Alcuin's day was the prelude to theology, not a way of turning men away from theology forever. It was not that there reigned in the minds of the leading educationalists of those times any narrowly utilitarian view of their tasks that would have made them treat theology as later generations have treated the study of natural science, or that they made their sovereign study their sole one also, but that their lives were ordered to a known end. Those who in modern seats of learning preach and practice the study of humanities have no such clear end, and even those who would not prefer that their pupils should come to accept the mood of Horace rather than that of Alcuin part company very soon from the eighth century. Yet there should be a keener sense of filial piety towards the men to whose labors we owe the preservation of Virgil and Cicero and nearly all the poets and prose writers of ancient Rome, except Catullus and Seneca and Tacitus.

Alcuin was born at York about the year 735. He was by birth of noble family, and one of his kinsmen was the Apostle of Frisia, St. Willibrord, whose life he wrote. But his spiritual descent is more distinguished, for the teachers who brought him up were themselves the pupils of St. Bede. Egbert, Archbishop of York and brother to the king, and his kinsman and successor Albert were the men who educated Alcuin and made the school and library at York. Albert made constant journeys to Europe for books, and he used to take Alcuin with him.

When Egbert died and Albert became archbishop, Alcuin became librarian; and when, in the fashion common among these men, Albert himself resigned his see to give himself a final period of cloistral retirement he called for his two favorite pupils and designated Eanbald to take over the diocese and Alcuin to take over the library. This famous collection of books, containing both the ancients and the Christian fathers, was the basis of Alcuin's learning, and he pays warm and vigorous tribute, in letters written years later, to all that the school of York meant to him.

It was in 781, when Alcuin was in his middle forties, that he met Charlemagne at Parma. Alcuin had just been to Rome to visit the Pope on behalf of his friend, the new Archbishop of York. He had met Charlemagne before, and his own fame as a teacher and scholar was by now well established. Charlemagne begged his assistance in the great business of spreading a knowledge of letters among the Franks, and in the following year Alcuin emigrated from York to France, taking with him several of the best scholars of York. He received three abbeys for the support of himself and his scholars, and Charlemagne continued for the next twenty years to give him all the material support he could need. But it was more important that Charlemagne himself became Alcuin's first pupil and set an example, together with his family, that no one should think himself above the pursuit of knowledge.

From the first Alcuin busied himself with editing as well as with teaching, because texts that were copied by hand easily became corrupt. Where there was little enthusiasm for learning, listless monks would copy manuscripts in a happy-go-lucky fashion, profoundly bored by the monotonous task assigned them by their superiors, and perhaps relieving their boredom by taking liberties with their texts. Alcuin found that in the realms ruled by Charles there were few good manuscripts of even the most essential service books, and his first task was to correct the books of Gospels and Epistles. He then set out on the great task of preparing a better text of the whole Bible. He was able to send to Charlemagne, in the auspicious year 800, when the Pope crowned the king as Emperor of the West, a complete Bible collated and purged from textual corruption. (This Bible still exists in Rome.)

The thoroughness and practicality of Alcuin's work is well displayed in the care he devoted to raising the standard of copyists as well as the amount of copying done. He would first of all himself revise the manuscript to be copied; picked scribes would then make copies which were distributed to the monasteries for further copies to be made. In this way libraries gradually grew up all over Western Europe, with books all originating with the court and court school of Charlemagne.

Alcuin wrote detailed rules for the guidance of the monks who were to copy the manuscripts, dealing particularly with the pitfalls of spelling and the difficult business of putting in the stops. A new handwriting came into use, and the manuscripts thus produced, of writers as little religious as Terence as well as of the fathers, have remained the great watershed to which textual criticism mounts. Many monks, copying out an uncongenial and very long work by an involved father, must have felt much less warmly towards Alcuin than we do today, and have seen with little enthusiasm how copying was taking root as a normal part of a monk's life. But it was also recognized that copying was obviously a work of charity and could be offered as a work of penance. "Lines" have always been a favorite form of scholastic punishment.

More spectacular was Alcuin's work as head master of the school which Charlemagne established and took with him when he moved his court, as he was forever doing. One of the pupils, from the country towards the Saxon border, by name Einhard, became the close confidant and secretary of the emperor and after his death wrote his biography. He has left a vivid picture of Alcuin's school. Such schools attached to courts were not novelties, but they had commonly troubled their pupils but little and had been ways of keeping the children of court officials and nobles safely supervised.

Schools are made by their heads, and education under Alcuin and Charlemagne was something strenuous and new. We read how Charles himself had a disconcerting habit of playing the part of school inspector, appearing suddenly and calling upon some random youth to say his lesson. At Alcuin's, as at later schools, there was a noticeable lack of performance on the part of the more nobly-born boys, who thought they need not trouble, but who were vigorously undeceived by Charles, who told them that he would reserve the first division posts for those with distinguished academic records, or words to that effect.

But a student, in proportion as he advanced, would find his days increasingly devoted to theology, and the memorable names among the pupils of Alcuin are the names of churchmen and monks. They belong, too, to the later years of his life when he dwelt at Tours, at the Abbey of St. Martin, which Charlemagne had given him, and conducted his own school there. It was in a way the most important thing which he did, because this school became the model of all monastic schools, as his pupils passed from his hands to become in due course head masters and abbots themselves.

Monasticism in England was passing from the vigor of the eighth century to the decline of the ninth. A hundred years after Alcuin and the glories of York, King Alfred was to be scouring what remained of Anglo Saxon England for learned men and to be finding the search much harder and more ungrateful than Charlemagne had done, when, on a similar quest, he had discovered Alcuin. But before the darkness of the ninth century England bequeathed through Alcuin the living example of the monastic school of Bede.

At Tours, Alcuin remained the friend and adviser of Charlemagne. He writes constantly to him, calling him "David" by a literary convention which is almost a mark of a literary renaissance by which scholars choose new and storied names to address each other by. Often the letters are concerned with the intellectual and theological interests of the king, but they deal also with the highest political matters and in particular with the state of the Church.

Alcuin's prestige as the adviser of Charlemagne, his past record, his spirituality, even the fact that Charles himself was no longer at hand to pale all other personalities by his presence, all combined to make Alcuin at Tours into a legend in his lifetime. Scholars flocked to him, particularly from his own country, and to have been the pupil of one of his pupils is a source of pride half a century later. The monks who had been sent by their abbots to study under Alcuin at Tours were marked out for important duties when they returned, and a few instances will show how the school of Tours continued its influence.

Thus Alcuin's favorite pupil, Rabanus Maurus, came to him from the famous monastery of Fulda in Germany. This monastery had been founded by St. Boniface himself to assist in the evangelization of the Germanic peoples, and in the fullness of time it played a great part. Rabanus Maurus—it was Alcuin who called him Maurus, and he retained the name—was recalled to his monastery in 803, the year before his master died. He was placed in charge of the abbey school with the order from his abbot not to deviate from the methods of Alcuin, and he attained great success because, in the manner of Alcuin himself, he grounded his pupils with great thoroughness in grammar. The school grew rapidly in fame and numbers, while Rabanus became abbot in 822 and Archbishop of Mainz in 847.

Among his pupils was a monk of Ferrières named Lupus, whose own abbot Sigulf, had been Alcuin's pupil. Lupus himself became abbot in due course and trained up another generation of monastic scholars. One of these, Hieric, taught St. Remigius of Auxerre, who was the great light of the tenth century and revived Tours as an educational center and finally established the schools of Rheims and Paris. His influence was comparable to that of Alcuin a hundred years before, and among those who came to receive from his hands the educational tradition which he had inherited was the young Odo who was to become St. Odo of Cluny, the founder of the reformed Cluniac order.

These names are but a handful from a heap, written here to show how widespread and continuing was the influence of Alcuin. In the ninth century, it is not too much to say, every monastery counted in the battle to save learning and humane interests. The Saracen marauders all around the Mediterranean and the Northmen who came up all the rivers of northern and western Europe wrought such destruction that no part of Europe was safe. The safest part, the region that is northern Switzerland today, where the great monasteries of St. Gall and Reichenau stood, was invaded a little later, in the tenth century, by the Mongols. Hardly a monastery in Europe but was devastated by one or other of these pagan bands. Much of the laborious copying of manuscripts proved but wasted labor and was destroyed in the conflagrations which marked the trails of the barbarians.

Not less disastrous was the destruction of continuity. Studies could not flourish in an atmosphere of peril. It was the dictum of St.

Edmund of Abingdon that a man should live as though he were going to die tomorrow, but study as though he were going to live forever. It was much easier for a monk of the ninth century to follow the first of these sayings. An obsession with material things or a concentration upon the sheerly spiritual were both nourished by the prevailing insecurity. What was not nourished was the patient building-up, in individuals or in schools, of a mastery of the arts and a foundational knowledge. That these proved to be sufficient, to the great good fortune of succeeding generations, was in large measure due to the vigorous use which Charlemagne and Alcuin had made of their good years, to the number of monasteries permeated by their influence, to the thorough training which placed, even in small religious houses, men able to carry on Alcuin's educational methods.

Those methods were excellently adapted to stand the coming strain. Alcuin was not a particularly original man. He was the teacher, not the original worker. His own mastery of the accomplishment of scholarship was workmanlike, not exquisite. Although he wrote poetry he is not remembered as a poet; his versification was but a facile means of expression, sometimes for teaching, at other times as an exercise in fancy, or as a little gift to please a friend. His predilection is for flowery compliments and ornate phraseology, and his letters to his friends often say surprisingly little in view of the distance such letters had to travel and the difficulty of sending them. He is content to write the most general exhortations and to wrap up simple sentiments in an elaborate garb of ceremonious and often fulsome flattery. These habits and tricks of speech have made his more literary writings unattractive to later generations, more displeased by crude prosody than interested in the life of which such letters afford us glimpses. But this convention of affectation in Alcuin's style must not be allowed to obscure his greatness as an educator, a clear sighted trainer of men whose symbol might well be the clear neat handwriting which his celebrated scriptorium made the standard for Europe for centuries. Where there had been darkness and confusion and weakness of purpose he brought an ordered lucidity, in life as on parchment.

He was zealous, so wide was his range, to collect and preserve the vernacular speech of the new peoples who came under Charlemagne's sway, being true in this to the tradition of Bede. Charlemagne, like Alfred after him, had this same desire to make education extramural, and to extend, beyond the cloisters and the few who knew Latin, some deeper knowledge of the Gospels and Epistles at least. The collecting of material for vernacular grammars and translations was a side of the educational work of the emperor which came to nothing after his death, for his son, Louis the Pious, destroyed the collection of German songs because they were full of the pagan gods; but Alcuin's interest bears further witness both to his wide vision and to his immediate practical view and educational effort.

Although he has attained his place in history as the leader of an educational renaissance, his resemblance to the typical scholar is only in superficial things. That he and Charlemagne and their friends should take new Latin names may remind us of the fifteenth and sixteenth century scholars—ashamed of the barbarism of their own good names—but these indulgences were for Alcuin and Charlemagne the little luxuries of men grimly preoccupied in a great struggle.

They were themselves, these makers of the Carolingian renaissance, not many generations away from paganism. The conversion of the Roman Empire, the steady spread of the faith through the second, and still more through the third, century, which paved the way for Constantine, is less startling than the subsequent successive conversions of the barbarian peoples. What the Angles and Franks had done, the Saxons and the Normans were to do, burning what they had adored, and adoring what they had burned. Alcuin and Charlemagne strove with book and sword to convert the Saxons, and felt the first rumblings of the storm the Northmen were to bring. Yet in a little over a century, could they have seen the future, those two barbarian peoples would be the foremost champions of the Christian creed, making of Saxony and Normandy the pillars of Christendom. But that future they could not see, and they only knew, as Alcuin in his letters is forever saying, that their lot was cast in a dark time.

To us, who know how rapidly the times were to grow worse, such phrases seem conventional. But to Alcuin the world was very evil, the imperial power corrupt and enfeebled at Byzantium, the papal power torn by faction in Rome, and the strong authority of Charlemagne the only foundation upon which to build. He wrote of the Holy See, "which judges all others and is judged by none," in words which make vain any attempts to claim him as an early Gallican or Anglican or as an opponent or belittler of the Papacy. But he took a very high view of the divine right of Charlemagne, and urged him not to shirk the largest responsibilities. In his letters we can see emerging the double conception of spiritual and temporal power which was to dominate Europe for centuries. But he withdrew himself from great affairs. His own tasks were more immediate, and he was neither a statesman nor a political theorist, but an educator attaining great practical results by faithfulness in little things and the planning and execution of year to year tasks.

He is among the more human and natural in the Church's roll-call of holy men, a man whose letters are interspersed with regrets that he is not in England, where he could get the good wine he cannot get—it is nearly twelve hundred years ago—in France. A contemporary, Theodulf, has left in a convivial poem describing the court circle of Charlemagne, a word picture of Alcuin. He gives us the picture of a large and hearty man, fond of the table and of talking loud and long. Alcuin had indeed a great gusto, which was one secret of his hold over his pupils, and particularly over his fellow Anglians, who flocked in such numbers to Tours that some local ill-feeling was aroused. But whatever he was by nature, he became by grace, as his life advanced, a man given over more and more completely to the supernatural life. From the time of his retirement to Tours his life was one preparation for death, and it is not surprising that he passed from his earlier love for the writers of pagan antiquity to a feeling that only too easily they became a hindrance to the soul and a bypath luring men from their appointed road.

It is to these later years that there belongs his letter to that favorite disciple, Sigulf, afterwards abbot of Ferrières, in which he recommends him to study scriptures rather than "the impure eloquence of Virgil," and that he reproved the Archbishop of Mainz for carrying Virgil about in his tunic instead of the Gospels. His whole life shows him to have been the least narrow of men, but he never, like so many later educationalists, failed to see the wood for the trees, or lost sight of his goal or confused his means with his end. He was a great teacher, not only of the seven liberal arts, but of the Christian life which those arts exist to serve, and so set his seal upon many of the foremost men of the next generation that his influence endured and he takes rank among the men to whom all Europe has been to school.

ALFRED THE GREAT (849–901)

by G. K. CHESTERTON

ALFRED OF WESSEX, ONE OF THE FIRST FOUR OR FIVE great men of the Dark Ages, was born in Wantage about the middle of the ninth century, probably in 849. He comes on the field of history, then almost continuously a field of battle, from under the shadow of the shield of Ethelred, his elder brother, already at war with the invading Danes; and there is always something about him indescribably humble and handy, like one who unpretentiously hammers away at an inherited task; a quality not at all inconsistent, but rather specially consistent, with his strong twist of personal originality.

All his house was devoted to the Catholic faith; but Alfred was a sort of accident, who added to that devotion a dexterity and military instinct which saved it, apparently against all the chances of war. Thus it was he, while still a cadet, who really won the Battle of Ashdown against the barbarians, while his royal brother was praying in his tent; and it is supremely typical of the time that the chronicler records the victory and says that it was doubtless due to the prayers of Ethelred. Various victories and defeats followed; until the whole barbarian invasion gathered itself into one vast wave under Guthrum out of East Anglia and swept the West Country from end to end like a sea, leaving Alfred clinging, as it were, to an islet in the pool of Athelney, and waiting for better times.

He gradually gathered round him the remnants of the Christian population, and in the spring of 878 appeared suddenly with an army before the Danish camp at Ethandune, possibly Edington; smashed in their palisades, captured their royal leader and his raven banner, and imposed on him the famous treaty of Wedmore, by which he and his people were baptized and withdrew their forces from Wessex, retaining only lands further to the north and east.

The rest of the story is sufficiently familiar; fresh outbreaks among the barbarians led to his extending his power over London and establishing a small navy in the Channel; and even obtaining a certain indefinite suzerainty over the north. But his best work was internal rather than external; and perhaps the best of all was the part that was purely educational. He clarified and codified the best laws of the West Saxon tradition; but he became a more important sort of legislator in the moral sphere when he translated Boethius for his people, with very characteristic additions of his own; and so brought into England the full tradition of Europe; the tradition of the Christian Creed resting upon the pagan culture. He had been troubled all his life with a recurrent and rather mysterious disease; and he died at the early age of fifty-two, in the first year of the new century. The night of the barbarian peril was already over, and he died in the dawn.

A thousand years of thanks and praise have rightly concentrated upon Alfred a light of unique and universal admiration. From the first words of the Anglo-Saxon Chronicle to the last wireless messages to the Anglo-Saxon clubs and dinners in Boston or Philadelphia, there has been a chiming unanimity, a chain of polite or popular compliment, in which there is actually no break at all. A Scottish rationalist like Hume, a romantic Tory like Scott, a Voltairean sceptic like Gibbon, a prudent Catholic like Lingard, an imprudent pro-Catholic like Cobbett, a practical and (spiritually) rather stupid Protestant like Macaulay, would all at any moment have testified to the solid and unquestioned moral reputation of Alfred. Men by the modern time had come to call him The Great; which was perhaps the only really true thing they knew about him. Everybody agreed to call him Great; and nothing perhaps has so completely obscured his greatness. He is one of two or three men who have been nearly obliterated by praise.

It would have been better for him, in the long run, or at least for his significance, if he had happened to be a cleric like Dunstan, that other maker of England in the Dark Ages; and so become, for a few foolish centuries, the butt of all the ravings of the anti-clerical superstition. Then there would have been subsequently, or eventually, a sort of excitement in digging him up from among the dead, and proving that he was not so unmistakably among the damned; the sort of pleasure felt by Ruskin or Rossetti in rediscovering medieval beauty in what had always been counted medieval ugliness. There would have been a thrill for the first Victorian thinker who maintained the paradox that a saint could be a good man. His real personality would probably be more vivid to us if he had been denounced by Hume and derided by Gibbon, and his real virtues dramatically rediscovered by Maitland or by Gasquet.

It would have been better for him, in the same sense if he had lived a few centuries earlier, when the night of barbarism was denser, as did the mysterious Arthur; so that sceptics might turn him into a myth and romancers into a romance. Then he, too, might have lingered in florid old French love stories merely as a jealous husband; until modern research re-established him for the first time as a just ruler. In that case, again, the good might have been interred with his bones in the ninth century and never dug up again till the nineteenth. The disclosing and cleansing of such sacred relics might almost have awakened a part of the interest accorded to the chips off the skeleton of a hypothetical ape. Or again, it might have been better for him in this sense if he had been a foreigner, even a great foreigner like Charlemagne; who from the first, however much he was admired, aroused that insular subconscious suspicion of any attempt to reunite Europe;

hating it if it excluded England; hating it more if it included England. So, when our national mood was narrowest, we hated in Austria even the flat and fading shadow of the Holy Roman Empire; and in Napoleon hated more vividly the return of the Romans. Then, once more, there might have been a belated understanding after a long misunderstanding; just as many are doing justice to the Austrian system after it has been destroyed; and there are even signs of a faint effort to be fair to Napoleon.

But Alfred was picked out from the first by converging and unwavering beams of the limelight of conventional laudation; he stands in a dazzling light that hides him like darkness; he is covered with a sort of white radiance that has all the effect of whitewash, and which has hidden from generations of the readers of our history the least notion of the twilight in which he really wandered and the light by which he was really led.

Perhaps the best stage of the story was that of the old chronicles, which duly and dully recorded good and bad kings; and very correctly recorded Alfred among the good. After that came a more narrow national motive, natural enough, but not exactly impartial, which presented Alfred as the inventor of the British Navy and the University of Oxford; and for twopence would have presented him as the inventor of the Union Jack and the Boat Race. But the patriotic partisanship which expressed the natural pride of a nation was a far finer and healthier thing than that queer and pedantic fashion which proclaimed only the pride of a race. Alfred really was in many ways extremely English, as we shall observe later; but, anyhow, he certainly was born in the British Isles and might be said to stand at the beginning of the British Empire. But, from the way the Victorian historians talked about Teutons and Saxons and the Germanic institutions, one might really suppose that Alfred was standing at the beginning of the German Empire. The whole thing was founded on a false conception of history; which supposed such a period to be the beginning of a glorious German or Germanic expansion, instead of the end and ebb of the old Roman expansion. Because it happens to be the beginning of our particular national history it is treated as if it were the morning of the world. The men who lived in that time felt it as the evening of the world; not to say the end of the world. And the greatest of the men who lived in that time certainly cannot be understood if that fact is not understood.

But in the familiar picture everything is accentuated that suggests only the new Nordic adventure. King Alfred confronts us, blonde and bland, with the battle-axe and helmet of a Viking, but the face of a rather sleepy Quaker; ready to found Christianity, cricket, the Anglo-Saxon race, the Anglo-American alliance, the Boy Scouts, or anything else that may require a friendly person in the ninth century to found it. Now, nobody in the ninth century, however friendly, felt in the least like that. It was not even anything so bright as the beginning of barbarism; it was, to all appearance, simply the end of civilization. In some ways, and especially in some places, it was even the end of over-civilization. The importance of Boethius is symbolic; the last of the old sages; the scholarly servant who already has a savage master.

But Alfred was not himself of the type that indicates merely a lusty or even a normal time. He was as brave as a lion and as wary as a wild fox; but he had nothing whatever of the serenity and solidity that makes up the perfect ideal of the Blonde Beast. He was an original as well as an origin. There is something even of the eccentric about him, evidently catching the memories of men when they speak of his speeches and actions; his abrupt and casual confession of mortal sins in his youth, long after they had doubtless been normally absolved; his abstractions and absences, due probably to the unknown disease that struck him on his wedding-day; presumably something convulsive or epileptic; anyhow, something isolating him from mere social routine. His outlook also was individual rather than racial or national; his additions to Boethius show how vividly he understood the vital issue of his age. "I say, as do all Christian men, that it is a Divine providence that rules, and not Fate." Then, even more than at most times, the fight with heathenism was the fight with fatalism. It was all the more so because all the Fates seemed to be on the side of all the heathens. In Christian psychology, if there were nothing else, Alfred is the type of a wiry and tenacious will, that wears down even Fate; for what we call Fate is only the fashion of this world that passes away, if any man can wait for it to pass.

But Alfred had no clear notion of what civilization he was founding; but only of what civilization his enemies were destroying. The real moral of his story is a moral for moderns. He himself lived in a world very like the modern world; that is, a world that had become much too ancient. Intelligent men like Alfred looked at that time on barbarism very much as many now look on Bolshevism: believing it to be wrong, but very much doubting whether it would be practically proved wrong, so far as anything can be proved by mere success. The Christian system was already coming within a century of its first thousand years; and many doubted whether it was not dying, as they do now, within a century of its two thousand years. The encouraging quality in the story of Alfred is the testimony to Christian tenacity in the face of such recurrent threats of decline. The final triumph of heathenism is not so near to us now as it was to him then. As he weathered the storm then, we have every reason to hope that we shall weather it now. But it was a very weather-beaten seaman who weathered it; and one wrinkled with the old age of the old civilization; a man not without subtlety and quite without optimism; a true genius of the ninth century.

So much it is necessary to say to wash away the vapid figure of facile virtue which was set up by the theorists of Germanic or Anglo-Saxon progress. But, inside all these things, there is a truth that is true in a much more subtle manner than they could understand. When all is said and confessed and contradicted, Alfred of Wessex is very English; not Anglo-Saxon or Saxon, but English; and he is a sort of testimony showing how early something distinctive in our insular culture had begun. It is very difficult to define these things in prose;

it would be better to attempt to describe them in poetry. But in all his policy we can see something that is a positive quality, though it might seem to some a negative lack of a quality. Perhaps the shortest description is a lack of the imperial logic. He had very little of that notion of rounding everything and everybody up in the circle of an *orbis terrarum*, which affected most followers of the Roman Empire, even when they dealt with something smaller. There is something in his action that smacks of the opportunist and patchy colonization of a commercial empire. He calculates how much he can certainly recover from the Danes; how much he can safely leave to them; and cares little for the mathematical unity of the pattern. He is conscious of achieving a broader kingdom, rather than of accepting a narrower empire. He is content to make Wessex wider; and has no appetite to make the world smaller. He would never have failed through a fatal afterthought of rounding off his work, as Napoleon failed by trying to round it off with Russia and Spain. His experiments are English experiments; especially in the fact of remaining experimental. There are many other aspects suggesting the same thing; as in the readiness with which tradition connected his name with legends of lonely adventure or casual human contact. It has truly been said that the story of the cakes would not have been told about a man without humor. But especially was he English in his relation to that great reality which can be real to all Europeans and to all human beings, and which yet realizes itself in forms so different and distinguished.

He was, if ever there was one, an English Catholic. He was supremely the type that proves to the world what is called a fanatical fixity of faith without fanaticism. He was of the type in which solitary and supernatural conviction expresses itself in energy, but not often in ecstasy. There is a sense in which it is true to say that, when once a man is a Catholic, he has no more need to be a mystic. In that sense, properly limited and understood, Alfred was all the more an English Catholic, because he only knew he was a Catholic and did not know he was an Englishman.

I was walking the other day round his statue that stands at Wantage, and reflecting that but for him not one of the things now standing there would exist at all. In the ninth century it was very doubtful whether there ever would be any Western civilization at all. It was quite probable that the wild Western lands would be left for dead and Continental culture turn eastward to Byzantium and Asia; with what consequences none can say. And if there had never been any monasteries or camps or cathedrals, there would certainly never have been any shops or hotels or petrol-stations. But I doubt if anybody but myself was at that moment looking at the statue, or even realizing the fact. Still, the statues are still standing in Wantage and Winchester; unless they have been since removed for the convenience of motorists.

SAINT WULSTAN OF WORCHESTER (1008–1095)

by DAVID KNOWLES, O.S.B.

SOME TWO OR THREE YEARS AGO THE COURSE OF MY reading took me to St. Wulstan, and to his Life, written by his English chaplain, Coleman, re-written by the great historian, William of Malmesbury, and printed in full for the first time in 1928.[1] Till then, I had only known the main facts of Wulstan's career, and I was not prepared for the revelation of his character that the Life gives. "Here is indeed a great saint," was my first thought; and then: "Here is indeed a great Englishman."

English indeed Wulstan was, by nature and by contrast. Let us take the contrast first, for it is the more familiar. Since our national history began, the course of English life has only twice been violently wrenched out of the straight—at the Norman Conquest and at the Reformation—and of the two, the Norman Conquest was the most complete break with the past in all save religious belief. Culture, the legal fabric, the social fabric, even the language, were all changed or modified profoundly, and within fifteen years of the Conquest almost every position of importance, temporal and spiritual, was held by a Norman invader.

Only one Englishman remained in the position he had held in 1066; not under a cloud, but with his reputation enhanced. Wulstan,

Bishop of Worcester, survived the Conquest, and survived it for almost thirty years, and while he acquiesced in the fact and indeed supported the Conqueror and was trusted both by him and his new Primate, Lanfranc, he remained a center of English thought and literature till his death. Only at Worcester do we find the transcription of Anglo-Saxon homilies after 1066; and Wulstan's *Life* by Coleman, written in English, is the last great prose work (exclusive of additions to the *Anglo-Saxon Chronicle*) to be written before English, as a literary language, was submerged, first beneath Latin and then beneath French.

And Wulstan was English by nature. Hard as they are to define, certain bold national characteristics are recognized by everyone when they are present in strength in some great character. Geoffrey Chaucer, Thomas More, William Shakespeare and Samuel Johnson are as clearly English as Jeanne d'Arc and Blaise Pascal are French, and John of the Cross and Ignatius Loyola Spanish. And different as Wulstan is from More or Johnson, he is clearly of their stock.

Like Shakespeare, Wulstan was born in the heart of England. His native village, whether Long Itchington or Bishop's Itchington, is within a few miles of the oak which boasts that it is the center of England, and within a few miles of the spire of Stratford-on-Avon. From the high ground there one looks over the vale of Evesham to the Malverns and Cotswolds that Wulstan knew so well on his bishop's visitations. He found his schooling, too, in the heart of England—first in the abbey of Evesham, which, with those round it, had not suffered from the decline that came to many in England at that time; and then in the abbey of Peterborough, which, so a chronicler tells us, was still called "golden town," by reason of its beauty and prosperity. Soon after his first return home he followed his father and mother

1. *The Vita Wulfstani of William of Malmesbury.* Edited by R. R. Darlington (Camden Society, Vol. XL, 1928). In the pages which follow I owe almost everything to Mr. Darlington's text and his excellent notes and introduction. I have throughout retained the current, less correct, spelling of the saint's name.

to Worcester, where both had entered monasteries, and became a member of the bishop's household. The bishop chose him for ordination, and for a short time he was the parish priest of Hawkesbury in Gloucestershire; then he became a monk in the cathedral priory of Worcester, which had been founded *c.* 970 by St. Oswald, the master of Wulstan's own father. The priory was small, and Wulstan, after passing through the offices of schoolmaster, precentor and sacristan, became prior at the age of forty. Under his rule the priory prospered temporally and spiritually; he won back many a village in the Severn valley which had been seized by the great laymen of the district, and he increased the number of monks; we are told that as prior he used to stand daily at the door of the church to give counsel to all who wished it; he preached to the people and baptized the children of the poor; men came from afar as penitents to him, and among them the great, such as Earl Harold.

In 1060 the Bishop of Worcester became Archbishop of York, and the two cardinals sent by Pope Nicholas II to arrange, among other duties, for his successor, spent a Lent as guests of Wulstan at Worcester. The prior's sanctity so impressed them that they recommended his appointment to the king, St. Edward, and Wulstan was consecrated at York in 1062, being about fifty-five years old. From henceforth till his death his life was one of almost incessant travel and activity. His diocese stretched south to Bristol, and eastwards over the Cotswolds and Warwickshire, and he was tireless in his visitations. Beyond this, he was constantly employed afield. Immediately after his consecration he was left in charge of the archdiocese of York, and later in 1072 he was given the administration of the diocese of Chester. We find him, before the Conquest, in the north, trying to induce the northerners to accept Harold as king, and in 1075 and 1088 he was actively engaged in suppressing the revolts of the barons against the Conqueror and Rufus.

William recognized his worth at once, and so, after hesitation, did Lanfranc, and councils in the early part of the Conqueror's reign, and courts throughout his reign and his son's, meant never-ending travel. At the age of eighty and more, Wulstan appears as witness to a royal charter at Dover, and his life is full of incidents of travel—now at Nottingham, now at Shrewsbury, now at Wycombe, now at Winchester. Like his Norman fellow bishops, he was a builder, and besides new churches throughout his diocese he rebuilt his cathedral at Worcester, and the crypt of his building still remains. He re-founded the priory of Westbury-on-Trym, and founded that of Great Malvern in what was then a wild and desolate district. Indeed, in an age of great bishops—of Lanfranc, of St. Osmund of Salisbury, of William of Durham, of Remigius of Lincoln—Wulstan of Worcester was second to none as an administrator, and foremost among all in sanctity. He died, aged probably eighty-seven, on January 20, 1095.

So far we have seen but the outside of the bishop, and a similar record might be made of many others of his century. Let us now look at the saint as he is shown us by a disciple whose account can often be checked by other documents and who is scrupulous in giving the witnesses of the events he relates.

Wulstan was not one of those saints whom God calls from a life of sin to sanctity. Grace gave him holiness young. Strikingly handsome as a boy, and an adept at field-sports, he felt the temptation to impurity as St. Benedict before him and St. Thomas Aquinas after him, and, as with them, his resolute turning from the semblance of sin was rewarded by God by an extraordinary outpouring of grace. Henceforward, he never felt the slightest prick of such temptations, and as a bishop he was wont to encourage others by the story of his own experience, so suiting his words, we are told, as to fit the age and circumstances of his penitents. Somewhat similar was his conquest of gluttony in the incident which, in legendary form, is all that many know of him. When he was a young priest at Hawkesbury his servants prepared a rich goose for his meal. Wulstan was not, as the story goes, saying mass, but absorbed in watching the preparations. At the last moment important business took him away before dinner was served;

the sudden disappointment brought home to him his momentary extravagance of thought, and he resolved thenceforth never to eat flesh-meat. As a young monk—again like so many of the saints—his prayers and penances were drastic in their intensity. We are told that every day he recited the penitential psalms with a pause at each verse and by night the longest of all the psalms, *Beati immaculati in via*; he slept often before the altar with his head on the altar step, or on the boards, with a manuscript for pillow.

Maturity, and the settled perfection of virtue, seems to have brought with it a marvelous blending of sanity and heroism. We have a number of personal details. His clothes as a bishop were simple, but not ostentatiously poor. When the worldly prelate, Geoffrey of Coutances, asked him why he wore woollen rather than the sables or fox-skins of other high dignitaries, he replied that statesmen might wear the skins of animals whose wit they matched; he was simple and would show it by his clothes. When Geoffrey urged that even the common cat-skin was better than lamb's-wool, Wulstan, with a laugh, remarked that the cat, so far as he knew, was not a liturgical animal, was not, like the lamb, a type of Christ. He dined, on principle, not alone but with his knights, eating a little fish, but by preference vegetables; a book was read in Latin, and then the bishop turned it into English for his retinue; afterwards, beer and mead were passed round, and only the cupbearer knew that Wulstan drank water.

Wherever he was, at Worcester, on a visitation, or on a journey, he always said the morning Office with his clerks in the nearest church, in spite of evil weather and miry ways. We are told of one occasion, at Marlow, when his clerks tried to dissuade him and then purposely led him into a bog; the bishop lost a boot, but had his way. He heard two masses every day before saying his own, and when travelling recited the psalms, the litany of the saints, and the Office of the dead; he refused to enter an inn before he had visited the neighboring church. Whenever and wherever he heard of a death, he caused those about him to say an Our Father, while he himself recited three psalms, and on every day but Sunday and the great feasts he had a mass of the dead celebrated. Out of devotion to our Lady he said her Office daily. It is surely characteristic that the only saints mentioned in his Life are the three great Englishmen—Bede, in whose honor he dedicated a church the day after his own consecration; and Dunstan and Oswald, whose Lives he carried with him as encouragement during his crucial trial before Lanfranc.

As a bishop he loved above all to preach on peace, and taught his chaplains to do the same—the peace of Christ, the chronicler tells us, sung by the angels at Bethlehem and given by the Lord to his disciples as he went to the Cross. From all over England penitents came to him, willing to tell to him what they would tell to no one else, for he never showed the least surprise or coldness at the heaviest story of sin and those who had once confessed to him were his friends ever after.

We have seen how his clerks were taught to follow his manner of life; that they loved him deeply is sufficiently shown by Coleman's zeal in preserving the memorials of his bishop. He had besides in his household a number of boys of noble family. Purity and gentleness were what he best loved to teach them; every day he taught them to wait on the poor whom he entertained, washing their hands and laying their table; the least service to the poor, he told them, was an act of honor to our Lord.

Coleman tells us that Wulstan's affection for these boys was deep, showing itself in a fatherly caress which recalls the gesture of Socrates passing Phaedo's golden hair through his hands when he sat weeping at his feet on the day the master was to drink the hemlock.[2] Nobility of feature, the bishop was fond of saying, was an earnest of nobility

2. That Wulstan's affection had nothing of weakness in it, is seen from another characteristic trait. He detested the long hair affected by the luxurious Saxons just before the Conquest. Whenever opportunity offered, he took out a small knife which he carried about him and with which he pared his nails and scraped parchment clean; with this he cut off a lock of the offending hair and laid the owner under obedience to cut the rest.

of character, and he added: "If God's creatures have such beauty, what must their Creator be!" One in particular, a young Saxon noble, Nicholas, owed everything to Wulstan. He was the son of friends of the bishop. Wulstan had baptized him, taught him letters, and then sent him to Canterbury to be finished by Lanfranc. He returned to Worcester and made its school second to none in England; he became at last prior of the cathedral monastery. He knew and loved the bishop more than all the rest and treasured his lightest words—among others these. As a young man he began to lose his hair, and when once Wulstan was affectionately caressing his forehead with his hand, Nicholas said laughingly to him: "You do your best to save my hair, but it is all disappearing." "No," answered the bishop, "not so. I tell you that so long as I live you shall not be wholly bald." His words came true, Coleman adds; Nicholas had hair over his forehead till the week in which the bishop died.

To anyone who has read the *Life* and loved its subject, the beautiful vales of Evesham and Gloucester will always recall Wulstan's journeys. Even in his day the district was one of rich orchards and harvests. The vines grown near Cheltenham rivalled—so William of Malmesbury tells us—those of France; the roads (as we learn from the story of one of Wulstan's miracles) were hedged and ran between plantations of fruit trees. Within the diocese were the great monasteries of Evesham, Gloucester, Winchcombe and Pershore, not to speak of the decaying Deerhurst and the newcomer Tewkesbury. The bishop was tireless in his visitations, and covered his diocese every year. At his exhortation new churches were erected, old ones repaired. He preached and confirmed without ceasing; we are told that often he confirmed two thousand, sometimes as many as three thousand in a single day, and if these figures (though Coleman had his witnesses for them) are an exaggeration, yet his statement that the bishop always confirmed fasting and spent the whole day at his task, sometimes tiring out eight successive clerks who were carrying the chrism for him, must be taken as literally true.

When he succeeded to the see of Worcester, almost all the altars in the country churches were of wood. Wulstan resolved to replace them all with stone, and while the change was in progress often consecrated two stones in two or three separate villages on the same day. It might indeed have been said of him that he loved the beauty of the house of God. He never passed a church on his travels without entering it to pray; we read of him in the little village of Blockley, in Worcestershire, on a Low Sunday, distressed to find domestic candlesticks, crooked tapers and dirty linen in the church; at Worcester, even as bishop, he used to go behind badly-dressed monks to set their habits in order and smooth out the creases. Above all, he loved chastity, and here he was relentless with those of his clergy who, like so many priests in the eleventh century, lived as though married. They must choose, he said, between their women and their churches; they could not have both. In this, it is probably safe to say that Wulstan was clearer in statement and more decisive in action than any other contemporary bishop in England.

His greatest act of reform has yet to be mentioned. The inhabitants of Bristol, then the chief port of communication with Ireland, had long been engaged in the slave-trade. Young men and girls were brought from all over England and sold to Irish masters. Even the efforts of the Normans were unavailing to check the crime. Wulstan set himself perseveringly to the task. He stayed long months in the neighborhood of Bristol again and again, going to the town every Sunday and preaching against the slave-trade. It took time, but he was successful in the end.

We have seen that Wulstan caused his young squires to feed the poor each day; we get other details from the *Life*. We read of a leper from Kent, who joined the other poor at the bishop's manor of Kempsey; and in another place Coleman tells us of the bishop's charity in Lent. Then, above all, he gave himself to the poor, every day he fed them and washed their feet, kissing the marks of their sores. On Maundy Thursday he washed, fed and clothed an immense multitude, giving himself no rest; when those around him said: "Rest now, my lord, rest; you have done your duty," he answered: "I have done nothing; but my will is strong to fulfill my Lord's command." That same afternoon he reconciled the penitents and blessed the Holy Oils and afterwards supped with those he had previously absolved.

On the last Maundy Thursday of his life he redoubled his efforts, knowing within himself it was for the last time. Twice was his hall filled with the poor who came to be washed and fed, and Wulstan had given orders that each episcopal manor was to provide clothing for one man, shoes for ten and food for a hundred. The bishop (he was eighty-six) sat on his throne utterly spent, reciting the prayers as the monks washed the feet of the poor. As the second crowd dispersed, the monks saw that the clothes were exhausted and the food nearly gone. They whispered to the bishop that it would be useless to allow the third series of poor to enter if they could do no more for them than wash their feet. Wulstan answered with the direct simplicity of the saints: "No. We must fulfill our Lord's command. That we can do. He must do the rest. My servants, it seems, are unwilling to perform this service for me. When I am gone they will wish to do so, but it will be too late." As he spoke the words, with one of those providential coincidences with which we are so familiar in the annals of contemplative convents, a series of gifts arrived for the bishop and he was able to send the third group of poor away dressed and fed like the others.

To anyone who reads Coleman's *Life* there comes an impression of continuous activity and travel. Wulstan was an apostolic bishop, and the picture that we get of him is of mature wisdom and beneficence that remains at once gentle and firm while incidents and passions are in a turmoil all about him. We are told that he was easy to live with, without idiosyncrasies, grateful for every kindness, thoughtful of the interests of others. We are also told that when he had to make a decision he decided promptly and pronounced his opinion at once. In his sermons he preached Christ and Him alone; even if it seemed to do violence to his theme, he brought Christ in. And in the midst of his activities he remained a contemplative. In every manor he had a small room made which only his servants were allowed to enter. Here every day after mass, when at home, he shut himself in and no one was allowed to disturb him, save a clerk who knocked on the door to warn him of the time of a meal or of saying the Office. Every Lent was for him a time of special retreat, and we have the word of Prior Nicholas that Wulstan was not only a lover of prayer himself, but most carefully watched over the prayer of others.

Nothing, indeed, to one who knows anything of the history of the times and of the activities of a bishop's office, is more instructive and moving than Wulstan's conduct when resident at Worcester. Though bishop, he regarded himself still as a monk of the house. It was then the custom, and is still at most Benedictine houses, for each priest in turn to sing the conventual mass for a week on end. When at home Wulstan almost always performed this duty, and we are told by his disciple, Nicholas, that the bishop was wont to say: "I am a monk of this house, and like the rest must do my week. As I am often away when my turn comes, I will do my office whenever I am here." He often attended the reading before Compline and went with the monks into church to give the night's blessing which comes in that Office. He was in choir for the night Office, and if he noticed that a monk was absent from oversleeping he said nothing at the times but when the others retired to rest once more he woke the defaulter gently, and together in the church they repeated the Office that the monk had omitted. Wulstan himself always remained in the church in the early morning while the monks were sleeping, and it often happened that a priest, wishing to say an early mass and unable to find a minister, was accompanied to the altar by his bishop.

At the end of his long life the fame of his sanctity had spread abroad. Thirty years before, Edward and Harold had valued his friendship; then came the Conqueror and Lanfranc; later, we are told, Malcolm of Scotland and his saintly wife begged his prayers. From overseas came letters, still extant when the *Life* was composed, from the Archbishop of Bari, from the Patriarch of Jerusalem, and from Pope Urban II. His last days are described in some detail. He fell ill at Pentecost, 1094, and at once sent for Robert of Hereford, who heard his last confession, which was followed by a penitential scourging. He remained, now better, now worse, till the beginning of the following year, when he was again visited by the Bishop of Hereford, by his old friend the great abbot, Serlo of Gloucester, and by the Abbot of Tewkesbury. The dying bishop reclined in a chair whence he could see the altar of his chapel; eight days before his death he was anointed by Prior Thomas, and every day after that till his death he received the Holy Eucharist as viaticum. He died about midnight on January 20, 1095. He was eighty-seven years old and had been bishop for thirty-three years; for the last twenty of these he had been the only pre-Conquest bishop of Saxon blood in England. His burial was attended by vast and sorrowing crowds, and not only his anniversary, but the day of the week on which he died, was long kept sacred by monks and townspeople.

Wulstan, one month before his death, had told his monks—as has many another saint down to St. Therese of Lisieux—that he would be nearer to them when dead than when alive. He kept his promise, and almost at once the monks of Worcester began to receive from him cures of bodily and spiritual ills. The first attempt at canonization was made fifty years after his death, but it came to nothing, Fifty years later, in 1201–1202, so many miracles took place that the bishop—the zealous and holy Malger—approached Innocent III. A commission was set up, including the Archbishop of Canterbury and the Bishop of Ely, and the members reported to Rome the genuineness of the miracles, sending to Innocent with their report Coleman's *Life of Wulstan*. The canonization took place on April 21, 1203, and the great Pope himself composed the prayer which is still read at mass in the English missal:

> Pour forth into our hearts, O Lord, the spirit of your love, that, by the intercession of blessed Wulstan, your confessor and pontiff, we may deserve to enjoy your sweetness in eternal bliss.

With St. Wulstan a long and not inglorious epoch of English history came to an end, the epoch which opened under Alfred the Great and which produced examples of sanctity in such great numbers—among them Dunstan, Ethelwold, Oswald, Aelfric, Edmund, Alphege, and Edward the Confessor. Professor Chambers, in an essay which deserves a far wider popularity than it will most probably achieve,[3] has shown us how this epoch is rich, too, in the works of craftsmanship and in masterpieces of literature. All this tradition, spiritual and literary, disappeared, lost beneath the flood of Norman culture; higher no doubt in the realm of the speculative sciences, and informed by a far more energetic spirit of organization and ordered progress, but still alien to England. Only the island of Worcester remained, and it is this isolation that gives to Wulstan his supremely interesting position in English history.

He was in fact the last great Englishman for many years—the last Englishman to be wholly English for some two centuries. Supremely attractive as St. Anselm is, and far as he surpasses St. Wulstan as a speculative theologian, he is not English at all, and the typical churchmen of the next century, even if technically Englishmen—John of Salisbury, Thomas Becket, Hubert Walter—are cosmopolitan, not in the sense that the Englishman in them is overlaid by the foreigner, but because the culture which formed their minds was that common to all Europe north of the Alps. Even St. Aelred and St. Gilbert of Sempringham have nothing of that massive force, that settled calm, that munificent benignity that are so characteristic of St. Wulstan, and which reappear in greater or less degree in so many of his greatest countrymen in succeeding ages.

3. *The Continuity of English Prose from Alfred to More* (Oxford University Press, 1932).

I fear that to some my sketch of him may seem to present a figure that verges upon the solid and the dull. Such is not my own mental image of St. Wulstan, and such is assuredly not Coleman's. Wulstan was not dull; he would have responded to any claim of affection or pity; his words would have had a divine wisdom. Yet there is this of truth in the suggestion—that as I see St. Wulstan he is not primarily the keen mind that could—tike St. Anselm or St. Thomas—mold an age's thought; nor yet a leader—tike St. Bernard or St. Ignatius—whom to know was to follow; nor yet a supremely attractive personality—like Newman or St. Francis of Sales—whom to see was to love devotedly; but rather a father in Christ from whom his sons received their portion, his flock their doctrine and his poor their food. Doubtless we see St. Wulstan through the eyes of two disciples—Nicholas and Coleman—for whom he had always been an old man, but even so I think that the impression they received was due to more than mere age on Wulstan's part. How different is the impression of St. Anselm that we receive from Eadmer! Yet Anselm was an old man when Eadmer knew him best, and Anselm at Bee had been a true father of many sons. But Anselm remained, like Newman, distinguished above all by his keen and sympathetic mind; Wulstan, like Ullathorne, by his habits of paternal rule.

But when all is said, what makes Wulstan most significant for us is his sanctity. I have not mentioned his many miracles; not, of course, because I doubt their authenticity (though from the nature of things it is impossible for us now to have strong evidence in any individual case), but because they do little to illustrate his character. But he undoubtedly worked miracles—and that in the pleasant villages under Bredon or the Cotswolds—he undoubtedly practiced the virtues and tamed his nature to a heroic degree, and he undoubtedly received from God the great and unusual gifts of grace that mark the saint. And, as we have seen, and as the reader of Coleman's *Life* would see in a hundred other examples, the mass, the Sacraments, prayer, the Office, devotion to our Lady and the saints, were to him what they are to the most saintly bishop of today. There is nothing puritanical, nothing *farouche* about Wulstan's sanctity; and that, for me, is its greatest charm. In the years when the great Hildebrand was consumed with hatred of injustice and treachery in the high places, St. Wulstan was tranquilly building more churches and replacing old altars with new in the heart of England. While a new intellectual movement was beginning to sweep over Western Europe, to be followed by a great spiritual movement which peopled the solitudes with men wishing to recreate the life of the primitive Church, St. Wulstan, an English monk with all his roots in the old world, yet not intolerant of the new, unperturbed and apparently uninfluenced by the stream of new life, preached Christ, the same yesterday and today, among the peasants and small landholders of Worcestershire.

SAINT AELRED OF RIEVAULX (1110–1166)

by BEDE JARRETT, O.P.

THAT ST. AELRED WAS ENGLISH WAS THE BOAST OF HIS contemporary biographers. By this they meant that he had no Norman blood in him. At a time when Normans were still dominant, Aelred though a Saxon, shared the culture, the firmness, and the gift of rule of the conquerors. But his name stood also for something gentler than the Norman, milder—more Saxon to the men of his time.

Actually his forbears for at least three generations had been priests; his father was Ellav, the Saxon, priest in Hexham. Somehow in those confused and ill-ordered times, the ruined abbey of the Austin Canons at Hexham had come into the possession of his family, but Ellav, moved by the growing sense of duty and of ordered and settled life, and by the increase of religious practice that the Norman conquest inspired, had put the ruins into repair and persuaded two Austin Canons to come and live there. On his deathbed (by then a Benedictine) in Durham, with the leave of all three sons—Samuel, Ethelwold, and Aelred he gave back all the property to the canons, bequeathing to them also his reliquary, a silver cross, enshrining the relics of St. Acca and St. Alchmund, famous Saxon saints.

But Aelred suffered no hurt in that irregular household as we should call it; in those days only a few were distressed at the public evidence of priest-families. The Normans were dis-edified by such sights, but the Saxons watched them untroubled. Thus Aelred never refers to this state of things as something he lamented. Yet because of his quiet home with his brothers, he was friendly, home-loving, all his days. His life indeed is a series of friendships.

The first move in his life that we know of came when he was chosen officially to go to the Scottish court as the boy friend of the nephew of the king. This interrupted his schooling so that he never quite caught up to his due standard, never learning all he should have done, when the time was for learning, and always in consequence spoke of himself as ill-educated, which was, however, not really true. Nevertheless this sudden seizure of him by David, brother and heir to Alexander, king of Scotland, to act as tutor and companion to Prince Henry, was the first break in his leisurely country life. David saw him at Hexham and was fascinated by him and carried him off. It was the opening adventure of all that was to follow. David himself had been educated in England, for he could be sent out of the country, being only the third son with little likelihood of succeeding to the throne. His mother, St. Margaret, dispatched him to the Court of Henry I to be trained there, not altogether an exile, since her daughter Matilda (known later as the "Empress Maud") was King Henry's wife, and would assuredly look after her smaller brother. Moreover, David's wife was a Saxon too, Matilda, the daughter of Waltheof, a Northumbrian earl, whose first husband was the Earl of Northampton. By this first husband she had a son called after her father, Waltheof. It was to act as companion to both her sons, Waltheof and his half-brother Henry, David's eldest heir, that Aelred crossed the Scottish border about 1134. Aelred must then have been about fourteen years old, a Saxon of Saxons; fair, blue-eyed, enjoying the material world and its beauties, sharp-witted, practical with his hands, not devoted to Norman tourneys nor to Norman books; a romantic boy with sentimental idealism, "desiring only to love and to be loved." His joy was friendship, his occupation was to be with friends.

Within a year of Aelred's arrival David succeeded his brother as king of Scotland, and Henry became the heir to the throne. Aelred was soon (how soon we do not know; nor, considering his age, dare we guess) made Seneschal, or High Steward, of Scotland, say the biographers. It really could not have been quite such an important post as that that was given him. All that later on he said himself about it was that he was put in the kitchen and had cooks for his companions; as likely as not he was equerry and major-domo and master of the household, and no more than that. But what most mattered was that Henry and Waltheof were his friends and occupied his attention; romantically, too, he worshipped King David.

This was the obsession of his life, this idolatry for the king, "whom I loved beyond all mortal men and who then was in the very flower of his age." Much later on, when he was abbot, he paid a visit to David, old and lonely since Prince Henry had died, and his coming stirred forgotten memories in the old king's heart: "How astonished they all were to see him kiss me when I went to take leave of him and to see his tears. But, as I saw this, I offered for his soul all the sadness that I felt at parting from him. And from the inmost depths of my being my heart shall remember you in that place where day by day the sacrifice of the Son is offered to the Father for the salvation of all men."

This second parting re-awakened all his old sorrows and reminded him of that romantic idolatry of his elder hero, which he saw now might easily have made shipwreck of him, had not David been "so humble, pious, chaste." It seems to have been David rather than Henry who held his affection, though Henry comes charmingly out of his pages: "lonely and quiet, shy, yet with a natural majesty, loved by all; chaste in body, grave in appearance, honorable in life, so frequent in church, so still at prayer, so generous to the poor, so reverent to age, so stern to injustice, that he seemed a princely monk or a monk prince. Braver than others in pursuit, keener in defense, slower in retreat, youth's hero, his soldiers' pride, the delight of his elders." This court of Scotland was his second home; he was there from the age of fourteen till he was twenty-three. He left it on business for King David with Archbishop Thurstan of York.

On his way back from York, when the business was done, he came through Helmesley, where he called in to see William d'Éspec, another of his heroes: "Huge, black-haired, long-bearded, with open brow, large eyes, broad face, trumpet-voiced." William was a perfect Norman, with his complete sense of Norman fitness to rule, and of the inevitable triumphant character of all Norman enterprise; the confirmed conqueror who could not help but win.

Like a true Norman, d'Éspec had founded a monastery near him in the vale of the Rye, which he already had called Rievaulx. Business done, Aelred was invited by the founder to see the monastery. It was interesting in itself, though the new style of building, or rather the new perfection of the older Norman style, had not yet been begun. There were then as yet only little huts. But the monks themselves were the interesting part of the foundations—a new type, Cistercians. This was their first house north of London, and was only just in its beginnings, founded in 1132, the year before this visit. It had been founded, too, by one of St. Bernard's own disciples, William, the first abbot, straight from Clairvaux; St. Bernard was still alive, having himself entered the order in 1113, and in 1115 having founded Clairvaux. Rumors had sometime before reached England of the new Cistercian movement, since the first beginnings of Citeaux were due, amongst others, to Stephen Harding of Sherborne, who eventually became abbot and whose Charter of Charity (1117) was the foundation of the new life in its permanent and final form. In 1129 Waverley, in Surrey, had been chosen for the first Cistercian monastery; Rievaulx, in 1132, was the second.

To this monastery Aelred came riding in the company of his host, and saw what had already been begun by the busy eager little band. Already in his ride from Scotland and its ruminations he had come to realize the narrowness of his life, the substitution in it of man for God, the diversion of his natural yearning for friendship from its true and complete object to a lesser one. Not that it was wrong to love man, but that it was right to love God. This new community pleased him; here was love of man and companionship, but here also was love of God. But was not love of God also to be found in the Scottish court? Certainly the King's mother had found God there. Why should not Aelred too? He could; but would he?

He went then with William d'Éspec to Helmesley, and next day started back north again out of Helmesley to the Border. As he and his companion rode back they reached again the valley of the Rye, and Aelred pointed it out to his companion, and suggested that they should inspect this monastery of which he had been speaking. Together they turned their horses to the west and rode down that valley, still harsh and unlovely, suffering from that harrying of the north by the Conqueror which had broken the resistance of the untamed English, still desolate; below were the little huts and the beginnings of the new buildings. Already sheep had been brought there; the poor soil allowed little else at first by way of cultivation than the grazing of half-wild sheep. Both of them went down and saw the life and joined the monastery there and then.[1]

Not for a long while did Aelred see again the king and the king's sons in Scotland: "The chains of my wretched habits held me, the love of my home held me, the bonds of good fellowship tethered me, more than all the knots of a certain friendship were straitened on me, sweeter to me than all the other sweetness of my then life." As he says of himself again in another place: "I was a prodigal son who had wandered; now I came back to my father's house, leaving behind me the husks of swine." What this "certain friendship" was, no one is likely to

1. Walter Daniel, who wrote his life, spoke of his first miracle as happening just after this. In the hospice, the day before he received the habit, he was sitting at his dinner when the monastery caught fire; a great commotion followed, shouting and the hurling of water. No lessening of the fire resulted. Folk rushed into the hospice to warn the postulants. Aelred sat unmoved and ate quietly on; at last he rose, gravely smiling, and seizing "a jug of English ale," threw it on the flames. The fire at once went out.

discover now. Why should we try to? But he has said that his friendship for King David was his greatest friendship: "Whom I loved above all mortals." God and St. Aelred knew to what he referred. Some modern biographers speak of an unknown lady-love. To have had a lady-love would have been foreign to all we know of him.

This was the beginning of his monastic life, and hard and difficult he found it: "My food is less, my clothes are less soft, my drink is only from the spring. At the day's end I lay my wearied limbs on an uncomfortable mat, my rest is broken, I fall asleep over my books. Only to three men, and that seldom, have I any leave to talk. But I see all about me charity, patience, fervor, zeal, affection, such as no Gospel precept nor apostolic epistle nor patristic homily nor ancient monastic practice could better." It was difficult, but not intolerable: "Our order is the cross of Christ," a sweet yoke, a light burden, yoke and burden sweetened and made light by love, divine and human.

Into the details of his life, its haps and hazards, it is of little interest to enter. We need do no more than mention them—novice master (his novices were famous for their sweetness and chastity), abbot of the daughter house of Revesby (from 1142 to 1147), abbot of Rievaulx at thirty-seven (1147), with occasional absences in London or York or France or Rome or more frequently, perhaps, in Scotland again. But the beauty of his life is the beauty of his friendships; for him they made his life, they helped him to understand life, they gave life the only value it ever had for him, even monastic life: "Externals only matter when they are the deliberate expression of love, divine and human."

He writes in his prologue to his book *Spiritual Friendship*: "When I was a little boy at school and the charm of my companions much pleased me, I gave myself over to love and friendship, after the ways and vices with which that stage of life is threatened, so that I found nothing more pleasurable, more desirable, more worthwhile than to love and be loved. Between these foolish loves and friendships, now for this boy, now for that, my spirit was pulled hither and thither;

not knowing what real love was like, I was often deceived by what was false. At length Cicero's book on friendship came into my hands, which at once seemed to me both valuable in the grave depth of its ideas and attractive for its easy eloquence; and though I did not deem myself fit as yet for so noble a type of friendship, I was glad to have found a formula for friendship by which I might reduce into order my disorderly loves and affections. Since however, it pleased the Good Lord to recall the wanderer, lift the fallen, cleanse the leper with the company of those in health, I put aside my worldly hopes and at last entered a monastery. At once I gave myself to study books of which till then I had been satisfied by looking at the bindings, and found that Holy Scripture delighted me and the little learning of my boyhood I dis-esteemed. I remembered, indeed, what pleasure I had had in Cicero's *Friendship*, but was astonished to find how little now it touched me. Already whatever had not first been sweetened by the sovereign sweetness of my most sweet Jesus, nor salted by the savor of Scripture, appealed no longer to my taste.

"Thinking this over, I began to wonder whether Scripture had any blessing to give to friendship, or was it only a thing which paganism had praised. However, I had already found that the letters of the saints were full of references to friendship, and I had already under the authority of this tried to make my friendships spiritual, but could not; so now I determined to write a book myself on spiritual friendship and to discover for myself the rules for a chaste and holy friendship. If any gather profit from reading this, let him give thanks to God and beg Christ's mercy on my sins. If any judge what I have written useless and superfluous, let him pardon my infelicity, which prevents me from setting down clearly all I have experienced and found to be true."

To Aelred, newcomer to the cloister, all the world was young, his monastery was full of triumphant youth. But his courtly life had ill-fitted him for the discipline of this new way; his eyes were restless, his heart was open to every impression, his wandering gaze round the faces of the community made his fancy dwell with relish on the comeliness of those he saw. Simon was the first of his new friends.

Simon[2] as a boy had gone over the hills from his father's castle to seek refuge with St. Bernard at Clairvaux, yet he was younger than Aelred when Aelred first saw him: "My son in age, my father in holiness, my friend in love." Against his father's wish he had walked across the hills to the Cistercian monastery, stumbling over the roads, eating and drinking what he could find—fruit and grass—losing his way only to find it again: "The boy Jesus went before this boy." "Most charming," Aelred found him when he met him at Rievaulx, him and Hugh his friend, who had both come from St. Bernard to join Abbot William's little band. How calm Simon was, how humble, how devout, with his guarded spirit, how recollected! Aelred could not but admire this type of youth that was new to him, "so wonderfully grave, so radiantly chaste, so silent, answering my questing eyes with no other answer than a smile; seldom speaking of his own accord, yet always answering if one spoke to him, but showing the while how sweet and fragrant he found his silence."

This reserve of monastic recollection deepened as he grew older; when Simon came near death, lingering long for eight years, yet dying suddenly at the end, he seemed to Aelred to be withdrawing himself from all about him, "forgetful even of me." Partly this was due to a delicacy of mind; he wished no one to be troubled about him. Neither Aelred nor Hugh was with him dying. Even the monk asleep in the next bed heard nothing. Partly it was because Simon's friend was God.

Simon's death was a great shock to him; he could not even cry, so stunned was he; could not believe he had lost his friend. He stood and watched the monks as they washed Simon's limbs before his burial; this was his Simon, he told himself as he looked, but his Simon could not be dead! From the beginning of his "conversion," as he called it,

2. F. M. Powicke suggests that this Simon is Simon des Sigillo, whose psalter was preserved at Rievaulx with St. Aelred's, happy memorials of their affection in prayer.

Simon had known him; of them all Simon he most loved. Never again would his friendships be quite so emotional as this one had been. In his latter years he thought that in his devotion to Simon he had let his sentimentality run away with him. But there was nothing wrong in that friendship, not even a shadow of wrong on Simon's side. Others, no doubt, had their own opinions about it and were shocked by it: "Shall you that are strong despise my tears?"—for the tears came at last. "Must you think our friendship was but carnal? Let them interpret my tears as they will. O Lord! You see and judge. Are my tears to be denounced, reprobated? Your tears excuse me, Lord Jesus, which you wept at the death of a friend." Had he had choice, he would have liked to have entered then with Simon to the embraces of Christ, but his wickedness forbade him: "Certainly he who was prepared entered to the spouse; to me in my misery the door was closed. Yet I shall follow you with my tears, with my poor prayers, with my affection, and in the unique sacrifice of my Redeemer daily at the dawn. And do You, O Father, greater in fatherhood than Abraham, open wide Your hands to receive this poor man, this other Lazarus; open wide Your heart to welcome him coming up from life's miseries, cherish him, comfort him! And to me, poor wretch and yet his friend, give it one day to share with him the peace and rest of Your heart."

Of his other friends we need only mention this Hugh, who had come with Simon from Clairvaux and whose friend Simon was before he was Aelred's: "Hugh more myself than I am." And then Ivo, who did not belong to Rievaulx, but to Wardon Abbey, whom he had met at Rievaulx, and who also died many years before him, yet whom he "forever remembered." Never can he fail "to see the mild eyes of Ivo and hear his pleasant voice." Ivo was certainly staying once at Rievaulx and was much troubled, as were so many of the young English monks, by this hunger for friendship, and its need. Was it wrong? Was it unnatural? Was it forbidden to love one or other of the brethren? The English youth of that time found in each other a refuge from the harsher and stricter Normans. Aelred talked it over with Ivo. "Here are you and I," so he wrote out afterwards the opening of their discussion, "and I hope Christ is in our midst a third. Here we have no man to break in on our talk, no man's chatter to interrupt us. I could not help noticing that as I sat with the brethren round me, all talking at once and all noisy, discussing, arguing, questioning, you sat by yourself, silent. When you did get ready something to say, it got no farther than your throat. You became shy and hung your head again. So I guessed that you hated noise and a large company, but that you did want to talk to me, only quietly and alone." So Ivo, who speaks of himself as "a boy," puts these questions that had troubled him: "What is real friendship?" "Is it allowable?" "And between men?"

The friend of Aelred to whom we are most beholden for our knowledge of all this is Walter Daniel. Walter wrote his life, and acted as his secretary; indeed, wrote out at least the dialogues of Aelred. Walter Daniel, like most of Aelred's friends, was also a shy, yet talkative monk, rather lonely and choosing solitary places for his walks and prayers and contemplation. Aelred opens a second dialogue with this remark to Walter: "I watched you rubbing your forehead with your hand as the others chattered, running your hand through your hair as you were impatient with their outbursts of shouting and laughter. I saw how angry you were when business people came and took up my time. It is true that these folk are a nuisance, but please remember that we need them sometimes, and their hostility can do us much harm." Towards the end of their talk the cellarer appeared, or at least was seen coming, and Aelred and Daniel and a third, who had joined them earlier, Gratian, Daniel's friend (a rather passionate young man, who like the earlier Aelred, "wants to be loved and love" and is not only Daniel's "friend, but everybody's friend"), go off out-of-doors to carry on their discussions undisturbed.

These are the monks for whom Aelred (now grown grey in divine service in monastic life) came to write his several treatises dealing with friendship; especially three—"The Mirror of Divine

Love," "The Dialogues on Spiritual Friendship," and the treatise on "The boy Jesus twelve years old." This last is addressed to Ivo. (He was about twelve years old himself when he met Prince Henry and King David and he loves the Latin word *duodenarius* and repeats it whenever he can; the rhythm of it pleases him.) He also wrote other books, chiefly historical, in which his English patriotism is most prominent. Thus in one he tells his gladness at the accession of Henry II, who represented the old Saxon line of kings: "Now we have an English king, and of the same nation we have bishops, abbots, princes, leaders of war." Some indeed were not purely Saxon, but "begotten of both bloods, to the honor of one and the consolation of the other." He speaks of Henry as "king of England by double right," and makes it clear that he thought Edgar Atheling rightful king and his niece, Matilda, Henry's mother, the rightful heiress. Henry is "the cornerstone in whom to our joy the two walls of the English and Norman race have been joined."

But to his monks the Normans were foreigners, and they grumbled when "foreign" monks came and stayed in the monastery and wanted to join them. His own monks' new-found patriotism made them anxious to forbid these a place in their midst; he explained humorously, however, that after all, if they only went far enough back, even the Saxons were foreigners, and once upon a time were newcomers. If the Normans were to be rejected because they were invaders, what standing would the Saxons have, who were invaders too?

Yet for all his genial sanity it must be admitted that Aelred's history is not quite convincing. His genealogy for King Henry would be difficult for the reader to believe in, however Saxon the reader happened to be; he traced it back through Matilda and St. Margaret to Edmund Ironside and Ethelred the Unready and King Alfred, and then by easy stages, through Wotan, the son of Beadwig, the son of Shem, back to Adam! It must be pleasant reading for the British Israelites to know that St. Aelred thought the Anglo-Saxons descended, like the Jewish people, from Shem and not from Japhet.

Still, though these historical works are entertaining and in part very valuable,[3] it is his teaching on the spiritual development of friendship which we wish chiefly to describe. We have said how his contemporary biographers insist on his being of "the old English stock." Because he was English he was able to deal with a widespread crisis in English monastic life, and he succeeded in appeasing it, to the quieting of consciences and in effect to the development of friendship as something not only to be tolerated in monasteries, but to be welcomed, to be encouraged instead of being suppressed.

The first thing to be remembered is not merely the natural tendency of a "converted" Englishman to Puritanism, but the actual Puritanism (devoid, naturally, of any heretical taint), which the Cistercian movement had accepted and which might well have led to the forbidding of friendship between monk and monk. It was the definite tendency of the Order to suppress whatever was superfluous. Would not friendship also be discounted in these monasteries, whence all other beauties seemed banished? The places chosen for Cistercian monasteries were to be remote and desolate. Their architecture was to be severe; there were to be no stained-glass windows, no statues, no paintings, in their churches. The furniture, vestments, sacred vessels were to be of the plainest. There was to be none of the newfangled ways of singing, as St. Aelred described them: "Making noises like horses, or women, or the dying, waving hands like mountebanks, preferring sound to sense." The habit was to be coarse, the food simple, the lodging of the monks austere. In such a society would friendships be allowed?

But it will be replied, perhaps, that the Cistercians loved beauty. Actually, the sites they chose for their monasteries are beautiful. They are beautiful now. But the beauties we see are the result of the monks

3. His authentic works are: *The Mirror of Charity*, *Spiritual Friendship*, *Homilies on Isaiah*, *Twenty-Five Sermons*, *The Genealogy of the English Kings*, *The Life of St. Edward the Confessor*, *The Battle of the Standard*, *The Miracles of the Church of Hexham*, *The Life of St. Ninian*, *The Nun of Watton*, *Jesus a Boy of Twelve*, *On the Soul* (an unfinished work).

settling where they did, and not the cause. Rievaulx is spoken of, when the monks went there, as "horrid"; the woods, the wide fields of pasture and tillage, the defending rivers, the "smiling" land was their creation—not deliberately, but none the less theirs. They made their sites beautiful. They set out to be skilled agriculturists; cuttings of trees, herbs, bushes, flowers, passed from monastery to monastery, passed overseas. Thus they made their places lovely. Nevertheless, the land was harsh when they found it. And they made it lovely, not because they meant to do so, but because they worked well.

Again, another danger that St. Aelred noted was the heavy toil of manual labor. He noted that the temptation that came to a monk as he worked with his hands was to grow bitter: "The bitterness of toil that let the enemy enter the cloister."

A third danger was the danger of worldliness; though the Cistercians were but young, their popularity gained them rich benefactions, and their industry developed the hidden wealth of their wide lands. The wool industry, which they did so much to increase, had been established in Britain by the Romans, whose finest and most expensive wool was imported from here. After a lapse of time the trade was resuscitated under Alfred, and again later was re-founded by Henry I. When in 1198 Richard I undertook to pay ransom for his freedom to the Duke of Austria, the Cistercians were induced to contribute one year's value of their wool crop, which amounted to £8,500. The contribution of the queen and the sheriffs of London together only amounted to a little more, £13,750. Thus later the wealth of the Cistercians became a byword. Already, however, St. Aelred saw, in consequence of this, the danger of cupidity in their life; he feared that those who were greedy of money would grow greedy of other pleasures. In guarding against greed, superiors might attack all pleasures. Might not friendships in the monastery fall under their ban?

His answer to all this was elaborate; in all it comprised the ingredients of a scholastic treatise which he gradually developed. The center of the argument is that charity is not merely the chief purpose of life, but the remedy and cure for all evils, the protection against threatened dangers; and charity consists in the love of God, out of which must come the love of self and the love of the brotherhood.

The love of God is the foundation of all spirituality; it is the basis also of happiness and peace. Then St. Aelred draws out the old monastic process by which the love of God normally developed; namely, by conversion, purification, virtue, knowledge, contemplation, charity. These are in order the stages of religious or spiritual progress: here Aelred is not following the normal teaching of St. Benedict and his school, but proposing a scheme of his own. Then comes love of self. Here St. Aelred ventures the proposition: "Whoever loves not his own soul certainly cannot love the soul of another." In the business of the self-love which he here indicates, and of the love of God he advocates certain practices, three corporal and three spiritual; first work, watching and fasting, then reading, prayer and contemplation. By these means a man can be led to love.

Thus at last he comes to his real point, the love of one's neighbor; he is writing as a monk for monks.

He insists, first of all, on the importance of the government of souls of a monastery being undertaken by whosoever is elected by his brethren to that office: "Falsely does he say he loves God who is not willing to shepherd His flock." He refers also to the difficult problem that such a superior has in knowing when precisely to be severe and when to be gentle: "Let them love me and fear me as much as You see to be expedient for them"; but: "Prelates must take care that neither their judgments be harsh nor their discipline slack. They should not be sad men, but joyous." Moreover, the superior who is less perfect as a monk yet is kind and gentle is more loved than that superior who is more perfect, but more austere. But the first is not more loved because he is less perfect, nor the second less loved because he is more perfect. They are loved more or less according to the love they give. And here he adds that youth and age in a superior have each its advantage; the young superior "is more eager, more joyous, more swift to act"; the older superior "more dependable, more dignified, more mature." These remarks are true in Aelred's own case. Daniel, who lived seventeen years under his rule, says that he expelled no one from the monastery, and that during his abbacy only four left, and of these three returned: "He exceeded all his fellow prelates in Christendom in patience and tenderness. He was full of sympathy for the infirmities of others, both physical and moral." Jocelyn of Furness, says: "He had wisdom in the world's affairs, he was witty, he came of the ancient English race, he was gentle, patient, compassionate to the infirmities of body and temperament in others above all the prelates of the Church of his day." Even Aelred himself speaks of "never having been disturbed or distressed, or losing charity or peace in the brotherhood. Never did the sun go down upon my anger." Walter Daniel adds that Aelred boasted that his monastery accepted everyone who offered himself, that "all strangers were welcome, that all men found room for themselves here like fish, in the breadth of the sea, the gracious, joyous, spacious peace of Divine Love." "That house," he said, "is not to be accounted a place of religion which has been too proud to bear with the weak."

Yet Aelred was insistent on the need of penance in his monastery: "St. Benedict spent many years on bread and water, and nevertheless escaped only with difficulty from the temptations of impurity. Almost was he overwhelmed. You heard that read in the lessons to-night." So for himself, he had a cistern built for cold water in which he bathed daily through the long winters and the summer. He found that this helped him to quiet his passions: "Stern means alone can tame wild powers."

Love of the brotherhood is a difficult task; some you love too little and some too much: "Yet no one has loved perfectly or truly who in this life passionately yearns for anything or anyone." Passion must be controlled. For this purpose, in every one Christ is to be sought for: "In every creature, even irrational or lifeless, I see the signs of Love having passed that way."

Still the love of the brotherhood is made easier by religious life: "What a wall its poverty is in this! What a tower its silence." Moreover, only by spiritual considerations can a man hope to keep his love as it should be: "For I would have you believe that he was never a friend who could hurt one whom he had once received to friendship. Never had he tasted of love's sweetness who can give up a love once cemented by love," and he adds: "As St. Jerome says: 'A friendship which can be broken was never a true friendship.'" Shakespeare's phrase is the same: "That is not love which alters when its alteration finds and bends with the remover to remove." Friends may be of all sorts, especially in a monastery, "where the lion lies down with the lamb, or, better, becomes a lamb." But friendship once made is forever.

But then friendships must not be made too easily. Since friendship is not a thing to be gone back upon, it must be entered after a deliberate and slow choice. Once it has been completely pledged, evil even must not be judged a reason for breaking it; though when it is beginning it can be gradually dissolved if the friend is found to be evil, i.e.: "Either he nags, or upbraids, or is proud, or reveals secrets told him, or practices detraction of his friend behind his back, or—most dreadful of all—corrupts one whom he loves."

In proving friends, the four qualities that most need finding out are: "loyalty, discretion, prudence, and the intention which the other has in entering friendship." And friendship itself includes: "First, a love that shares what gifts it has; and secondly, an inner affection which is the pith and marrow of it; and thirdly, a sureness that knows nothing of fears or jealousies in love and that trusts absolutely the beloved; and fourthly, a joyous acceptance of whatever the beloved does or does not do." "You ask too much," said Walter Daniel to his abbot; "it were better to have no friends if they are to cost so high." "Ah, wonderful must be he who can afford to do without friends and without love! More wonderful assuredly than God Himself," was Aelred's answer.

Rather, he answered, it is love alone that makes life worthwhile. "God," added he, "took Eve from Adam's side to prove love to be collateral," a heavy pun.

For him this spiritual love is possible only because God is seen in every one. Because God is in them, you love even the unlovable; because He is in them, you love and will not profane your love. Your friends are the shrines of deity; remembering that, you keep your reverence for them and restrain your passion towards them. Thus on earth you live in heaven, for what is heaven but the consummation of all love, human and divine: "For who would wonder that Aelred could not live without Simon, save he who did not know how sweet a thing it is to live with a friend; how sweet it will be to meet him again in Paradise."

Thus over all must be the figure of the Crucified, "a third" in all friendships—the perfect friend: "To me makes more appeal, Lord Jesus, your sadness than the joy of all the world; more sweet to me are your tears at the death of a friend than that fortitude of the philosophers that left them unmoved by affection's loss. Sweeter to me your eating and drinking with publicans and sinners than the harsh fasting of the Pharisees. Truly is the fragrance of Your ointment above all spices! How it touches me when I see the Lord of majesty showing Himself in things of the body and of human affection, not like the strong, but like the weak. In my weakness this comforts me."

Hence grew Aelred's great devotion to the Eucharist as love's sacrament: "In this manger under the appearances of bread and wine is the true body and blood of Christ. There in swaddling clothes is our Christ, in the swathed bands of bread and wine, invisible but real. We have no memorial so great of Christ's nativity as the daily reception of His body and blood."

For the last ten years he suffered from arthritis and other painful symptoms, and had to obtain leave from the General Chapter to eat and sleep in a little room near the infirmary. A little thatched house was built for him near the large ward of the infirmary, "in the apple-orchard," and there all day long the brethren trooped down to see him and talk with him, and no man forbade them. They talked and chattered about everything under the sun: "Sons, speak what you will, only let not any base word fall from your lips, nor detraction against the brethren, nor blasphemy against God."

Meanwhile some troubles arose which required settlement and which he was able to adjust, a threatened quarrel with a very near neighbor, the Cistercian abbot of Byland. Again, in 1162, he went north to Scotland to settle quarrels between Fergus of Galloway and his sons; "a terrible land," he found it, for all his love of Scotland. He settled the quarrel so well that Fergus became a canon of Holyrood. Before this in 1148, Aelred found his old friend Waltheof, once a lad with him and Prince Henry at the Scottish Court, now abbot of Melrose. He visited him. He also visited the daughter house of Dumdrennan and then came home again. Waltheof died in 1159.

Here other troubles for a while came on him. Since all Cistercian houses were suffering at the hands of King Henry II, who was furious with the Order for having given hospitality to Becket at Pontigny, Rievaulx also suffered. But these troubles he could do nothing to assuage; the Mowbrays and others of the king's men ravaged his estates.

In 1166 his pains had so much increased that he prayed at Christmas for death and told his monks so at Chapter on Christmas Day. He was present at the feast-Mass and at Vespers, seated by the presbytery; after that he was carried back to his cell, where he lay unconscious for two hours. In the first days of 1167 he felt death nearer and sent for his monks to say farewell to them. He reminded them that he had before said farewell to them, when he was leaving for France or elsewhere on the affairs of his Order or for the king. This was just such another leave-taking, only now they were to think of him as an exile who was leaving them for his home, namely, "God who redeemed me by Himself, who by His grace bound me to Himself in this life of the cloister without my merit. To Him I go."

In a portion of his cell a chapel was arranged, an altar and a crucifix above it, and the figures of his most beloved saints about it. A fire was lit in the cell; over this he crouched in his great pain; stone, kidney trouble, all manner of diseases assailed him! His comfort lay in the Mass and in his well-loved books, the psalter with his own marginal annotations, the gospel of St. John, and the *Confessions* of St. Augustine (his dearest author, whose writings were the foundation of his own, whose *Confessions* could always make him cry, and who was referred to by the monks chaffingly whenever they quoted him to St. Aelred as "your St. Augustine"). These three had always been the staple food of his thought and prayer. With these and his prayers he would spend his days save when the monks came to talk to him. As the early days of 1167 advanced he had to give up sitting on his bench at the entrance of that part of his cell which had been fitted up as an oratory, "thinking how he was but dust." Instead he had to keep his bed. On January 5th he was anointed by Abbot Roger, of Byland. His pains steadily increased. When death actually came it could not come quickly enough for him: "*Festinate*," he kept repeating. "Make haste, make haste, for Christ's love." This he added in his own Northumbrian Saxon tongue, dwelling on the words "For Christ's love." It seemed sweeter to him in English; the very words were music to him, "Christ's love," "Christ's love." Walter Daniel, who wrote his life, was with him, and pointing to the oratory, said to the dying abbot: "My Lord, look at the cross; let your eye be where your heart is." Aelred burst out anew: "You are my God and my Lord. You are my refuge and my savior. You are my glory and my hope for eternity. Into Your hands I commend my spirit." It was 12th January 1167 when he died.

When he had ended his dialogues on Spiritual Friendship, he had spoken openly to Walter Daniel of his last and most perfect friendship, with a boy whom he trained to religious life and holiness, who was so devoted to him, and so frank, so kindly critical, so straight, tender, true. Of this affectionate union of theirs he had used words which showed how this love of man was for him the image of a greater love, and how friendship was to him no less than a sacrament: "It is part of the very bliss of heaven thus to love and thus to be loved.... If you but knew how to clear your mind of aught else and see that Jesus Himself is God, you would see revealed face to face Love's perfect rest." Into that very bliss of perfect rest he passed.

FOR REFERENCE it will be sufficient to notice:

The Works of Aelred, J. P. Migne, P. L. Vol. CXCV.

Lives of the English Saints, John Dobree Dalgairns (London: 1903).

Aelred of Rievaulx and His Biographer, Walter Daniel, F. M. Powicke (Manchester: 1922).

SAINT THOMAS OF CANTERBURY (1118–1170)

by HILAIRE BELLOC

The life and death of Thomas à Becket, Archbishop of Canterbury, may be put in the phrase "Constancy and its Fruit." Now the fruit of constancy is not what the constant agent himself immediately desired. This is because man is a subordinate. He cannot fashion the future to his will; he is used by God.

Men are used. The purposes of God, which guide the universe, cannot be the purposes of one man. But if that one man's purpose is humble and direct, open and good (which means in unison with God's purpose), then he would rejoice at the fruit of his constancy. Though it should not be that which he had desired, it will be consonant with what he had desired. It will be found larger than what he had desired. It will be found more permanent than what he had desired. He will serve God in a sense unwittingly, though wittingly in purpose. But he will glorify God in the result.

Each man who has achieved, has achieved something other than he intended. Each man who has achieved, has achieved something in the same axis with, along the same direction, as his intention was—in proportion as his intention was good.

In the history of Western Europe the episode of the martyrdom at Canterbury is a capital example of constancy. It stands out the more vividly because, in that very place, in that very See, the purpose for which St. Thomas died has been conspicuously denied, ridiculed, frustrated, and (locally) destroyed.

The principle for which St. Thomas suffered martyrdom was this:

That the Church of God is a visible single universal society, with powers superior to those of this world, and therefore of right, *autonomous*. That principle is the negation of the opposite, of the base, ephemeral, thing already passing from Christian life, sometimes called pedantically "Erastianism"; the principle that the divine and permanent is subject to the human and passing power. St. Thomas died for the doctrine, the truth, that the link with eternal things must never be broken under the pressure of ephemeral desires, that the control of eternal things cannot, in morals, be subjected to the ephemeral arrangements of men.

But note this—that his constancy was exercised for a particular form in which that truth applied to the society of his own time. The specific detailed formula for which he laid down his life, later lost its meaning because in the perpetual flux of human arrangements words and conditions changed. The ultimate principle remained unchanged. He fought against an attempt of the civil power in his time to subject the Church of God to its jurisdiction in a particular fashion which since then has ceased to be of moment, and almost ceased to be of meaning. On which account it might be asked whether it were worthwhile for him to have fought at all. But he gained a victory for the essential principle, to that in his image one man after another arose (and shall in future arise) who have and will—God granting them grace—maintain, that same principle: that the things of God are not subject to the judgment of men.

St. Thomas fought against what was in his time a certain innovation, but an innovation apparently so slight, certainly so subtle, and above all so convenient to the general spirit of the time, that it seemed—though an innovation—a piece of common sense which only an obdurate, fanatical man would resist: someone anchored in the past or wedded to a dead ancient formula. He fought against an innovation put forward in sixteen articles, called "The Constitutions of Clarendon"; of which sixteen articles many were tolerable enough, and all arguable, and every one of which in one form or another has lapsed from the area of conflict into that of agreed things.

The two conspicuous points upon which he resisted were: (1) the judgment by the civil courts of clerics of whatever rank when first accused of a crime—a privilege still existing in Canon Law but in practice everywhere abolished, and (2) the rule that there should be no appeals in spiritual matters to the sovereign pontiff without leave of the king. On this second point the position has been turned by the fact that the non-Christian modern governments (whatever may be true of the future) do not recognize the Supreme Pontiff, nor indeed any such thing as a spiritual court. So our appeals may go forward merrily enough, only Caesar does not admit any jurisdiction in the final court to which they are preferred—nor, as a rule, any matter for appeal. If I desire my marriage to be declared null I may appeal to Rome without leave of the state, because the state does not admit as yet in modern countries that Rome has jurisdiction in such affairs. And though Rome declare my marriage null I am, under Caesar's modern law, bigamous if I marry again, or (what is much more probable) if Rome declares me bound to my wife, I am no adulterer in Caesar's eyes if under Caesar's law I marry another.

How then can it be true that St. Thomas—having apparently technically succeeded by his constancy upon two points which even in his own time seemed to many dubious, and these points having in practice become devoid of any practical meaning today—achieved, and that his constancy bore fruit? In this way. That his heroic resistance prevented the assault of the temporal power against the eternal from being fatal at the moment when, precisely, it might have been fatal.

To put it bluntly, he saved the Church. He came, he was raised up, he was murdered for God, just at the moment which might have been the turn of the tide towards secularization. He checked it for four hundred years. The tide flowed on, but not to the complete destruction of Christian unity. The great intellectual and therefore skeptical movement of the twelfth century was prevented from disrupting Christendom; the tide flowed on, then slackened. The organization of the Church grew old, the arteries of its human organization hardened; by the end of the fifteenth century, more than 300 years after the killing of that man at Canterbury Cathedral, the time was ripe for a greater assault, and the assault was delivered. In part it conquered, but not *wholly*, as, but for St. Thomas, it might have done far earlier.

Fools or provincials would say that the last assault conquered altogether. It certainly has not done so. The extent of its conquest is still debatable. But had not St. Thomas died, even the occasion of this modern debate would not have arisen, for already, at the beginning of the great medieval spring, the Church would have failed.

That, in saving the Church, he saved society itself, was instinctively felt by the common people, through whose spontaneous piety Almighty God achieves his purposes more widely than through any other channel, save perhaps through the channel of individual holiness and courage. The common people, not the clergy (though it was to their interest) in a burst of enthusiasm imposed the worship of the martyr upon Christendom. They felt it in their bones (and they were right) that if the laical state—the seeds of which were being sown—should once rise to maturity and complete power, they would be what they have become today, halfway to slavery. The independence of the Church was the guarantee of their customs and of that spirit whereby Christian men grope towards, in part always enjoy, and necessarily and always proclaim, freedom. It required the imbecility of modern Dons to wonder why St. Thomas should have so suddenly become a popular saint—why Canterbury should have become one of the great shrines of Christendom—and to decide that it was due to some odd mechanical conspiracy on the part of the priests! It was one of the most unplanned things that ever happened in history. It rose like a spring out of the earth exactly as, in a quite different field of spiritual appeal, there sprang in our own day the recognition of St. Therese of Lisieux: a young woman high among the Saints of God.

There is another major consideration in the matter of this great saint. Is it better to be direct or subtle? I mean, is it better for the purposes of God to be direct or subtle? Which is the better for one's own soul, there can be no doubt. But is it better to be direct or subtle for the achievement of the Kingdom?

Now to that unending doubt there are, as to all unending doubts, two answers equally valid. For there are conditions under which to be subtle is essential, when, without subtlety, there is nothing but disaster, even in the matters of the soul; and there are also conditions under which (and this is more easily forgotten by the tortuous and fallen spirit of man) for the achievement of the Kingdom it is better to be direct and to challenge.

Were not the first method admissible human affairs, and therefore the affairs of God on earth, would be a chaos and would fail. But for those who ridicule the second method as something impossible or, what is worse to the intelligence, grossly insufficient, St. Thomas provides an example. It happened to be his business, it happened to be his duty, it happened to be his triumph, to be direct. As against the multiple, to be single; as against the diverse, to be absolute; as against maneuver, to charge.

There is yet another question arising from this great story. It is the most searching question of all. "What about pride?" All challengers suffer, of necessity, the temptation of pride. They are of the breed of certitude and of simplicity; being simple and certain they will brook no contradiction; they are as it were blindly convinced of the right—and the right is their right. Now to make certain that you are always right is to put yourself in the position of God, and in so far as you put yourself in the position of God you are suffering from the weakness and nastiness of pride. These protagonists have always been accused of that fatal flaw in themselves. What is much more important for the comprehension of their very selves, they have always been at least *tempted* to it: now a permanent temptation is part of character, but by the Grace of God it is not necessarily a mastering part.

It is true, then, that all the great protagonists have had pride for a companion. To yield to it is their temptation, but it is a constitutional tendency and not a motive of their energy. They are sure. None shall deflect them. Yet their object being something outside themselves, they have in them a solvent of the evil thing; and I will believe that those who appear before the throne of God after heavy battles in the right cause, yet clouded with too much opinion, will have it easily forgiven them; especially if they have been defeated in the battles of the Lord.

Yet let this also be noted: that the instruments which are chosen for work of this land, those of the Tertullian spirit, cannot but be of that human sort which is imperfect through aggression and assertiveness and edge. They are sent out to dig like chisels; they must of necessity offend on that against which they act; for every permanent work is done in hard material and against the grain. Were they not what they are, nothing would be achieved for the Kingdom—or, at least, all would be only half done.

If these things be so (and they are so) let us consider the process whereby this great saint came to his glory.

What we today call England, a certain unmistakable unit, a nation, was created by the success of the Bastard William of Falaise, called "The Conqueror," when he confirmed by arms his claim to rule the country. (The word "conquest" is deceptive. There was in his day no modern idea of the violent unjust rape of one territory by the people of another—but to discuss all that would take too long.) What we call England was made, grew from, began, upon a Sussex hill in 1066. Not that the blood which we call English began then and (God knows) not the landscape nor the deep things which inhabit the native soul. All these are immemorial; the English imagination, the English humor, the English Englishry is from the beginning of recorded time. The pirate invasions from the "Angulus" or Bight of Denmark, their few colonies on the eastern coast, never profoundly affected this island. Nor is language a guide. But just when Europe was turning to a crystallization of nations out of that circling cauldron of the Dark Ages, England also was crystallized; and it was the Norman influence which precipitated her thus from a boiling into a crystallization. The process had not gone on a lifetime when St. Thomas was born.

We do not know the exact date of his birth. It was almost certainly between fifty and fifty-five years after the decisive battle which put the Bastard of Normandy, William, upon the throne at Westminster. It is thought that the year 1118 may be the most probable guess. St. Thomas was born in London, in Cheapside, at the end of December, the son of a London merchant, who had begun business upon the other side of the channel in Rouen, and had there secured wealth. It was a time when, for now nearly a hundred years past, the directing classes of England had been more and more mixed with the Continent and in which they had more and more come to be French-speaking—as must have been St. Thomas himself and all his people. The distinction between the gentry and merchants had not re-arisen (it is the nature of society, and crops up period after period).

His father was of gentle blood in the sense that the family had been territorial in Normandy, nor did St. Thomas ever feel himself to be other than the equal of those with whom he mixed. He was a huge powerful young man, good at every bodily exercise, a fighter on horseback; he certainly had ambition, and he was helped therein by those through whom he rose. He was of a world alive and eager, and when after his first advancements, partly perhaps through the wealth of his father, much through the recognition of his abilities, and more from the protection of the first man in the kingdom, the Archbishop of Canterbury, who promoted him, he rose. He took the Plantagenet side in the days when the young Plantagenet heir who was to be Henry II, at least ten years younger than himself, came by certain accidents to be the King of England. This Henry II of England sprang from the famous house of Anjou; packed with vitality, showing sparse red hair, intense, violent, exact; and the two men of similar energy became closely bound together. Now this Henry II of England, this new king of the new Angevin stock, great-grandson of William the Conqueror, married the divorced wife of the King of France. She was the heiress of all the west and the south, and her young husband became not only King of England but, under a sort of feudal homage, real ruler beyond Normandy (which he had inherited on the English side), also of all the South and West of the French kingdom. He was thus in his active and battling youth possessed of a greater recruiting field and a greater revenue than the French King, his Sovereign; and upon his will the future of Europe would largely depend.

Therefore St. Thomas as his bosom friend and fellow-in-arms stood out also before Christendom. Thomas fought for his junior, the King, during the expedition into Southern France in 1159, seven years after Henry's accession; he became glorious through a single combat with another man, saddle to saddle; he was the soldier of his day. His young master and friend determined to make him his all-sufficient minister, the title of such in that day being "Chancellor."[1] That young determined king of so much, and lord of half the West, did more for him. Henry being thirty years of age and St. Thomas about or over forty, the king determined to make him Archbishop of Canterbury, and thereby to make him also the first man in the Kingdom.

It is essential to understand what this meant. In theory the monks of Canterbury could elect their Archbishop; in practice for centuries, the king really nominated him.

The Church throughout the West was one body; the English province of the Church—or rather the two provinces of the Church in England, York and Canterbury—had been but part, for four hundred years at least, of Western Christendom. The unity of the Church had

1. The term, though preserved, has of course nothing in common with the modern title of Lord Chancellor, which applies to some chance lawyer or other who has worked his way through Parliament.

survived an anxious disruptive period after the death of Charlemagne more than three hundred years before, when, for the better part of two centuries, all manner of disturbances and quarrels had threatened to overwhelm Christendom. In that interlude—that interregnum as it were of our civilization—all manner of disruptive forces threatened us. The Moslems, who had swept over half Christendom, perpetually attacked in the South; Mongol and Slav Pagans from the East; Scandinavians from the North; the great landowners made themselves masters over their districts, and there survived of the imperial authority almost nothing, of local royal authority very little. The revenues of the Church, fixed in ancient endowments of land, fell in part a prey to the great families. But the structure of society held fast; the Mass, all the Liturgy, the hierarchy, the framework—clerical and lay—stood.

About a hundred years before St. Thomas's birth, the energies of Christendom began to raise a new dawn; and for that century those energies proceeded to a rapid extension of architecture and letters and learning. We have the vast adventure of the Crusades; we have the revivified powers of the Papacy, always admitted and always in the very nature of our society, but now to be fully exercised. With all this there went a new discipline throughout the Church; the enforcement of the long lapse in the matter of celibacy and an increasing clarity in the organization which would bind Christendom together. But at the same time there came necessarily, with greater wealth and clearer thinking and more eager ambitions, the growth of power in the Princes—of whom Henry II of England was among the very first.

It was in such a conjuncture, with the power of the Pope now well and consciously organized, with all Christendom knowing that on it, and the full society of the Church in hierarchy below it, the future would depend—for that civilization was at stake in a rising quarrel between the independent universal Church and the local magnates—it was just at such a crisis that "Thomas of London" as he signed himself, was, on the insistence of his companion-in-arms and deep friend, the younger man Henry, put into the See of Canterbury.

He was consecrated on Sunday, June 3rd, 1162, to the See which his old patron had occupied and which had been vacant for a year. It was a Sunday which St. Thomas in memory of the event turned into that Feast of the Trinity, the name of which has been preserved ever since. We must never forget that it was from Canterbury that the Feast of the Trinity proceeded, as did that other solemn Catholic custom, the Elevation of the Host after consecration at Mass.[2]

Immediately upon St. Thomas's elevation to the throne of Canterbury the inevitable clash between his strong character and the strong character of his junior, his close friend, his king appeared. For St. Thomas, authoritative, determined and always laying upon himself a clear course and always holding a clear definition both of his rights, but still more of his duty, was now the unquestioned head of the Church in England, and the Church was not a part of the State, was not indeed a part of Christendom; it was the soul of Christendom, superior to any local government and independent of any temporal government, not only in all that concerned doctrine but in all that concerned its own discipline and personnel.

With the awakening of a new and greater civilization in this twelfth century and with the revival of the old doctrines of imperial right under the lay imperial code of the Roman Empire, this superior, intangible, autonomous character of the Church was challenged. An effort could not but arise on the part of the lay power to make the Church within that power more and more subordinate to the earthly monarch of the realm. England, the best organized state of the time, and Henry its King, now lord of Normandy and all Western France as well, Henry, who was upon the whole the strongest monarch in

2. Landfranc, St. Thomas's chief predecessor and first Archbishop of Canterbury in the new England, was the great defender of the Real Presence, when the first doubts began to be cast upon it in France during his youth, and in reparation, or by way of especial homage, he would hold the Host reverently in his hands after consecration, lifting it somewhat in front of his face, and it seems that it was from this gesture that the full Elevation developed.

Christendom, still young (little over thirty) and of a fiery energy, could not but move as he did. He began an attempted control over that part of the universal Church which lay within his frontiers. Had he at once and wholly succeeded, the disaster, which was as a fact postponed for four hundred years, would have begun in the twelfth instead of the sixteenth century and—what is much more important than a mere postponement—it would have been universal, it would have affected the whole structure of the Church and condemned that structure to decay; it would not have been a mere division of Christendom, leaving a Catholic portion saved and sound, but a sapping of the vital principle of Christendom throughout Europe.

The moment for the revolutionary change proposed by this first Plantagenet was after a fashion inevitable, for it corresponded to another change which had come upon the Church itself. The main body of the Church officials, the "clerics," from its earliest days to the close of the dark ages, was composed of the hierarchy: priests and bishops. Less than the priests, but usually on their way to becoming priests, were the deacons and sub-deacons. There were also many who were in lesser orders and were still called "clerics," though not, properly speaking, of the sacred hierarchy. The general tone was given by the priest, he was the *typical* cleric; the lesser clerics were only a fringe. The determining number which gave its color and tone to the mass of ecclesiastics, those who would be generally recognized under the term "clergy," were the fully qualified priests who alone could consecrate and offer up the sacrifice of the Mass. The great bulk of them were settled as parish priests, though there was also a large number who were unattached, candidates for endowment who had not yet received it and might never receive it.

Now at the end of the Dark Ages and the first stirrings of the high medieval civilization, that is, with those last years of the tenth century when it was clear that Europe had saved herself from barbarian and Moslem pressure and the great siege was at an end; when one reform after another, each more thorough than the last, was leading up through more than a lifetime of effort to the Cluniac movement and at last to the glorious achievement of St. Gregory VII, when the origins of the Crusades had appeared in Spain, when a new culture was beginning in the schools and an administration more and more developed in the local courts, the clerical members were vastly increased.

They were so increased *not* by the addition of a great number of new priests, but by a great number of new men whose activities were secular, though they were tonsured and affiliated to the clerical body. These kept the accounts, they studied and systematized the old and new laws, they were the writers, the negotiators and the calculators; they filled the growing mass of minor posts which the new civilization had produced; they fulfilled nearly all the duties which could not be fulfilled either by the fighting class or by those who cultivated the soil or by the artisans. It is from this great mass of non-priestly but clerical men that there has been derived our word "clerk," and in general the identification of the word "clerical" with the whole business of writing. Those who taught were clerics, most of those who negotiated between princes were clerics, those who looked after the papers of public or private wealth were clerics.

The consequence was that the State was now—by 1162—newly faced with the presence of a new vast clerical body, fulfilling the functions and liable to the temptations and accidents of the layman. It was newly faced with thousands of individuals who were technically part of the clerical—that is to say, the Church—organization, and therefore amenable only to the Church law and the Church courts, and yet in daily roles typical of what today we should call laymen.

This state of affairs was not only the excuse, but in part the cause of the king's novel attempt: but he made no distinction between the various parts of the clerical body, and if his policy had won, any priest, however exalted his position, would have fallen (as he has fallen in modern times) under the lay power. The medieval autonomy of the Church would have disappeared, and with it, soon, religion and the unity of Christendom.

In the first year after the new Archbishop had been enthroned the great quarrel broke out. At Woodstock, in that royal manor on the land which was later made over to Marlborough as a reward for Blenheim, the king published "The Constitutions of Clarendon." Here we must note very carefully what these were and—a very different thing—what they purported to be.

The document purported to be "a record or recognition" of his grandfather's (Henry I) *customs* in Church matters, the *accepted* Church law of the realm. It is of the first importance to mark that. There was no admitted innovation. Such an idea would have been abhorrent to the time. The only test of right was custom; and to effect this beginning of revolution a pretense had to be made that it was an old custom which was being claimed and which furnished the moral basis for the action which the king proposed to take. But the thing was a falsehood. Although the document includes in its sixteen clauses not a few customs which had indeed tradition behind them, it also contains two of the utmost moment, both of which were revolutionary. These two clauses were the third and the eighth, and it is interesting to note the subtlety with which those who served the king attempted to give to a novelty (and a subversive novelty at the time) an excuse.

The eighth clause lays it down that no ecclesiastical appeal could be carried beyond the king's court (that is, to Rome) without leave of the king. Appeal could be made from the archdeacon to the bishop, from the bishop to the archbishop, and from the archbishop to the king, but the further appeal to Rome was declared to be against custom and right save when it was especially permitted by the Crown. Observe here this question of the old custom and right, at any rate since the Conquest. The Crown had claimed, the Church had never admitted, the right to prevent *recorded pronouncements* passing into or out of the kingdom without the royal leave. Thus a Papal Bull could not be introduced into England after the Conquest save by leave of the king; but it had never been admitted, I say, as a moral right by the Church: it could not be so, for to admit it would be to make the unity of the Church dependent upon the will of a local sovereign. It had been a custom of force and not of agreement between the two separate powers. But this new eighth clause in the Constitutions of Clarendon said something quite different. It said that there was no constitutional right of appeal from English ecclesiastical courts to Rome; they laid it down that *custom* so deemed; and so to lay down the custom was a falsehood.

Much more important in practice (because in practice appeals would have constantly been allowed anyway) was the third clause of the sixteen, which was the one round which in reality all the battle was to rage. By this clause the personnel of the Church, the members of that international and super-national body coincident with the Papal authority and with all western Christendom, was to be treated—in this realm at least—as the laymen were treated, and to be regarded in the administration as subjects of the king, and not as officers of a universal church. Hitherto any cleric accused of a crime could be tried by his ecclesiastical superiors only. They could for a grave crime degrade him, were he to offend again he would then be tried of course as a layman, his privilege of clergy had gone. But the principle was clear and universal, that while he was still a cleric he was amenable to clerical jurisdiction alone.

The introduction of this capital revolution was effected, as I have said, with great subtlety of phrase. "Clerics accused in any matter" (it ran) "being summoned by the king's justice and the Ecclesiastical Court, it may be seen what matter should be replied to in that Court...so that the king's justice shall send into the Court of Holy Church to see for what reason the matter is being dealt with there. And if the cleric be convicted or shall confess, he should not further be protected by the Church."

This is on the face of it much more tentative and much more of a compromise than we are usually told in our textbooks, where we are informed that the king proposed purely and simply to take jurisdiction out of the Church's hands. The form of words was such that a well-meaning ecclesiastical authority might be deceived and that men too timid to resist might salve their consciences.

It was clear that the intention was—it would at any rate soon be made the effect of such a clause—that clerics accused of a crime should in practice be withdrawn from ecclesiastical jurisdiction and treated as laymen. But it might be argued from the form of words that all that was going to happen was a courteous discussion between the lay and ecclesiastical power as to what the man was had up for, and whether it really did concern the Church, etc., etc. It is of capital importance to remember this in the story of what follows.

This document containing these revolutionary proposals, the Constitutions of Clarendon (it is a short thing, less than 2,000 words in length) is drawn up in the form in which it had been assented to by the magnates of the kingdom, including the bishops, and at the head of the list of those who assented was the name and title of Thomas, Archbishop of Canterbury, the first man in the realm and the head of the English province of the Church Universal. *The Constitutions were accepted.* The lay lords accepted them of course, but so did the bishops, and (possibly under a verbal misunderstanding) the Pope.

St. Thomas himself accepted them, but he had already grasped the core of the matter; he accepted grievously and with grave reluctance after a delay of three days, saying that he must obey the Pope, but that such obedience was compelling him to perjury—meaning presumably that he never could in practice agree to the changes proposed. All had begun in the summer of the year after St. Thomas's enthronement as Archbishop, in the month of July, 1163. In October a Council at Westminster confirmed the Constitutions. But the resistance of St. Thomas was beginning. When the bishops agreed, they had only agreed (presumably under St. Thomas's influence) with the clause added, "saving our order." The bishops in their turn had influenced St. Thomas in his agreement as late as January of the next year, 1164, when all the great of the realm were again summoned to Clarendon.

But St. Thomas believed that he had acted like St. Peter; his conscience would not let him rest, and Henry knew that it would soon be open war between them.

He saw the Archbishop twice, he understood what resistance he was to be prepared for, and he summoned for the October of that year (1164) another great council at Northampton. Instead of sending a special summons to the first man of the realm—the Archbishop and Primate—he sent for him by orders to the officers of the County of Kent, a planned belittling, and an insult to one whom he now regarded as an enemy.

St. Thomas came to that great meeting, and was there an isolated man. He appeared in the outer hall, with his huge figure standing out above them all, grasping his Cross in his own hand instead of having it borne before him, as though for a symbol that he alone, Thomas the individual soul, was standing out with none to befriend him or support him.

The bishops of England, some of whom were his personal enemies, but most of whom at heart knew that he was doing right, begged him to yield. He retorted by solemnly telling them that it was *their* duty to obey *his* authority.

The quarrel grew fiercer, Henry forbade an appeal to Rome, and told the council to denounce the saint for a traitor. The king's attitude was modified for a moment through the hesitation of the bishops, when they saw how grave the matter had become; he allowed the appeal to Rome, but he carried out a policy of violent financial persecution, demanding huge sums from the See of Canterbury upon various pleas of chicanery; and on All Souls' Day of that year (1164) St. Thomas secretly sailed from Sandwich to take refuge upon the Continent, to see the supreme Pontiff of Christendom in person and to be free from the peril of direct constraint. Before the end of November he had seen Pope Alexander III at Sens. He laid at the feet of the Papal authority two things; the text of the Constitutions against which he was holding out, and his archiepiscopal ring—the tender of which meant that he was willing, or rather anxious, to resign his See and so leave the decision to his successor, and the Pope free.

At this point we must particularly regard the attitude taken by Alexander III, the Pope of the day. It can be too much excused, but it can also be maligned.

Alexander III was one of the great political Popes who have, in the Providence of God, been preservative of Catholic political power in the world. He was engaged in a struggle against the greatest of the Emperors, Barbarossa, and was defending not only the liberties of Rome and the Church, but of the Italian cities. The Emperor and his Germans had set up against him an anti-Pope, and Alexander was at this moment in France because he was virtually exiled from Italy by the strength of his opponent. It was of the highest moment that so powerful a king as Henry should not join forces with the new German schism. Anyhow, whether he is to be praised upon the whole or blamed, the Pope, deliberately considering all the circumstances, chose to temporize. He would not allow St. Thomas to resign; he said that the Constitutions of Clarendon were not to be accepted as a whole, but that six of them were acceptable—"tolerable" was the word—that is, to be accepted if necessary. In general, his support of St. Thomas was lukewarm. He aimed at a reconciliation, and what is more, it seems that he still thought the issue to be only a verbal one, a question of formulation, of interpretation. If that were so, he was wrong and St. Thomas was right; it was not a verbal matter but a matter of vital principle, as the event would certainly show if ever the proposed changes were accepted.

There followed for years a swaying struggle, in which at moments St. Thomas was nearly reconciled to Henry—on condition of course that he was not made to accept the obnoxious thing—in the course of which Henry nearly yielded twice, but also in the course of which there were moments of acute tension and almost of violence. Thus, when St. Thomas took refuge with the Cistercians at Pontigny, Henry threatened in revenge to expel all the Cistercians from England.

Towards the end of those uncertain years of St. Thomas's exile Henry went so far as to have his young son crowned by St. Thomas's especial enemy, the Archbishop of York, Roger de Pont l'Eveque—although the Primate alone had the right to crown the kings or heirs of England. To meet the threats that were taking place against ecclesiastical property and the usurpations of his enemies in his absence St. Thomas began to issue excommunications. He had even threatened that if Henry did not amend before Candlemas of the year 1170 he would be put under an interdict.

It was in the June of that year that Henry committed the blunder and the outrage of having his young son crowned by Roger of York, though, not only St. Thomas but the Pope himself had forbidden such action. The king feared he had gone too far, and began to go back. A few weeks later, at Frètèval, he was so far reconciled that he promised to be guided by the Archbishop's counsel, and to keep silent upon the whole revolutionary policy of ecclesiastical jurisdiction. He even openly proposed to return to England in the company of St. Thomas. But he delayed, and made shifts for further delay, until at the end of the year, in the November of 1170, St. Thomas proceeded to the final actions which culminated in his martyrdom.

It was proposed to send the saint back to his See, the property of which was to be restored and the administration put again into his hands; but as a sort of warder over him during the journey was set John of Oxford, a notorious enemy with whom he would not have been safe, and he learned that Roger of York and the Bishops of London and Salisbury, who were also especially opposed to him, were plotting to prevent his landing. St. Thomas had obtained from the Pope letters inhibiting and conditionally excommunicating those who opposed the Primate. He sent these letters across the Channel in advance of himself, dispatching them on Sunday, November 29, while he sailed on Monday, November 30, from Wyssant—the little port between Calais and Boulogne then often used—and on the next day, Tuesday, December 1, he landed at Sandwich and proceeded to his palace and cathedral at Canterbury. He there reiterated his position again fully and awaited whatever results might follow from his firmness. Those against whom he had moved the Pope to act demanded unconditional absolution. He replied that he must await the Pope's further letters. And they proceeded to the king in order to lodge their appeal. Meanwhile, the property of the See was not restored, as had been promised, and to the burning indignation of the Archbishop, the immediate lands of the archbishopric were in the hands of robbers and despoilers, notably a lawless brigand of a fellow, De Broc, who had seized one of the archiepiscopal castles, Saltwood, and was making it a nest of robbers.

On Friday, Christmas Day, St. Thomas excommunicated De Broc, and four days later—Tuesday, December 29—appeared those four knights who had acted upon the king's passionate words, and were ready to slay. They bade St. Thomas absolve the bishops. He was steadfast, and refused. It was the afternoon of that winter day, and the sun was already sinking, when they came back armed and with them De Broc, determined to save his booty and to that end to extract his own absolution by force. In the presence of these five men, now armed, the monks dragged their great master with them into the cathedral through the cloisters by the north door. They would have barred the door, but St. Thomas forbade them to do so. The light was now failing and the great church was half in darkness when the armed murderers burst in by that north door. All fled save one Grim, who stood by his master, holding the Archbishop's Cross in his hand. The swords were drawn, and with one of them the Archbishop's cap was struck off. He knelt upon the stone floor of the North Transept, not far from the corner pillar thereof where one turned into the Ambulatory round the Choir. So kneeling he covered his face with his hands. He was no longer throwing back angrily into the teeth of his opponents the insults they had given him: he saw that death was upon him. And as he so knelt, with his hands before his face, he murmured, "To God and Blessed Mary, to the patron Saints of this Church and St. Denis

I commend myself and the cause of the Faith." He bowed his head and awaited the blow. The first that struck was Fitzurse; Grim put up his hand to shield his master, but his arm was broken and the sword gashed that master's head. Another blow followed, and he fell. A third cut off the crown of the skull and with the sword's point the brains were scattered upon the stones. Then, having done these things, they left the body where it lay and fled out into the now dark winter air.

Those few moments of tragedy in the North Transept of Canterbury had done what so many years of effort had so far failed to do. The whole movement against the autonomy of the Church was stopped dead. The tide ran rapidly backward—within an hour St. Thomas was a martyr, within a month the champion not only of religion but of the common people, who obscurely but firmly knew that the independence of the Church was their safeguard. A tale of miracles began, and within a year the name of St. Thomas of Canterbury was standing permanently above and throughout Christendom. Everywhere there were chapels and churches raised to his name, and then came the great uninterrupted pilgrimages to his shrine year after year, until it rivalled St. James of Compostela, becoming the second great center in the West and loaded with gems and gold and endowment.

DAME JULIAN OF NORWICH (1342–1413)

by E. I. WATKIN

Habent sua fata libelli.[1] Most writers address only their contemporaries. A few find audience of future generations. But there are also those whose message is apparently lost, and who must wait for their audience until a more or less remote posterity. Of these were Henry Vaughan and Gerald Manley Hopkins among the poets and among the mystical writers Dame Julian of Norwich. Within a restricted circle, indeed, she possessed her contemporary disciples. But that circle can never have been very large and must soon have passed. But four manuscripts survive, of which only two are anterior to 1600, and it was not until the 17th century that the record of her religious experience was first printed by Serenus de Cressy in 1670. And it was only in the closing years of the last century that her book became at all widely known. Now interest is awake; her readers are many. Evidently Dame Julian's message is specially adapted for our reception, is a spiritual food which our constitution is peculiarly fitted to relish and assimilate.

Of Julian's biography we know little that is certain. Two or three days of a life covering at least seventy-one years stand out in vivid light. The rest is darkness. Of her origin we know nothing. An allusion to "the sea-ground" with "its hills and dales green seeming as it were most growing with seaweed and gravel" suggests perhaps that her home had been on the Norfolk coast.[2] If the manuscripts correctly report her Latin exclamations, *Benedicite Domine*, or *Dominus*, her description of herself as unlettered was not altogether humility. On the other hand, she was certainly acquainted with the New Testament, directly or indirectly, in an English version. "The place in a high manner dignified by her abode" as her first editor, Serenus de Cressy, writes, "and by the access of her heavenly guest, was the City of Norwich." She was an anchoress living in a cell against the south wall of St. Julian's Church. The majority of anchorages were placed on the north wall. It is pleasant to know that Julian whose writing is so remarkable for its spiritual sunshine of confident joy was not debarred from the cheer of physical sunlight. The cell was demolished in the 18th century by those who did not share Fr. Cressy's view of the dignity conferred by her inhabitation. Its foundations however have been laid bare. It is usually supposed that this cell was the scene of her revelations. But Miss Underhill in her valuable study of "Julian of Norwich" in the *Essentials of Mysticism* points out that the presence in her room of many persons makes it more probable that this experience occurred before she entered the anchorage, and suggests that she was then a nun in the Benedictine Abbey at Carrow. For St. Julian's cell was in the gift of the Abbey. It is, indeed, extremely unlikely that even at a death bed the cell of an enclosed anchoress would have been open to a large number of bystanders—including Julian's mother and "a religious person" other than her confessor. When Richard Rolle visited his friend the recluse, Margery, in her illness he did not enter her cell. On the other hand, there is no mention of an Abbess as

1. The writer desires to thank the editor of *The Catholic World* (New York) for his courtesy in permitting the publication of portions of an article on Dame Julian of Norwich which appeared in that review.
2. If I am right in concluding that her home was the scene of her illness and revelations (see below), it was probably in the neighborhood of some house of male religious to which her visitor belonged.

present, or of any nuns. Her mother closed Julian's eyes when she was believed to be dead. Surely the Abbess would have performed this office for one of her nuns. And it was not a convent chaplain, but the parson, "my curate" (i.e., parish priest) who was summoned to her death-bed. Surely Carrow is unlikely. If the sickness and visions took place neither at Carrow Abbey nor at St. Julian's anchorage, we may conclude—a conclusion borne out by the mother's presence and prominence—that they occurred while she was at home. Possibly it was in consequence of this episode that she embraced the eremitical life or was at last permitted to do so.

Her age, thirty and a half, is indeed, as Miss Underhill remarks, an objection to this hypothesis. But it is far from decisive. Some circumstance of which we know nothing—perhaps her mother's opposition or need—may have kept her at home. And if Julian speaks of a youth consecrated to God, she regarded herself as definitely young at the date of her revelations—though twenty years later we hear of servants attending upon her in her old age. In any case it was certainly in the solitary confinement of her cell that Julian came to understand the meaning of her revelations as she explains them in her book. The cell at St. Julian's was at least her theological college. She was still alive in 1413. The date of her death is unknown. In place of epitaph on her equally unknown tomb we may inscribe the judgment of a 17th century French Protestant, Pierre Poiret, in his catalogue of mystical writers—*Theodidacta, profunda, ecstatka*, Taught of God, Profound, Ecstatic.

Julian tells us that in her youth she desired "three gifts by the grace of God." The first was "mind of the passion." By this she meant not only an intense realization of the Passion but even an actual vision, "a bodily sight." The second was an illness grave to the point of dying without actual death. This illness she desired for the age of thirty. "And this meant I, for I would be purged by the mercy of God, would after live more to the worship of God because of that sickness." The third was to receive three spiritual wounds, a number suggested by the three bodily wounds of St. Cecilia's martyrdom. These were true contrition, kind compassion, i.e., a feeling of Our Lord's suffering, and "willful longing to God." This willful longing is for Julian the substance of religion and of prayer. It is "the affectuous stirring of love to God for Himself," the "sharp dart of longing love" on which the anonymous mystic, contemporary and fellow countryman, who wrote *The Cloud of Unknowing* lays equal stress and of which he says "this is only by itself that work that destroys the ground and the root of sin" and that "all virtues shall truly be, both perfectly conceived and feelingly comprehended in it, without any mingling of the intent."

In the May of 1373, when Julian was thirty and a half years of age, the illness she desired was granted.

Six days and nights she lay ill, during half that time in a critical condition. On the seventh night death seemed certain. On the following morning, Saturday, May 8th,[3] her body was paralyzed from the waist downward. She was propped upright in bed and the priest set a crucifix in front of her eyes. As she gazed on the crucifix, the room grew dark about her "save in the image of the cross wherein continued ordinary daylight, and I know not how." If this was a pathological symptom, it was a symbol also of a world whose meaning is dark, except for the light yielded by the Cross. The paralysis crept upward. Julian was now scarcely conscious, when suddenly all feeling of pain passed away (she had suffered from difficulty in breathing) and from the waist upward "I was as whole as ever I was before." The second spiritual wound came into her mind, her desire for compassion with her crucified Savior. But she no longer desired any "bodily sight." All this while her gaze was focused on the crucifix before her. "And in this, suddenly I saw the red blood running down from under the garland, hot and freshly, plentiful and lively, right as it was in the time that the garland of thorns was pressed on His blessed Head." "And in the same showing, suddenly the Trinity fulfilled my heart most of joy;

3. May 13 rests on a mistaken reading of the Paris MS., xiii for viii.

and so I understood it shall be in heaven without end for all that shall come there."

This was the double beginning of a series of revelations which lasted from four in the morning "till it was noon of the day or past."[4]

When they were ended and Julian left to physical pain and the listless aridity of an exhausted nervous system, she began to doubt their reality and told a religious who visited her that she had raved. It would seem that the chief matter of her doubt was the series of sensible visions of the Passion. But she is careful to add, "I believed truly for the time that I saw." That night another "showing," an intellectual apprehension of Jesus' presence in the soul together with a comforting utterance reassured her belief for the remainder of her life.

"All this blessed teaching of our Lord God" Julian tells us, "was showed by three parts; that is to say, by bodily sight; and by word formed in my understanding, and by ghostly sight. For the bodily sight, I have said as truly as I can: and for the words I have said them right as Our Lord showed them me; and for the ghostly sight, I have said some deal, but I may never fully tell it." These words may conveniently be grouped with the bodily visions to which they are psychologically akin. There are thus two distinct categories of "showing," the apparently physical, whether seen or heard, and the spiritual vision. Of the former the vision of the bleeding face of the image is an instance, of the latter the joyful intuition of the Trinity. Some of the showings lack any "physical" vision, and consist wholly of spiritual intuitions.

As Miss Underhill points out, these physical "showings" reflect contemporary art and devotional literature. Moreover, modern studies of subliminal activity have shown that the images out of which visions and locutions are woven, and even the concepts that explain them already existed in the sub-consciousness of the visionary, and

4. Or perhaps "it was nine of the day overpassed," as Miss Warrack's edition reads from another manuscript.

are derived from environment, education, or reading. But this fact does not disprove an objective contact with God as the ultimate stimulus giving birth to these visions, words and ideas and even to some extent determining their arrangement. Whether or not this Divine stimulus or arrangement is present, and if so, to what degree, can be judged only from the religious value of the teaching thus conveyed, or from the spiritual effect on the mystic or his disciples. Since we are embodied beings, intuitions of the Divine are likely to clothe themselves in the sense-derived images and concepts laid up for their vesture in our subliminal wardrobe. The extent to which mystical experience thus translates itself will no doubt vary with psycho-physical constitution. But if we are theists, we shall see no reason to deny that it also depends on the purpose of God.

The supreme revelation of God's love in face of the evil in the world is the crucifix. Therefore Dame Julian's "Showings" begin with a vision of the Crucified and continue with a series of visions of the Passion. Of these there were five.

"Our courteous Lord," Julian writes, "showed His passion to me in five manners. Of which the first is the bleeding of the Head; the second, discoloring of His blessed Face; the third is the plenteous bleeding of the Body, in seeming of scourging; the fourth is the deep drying of our Lord's Body on the Cross by an inner parching of thirst and a drying wind." (This feature was probably suggested by the withered and meager figure of the medieval crucifix.) "And the fifth is that was showed for the joy and the bliss of the Passion." This fifth vision was the sight of a sudden change in the dying Christ to "a blessedful cheer." With this change she heard the words "Are you well-satisfied that I suffered for you?" "I said 'Yes, good Lord, thank you; yes, good Lord blessed may you be.' Then said Jesus our good Lord 'If you are satisfied, I am satisfied: It is a joy, a bliss, and an endless liking to me that ever I suffered passion for you: and if I might have suffered more, I would have suffered more.'" And here we must remember that as Dame Julian tells us elsewhere, the "you" for whom Our Lord would if possible have suffered even more than He did is not the individual Julian but each and all of the saved. "All that I say of me, I mean in person of all Christians."

The passion series closes with a vision already half an intellectual apprehension, in which was shown to "the understanding" the wounded side of Jesus opened to provide a "fair and delectable place large enough for all mankind that shall be saved" and within the wound "His blessed Heart cloven in two."

The second mode of revelation experienced by Julian is purely intellectual or spiritual. Supreme in this mode is the immediate experience of the Absolute Godhead—mystical experience in the strictest sense. For this is the intuition-union of God which is the essence of mystical prayer. Inextricably blended with this intuition in Julian's revelations is a series of distinct conceptions, "understandings" of the Divine Attributes and the Divine Action in man and creation as a whole. These intellectual visions blend in their turn with the visual or audible "showings" already considered. Julian's revelations are a gospel to her "even-Christians" rather than an account of her personal union with God, or of the way by which she attained it. She, therefore, says little of the formless concept-transcending prayer-union which exceeds even these intellectual apprehensions of the Divine attributes. For, of its very nature, it lacks a content communicable to others. But she speaks of "an unperceivable prayer" which is evidently this indescribable union, and hints at it as underlying her inability after years of reflection to express her "ghostly sight."

We cannot suppose that all the significance she finds in her intuitions of Divine truth was distinctly present to her mind in those first hours of their apocalypse. Their interpretation is largely due to later reflection upon an intuition originally too full and too indistinct for clear understanding. A shorter version of the Revelations has been discovered in a 15th century manuscript and published by the Rev. Dundas Harford. In this version, the theological developments of her "showings" are for the most part absent. There is nothing corresponding to Chapters 44–63 of the longer version, the section most exclusively a theological treatise. The editor contends that this version is the more primitive form of the revelations before later reflection had worked over their material. This is most probably true. For this shorter version contains several homely details absent from the longer, for example that the priest brought his serving boy, that Julian was propped up *with clothes*, that her mother was present and "lifted up her hand to lock her eyes" believing her dead, that the bystanders bathed her temples. There are also a few bold sayings and ambiguous phrases absent from the longer version. On the other hand, many of the absent passages are spoken of in the longer version as direct revelations. It is likely that in the years of prayerful contemplation during which her revelations were pondered by Julian many of their interpretations came to her not as conscious reflections of her own mind, but as intuitions or illustrations apparently the direct gift and illumination of God. In any case we are bound to ascribe a considerable portion of Julian's theological explanations to her own reason whether operating consciously or subconsciously. But we should not conclude that this "use of natural reason" led to an arbitrary remodeling or misinterpretation of the intuitional material. For, as Julian says, the intuition, the immediate experience, "the inward gracious teaching of the Holy Spirit" and "the use of man's kindly reason" are both "of one God." And as regards the human medium, a psychology which forgets the unity of the soul and draws too sharp lines of demarcation between the intuition in the central depths raised into consciousness in their peculiar contact with God, and the normally more conscious activity of discursive reasoning, must be artificial and sterile—a dissection, not a picture of the living organism. Without these abstractions and dissections we cannot indeed understand the organism. But they are unable to reveal its living reality. Its unitary and individual life eludes their analysis.

Julian's attempt to translate her obscure but vivid intuition into terms comprehensible by the understanding sometimes takes the form of a parable. These parables range from simple illustrations that occurred to her mind, "came into her head" as we say, to visions or locutions that appeared to be the direct work of God. They deserve our special attention since they are not only one of the most attractive features of the book, but present in an imaginative, and therefore easily intelligible, form its sometimes difficult and always profound theology.

"As the body is clad in the cloth and the flesh in the skin and the bones in the flesh and the heart in the bulk, so are we soul and body clad and enclosed in the goodness of God."

"He showed a little thing, the quantity of a hazelnut, lying in the palm of my hand…and it was round as a ball. I thought 'What this may be?' and it was answered thus 'It is all that is made.'"

"He showed this open example: 'It is the most worship that a solemn lord or a great king may do to a poor servant if he will be homely with him: and namely, if he show it himself of a full true meaning, and with a glad cheer both in private and openly.'"

"In this time I saw a body lying on the earth: which body showed heavy and fearful, and without shape or form, as it were a foul stinking mire. And suddenly out of this body sprung a full fair creature, a little child full-shaped and formed, swift and lively and whiter than the lily, which sharply glided up into heaven. The foulness of the body bespoke great wretchedness of our mortal flesh; and the littleness of the child bespoke the cleanness and the pureness of our soul. And 1 thought with this body remains no fairness of this child, as with this child dwells no foulness of this body." A picture curiously reminiscent of Blake.

And there is the parable of Motherhood, too long for quotation, which occupies the sixtieth and sixty-first chapters. The services of a mother to her baby are applied to the service of Jesus to us in the birth and infancy of our supernatural life. But the most developed and the most important parable—a parable which condenses Julian's central teaching—is the parable of the lord and the servant. To this we must return later. The majority of these parables are wanting in the shorter version. Perhaps some of them suggested themselves later, perhaps

Julian was afraid these secondary pictures might distract her readers from the primary visions and teaching.

Such then are the media of Julian's revelations—intuition, speculation, conscious and, far more important, subconscious art. It remains to consider the religious doctrine that they convey.

To the double character of the revelations, in part sensible visions and words, in part intellectual contemplations, correspond roughly the two poles around which their doctrine revolves. One pole is the incomprehensible and infinite Godhead, eternal and immutable; the other the redeeming humanity of Christ with Its extension the Church. This bi-polarity is the distinctive feature of Christian mysticism. For Christianity is the religion of the Incarnation of Godhead in humanity, of the Absolute in the relative, of Eternity in time.

The Eternal Godhead, Its incarnation in human life in Christ and His Church-body, are thus the two poles alike of the universal Christian revelation and these private revelations of Dame Julian. This is evident already in the first showing where the joyful apprehension of the Trinity represents the pole of eternity, the vision of Christ's bleeding Head the pole of time. This double vision of eternity and time—not of eternity as absorbing time and reducing it to nothingness—nor of time as possessing a value independent of its manifestation and incarnation of the Eternal Good—runs through the revelations. Julian's treatment of the soul, of prayer, of redemption, of the problem of evil is unintelligible unless this twofold point of view is always before the mind. The same problem or fact wears a different aspect, as it is regarded from the lower standpoint of time—its phenomenal aspect, though real enough in its sphere—or from the higher standpoint of God's eternity—its ultimate and therefore truest reality. And both aspects are seen to be harmonious and complementary, though Julian not possessing the unveiled vision of God cannot always explain how the harmony is effected.

To eternity belong "the substance of the soul" and God's "higher judgment" upon it; to time "the sensuality" of the soul and the lower judgment passed upon it by the Church on earth. Unless this double standpoint is grasped, Julian may seem to teach doctrines which she would in fact have abhorred. Keeping it always before us, we will consider her doctrine of God, of the human soul, of evil and its redemption, and finally of prayer.

Julian sees God immanent in all things. "I saw God in a point; that is to say in my understanding (I saw Him thus) by which sight I saw that He is in all things." The point here represents, I believe, not the center of the universe, but the least portion of being.

But if present everywhere, not in equal measure. The soul being most Godlike—capable even of the beatific vision of His Infinite Being—is His special seat. In the sixteenth revelation, Julian sees Christ both in His Godhead and in His Manhood specially present in the human soul (Ch. 68).

As God is immanent in all things, so is He their value, their positive being (Ch. 26). It is indeed their inherent limits as contingent and relative beings which constitute them creatures essentially distinct from God. As God is thus the goodness, the ultimate and truest reality of all things, He is also the agent of their activities. "I beheld that He does all that is done. Wherefore all things that are done, are well done; for Our Lord God does all: for in this time the working of creatures was not showed, but of Our Lord God in creatures and all He does." "Man beholds some deeds well done, and some deeds evil: and Our Lord beholds them not so, for as all that has being…is of God's making, so is all thing that is done, in property (i.e., really, in the ultimate truth of it) of God's doing…." "See I am God: See I am in all things. See I do all things…. How should anything be amiss?" Analyze the limited existence of creatures, it is unintelligible save as contingent upon and grounded in Absolute Being. Analyze causation and activity, and they also are unintelligible as independent and self-explanatory. They are essentially contingent upon and relative to the One Absolute Cause and Agent. And the positive existence and activity of creatures is good. For as positive value and energy they are the communications of the being and activity of God.

If Julian sees God in all things and especially in the human soul, she also sees all things and especially the soul in God who transcends their being which He gives and preserves. "As the body" to recall the little parable already quoted "is clad in the cloth and the flesh in the skin—so are soul and body clad and enclosed in the goodness of God." "God is more near to us than our own soul—for He is the ground in whom our soul stands.... Our kind is in God whole (i.e., our specific and our individual nature are contained in His universal being); in which He makes diversities flowing out of Him to work His will." "Verily I saw that all our substance is in God." The complement of the vision of God in a point is the vision of the universe as a ball, the size of a hazelnut, lying in the palm of the Divine Hand. "I marveled how it might last, for I thought it might suddenly have fallen to pieces for littleness. And I was answered in my understanding. It lasts and ever shall: for God loves it. And so has all things being by the love of God. In this little thing I saw three properties. The first is that God made it. The second is that God loves it. The third is that God keeps it." Our immanence in a transcendent God is for Julian a more valuable truth than the immanence of God in us (Ch. 54).

Julian distinguishes between "the substance" of the soul grounded and dwelling in God and "the sensuality" of the soul in which God dwells. The sensuality is the soul as informing the body, its life principle and the subject of our psycho-physical experience. Hence it begins to exist "when our soul is inspired in our body." Her concept of the higher part of the soul, the substance, is more difficult.

After comparing different passages I believe that by "the substance of the soul" she means its inmost depth or center from which the will and understanding take their rise. The ground of the soul, the apex of the soul, the synderesis [the innate moral consciousness] are other terms current among medieval mystics. This center, normally subliminal, is, mystical writers agree, the peculiar seat of the mystical contact with God. For it is most free from the limitations of the more or less superficial psychical functions and their sense-conditioned experience.

For Julian the substance is so immediately united with God that in those who will be saved it is never separated from Him, however grievously the soul sins in her sensuality. In the shorter version she says "Prayer ones the soul to God. For though the soul is ever like God in substance, it is often unlike in condition through sin on man's part. Then makes prayer the soul like unto God when the soul wills as God will. And then is it like to God in condition as it is in substance." She even says (in the longer version) "I saw no difference between God and our substance but as it were all God." She hastens, however, to add that "my understanding took that our substance is in God, that is to say, that God is God and our substance is a creature in God." To the substance belongs a "godly will that never finally assents to sin and never shall, that may never will evil endlessly but ever good." This is opposed to a "beastly will in the lower part that may never will no good." The latter statement is, however, a passing exaggeration; for Julian elsewhere implies the truer view that the lower will is sometimes good, sometimes evil. Hence arise the two judgments mentioned above, God's higher judgment of approbation on the good will of the substance, the Church's lower judgment of censure on the sinful will of the sensuality. This doctrine of an indefectible union between the elect and God in the fundamental orientation of the will is, as far as I know, peculiar to Julian among Catholic mystics. It may even seem identical with the Protestant teaching of the indefectibility of grace. But Julian also teaches that a soul that shall be finally saved may fall into mortal sin, "I saw how sin is deadly for a short time to the blessed creatures of endless life." This seemingly inconsistent doctrine of a substantial will-union persisting in spite even of mortal sin is, I believe, Julian's vision of the ground of the soul as outside the time series in the eternal Now of God. However a soul may sin in time, if it is finally saved for eternity, in eternity and therefore in the present vision and *reality* of God—more real than the time series and its phenomena—it is now what it will finally become. *Sub specie aeternitatis* and, therefore, in God the will is essentially and fundamentally its final choice. Moreover, as we shall see, Julian does not separate any elect soul from the solidarity of Christ and His Saints. God sees all souls saved in Christ as an indissoluble unity, one "man" with and in Him and therefore as good and united to Himself in the one will of the Mystic Christ.

Flemish and German mystics had spoken of the Divine Idea of each soul as its uncreated ground or substance. When a soul has fulfilled God's purpose in its creation, it corresponds and is perfectly united with its type-idea in the Divine Mind. Since the substance is the expression of an idea of the Divine Wisdom, the created substance thus the reflection of the uncreated, and since that Wisdom for Christian theology is the Second Person of the Trinity incarnate in Jesus Christ, that Divine-Human Person is for Julian "our Mother in kind, in our substantial making, in whom we be grounded and rooted."

Julian has perhaps confused to some extent the uncreated substance with the created. Hence she speaks of the work of redemption as a re-union between the sensuality and the substance. But there are two distinct unions—the re-union between the created and uncreated substance in the beatific union with God—and the perfect subordination of the sensible functions of the soul to its central ground. She also speaks as though supernatural gifts, especially faith, come from the substance of the soul. This can only be true of God as the ground and *ideal* substance of the soul. Of the created substance, it is true only in the sense that faith—with hope and charity—is directly given to the root of the soul's central functions and thence attains the more superficial phenomenal functions. Further, Julian once says the substance was "made without beginning" a statement true only of the uncreated substance—its Divine Idea. Yet we have noticed her explicit statement, that the substance of the soul is a creature distinct from the eternal Godhead. This portion of the book leaves the impression that she has been unable to achieve a perfectly clear understanding and expression of her intuition. Perhaps she has misunderstood hard sayings of mystical writers read or heard during her years of reflective elaboration. We must remember that the fourteenth century German-Flemish school with whose teachings Julian, as Miss Underhill shows, must have been directly or indirectly acquainted, derives from Eckhart who did speak of the ground of the soul as somehow uncreated and Divine. And his pantheistic error[5] though abandoned by his disciples[6] left its traces in their phraseology.

But there remains clear enough for Julian's readers the teaching that our true nature and personality consist in the union with God and life in Him which we are created to achieve. We came forth from God to express in our unique individuality, a unique aspect of His wisdom. However we fail, unless we finally and totally reject Him we are in the center of our being united with Him; if the root of our will cleaves to God, our feelings about Him matter little. The process of redemption is thus a return to our origin, a return by grace to our true nature, that aspect of Divine Reality eternally present in the Wisdom of God which from eternity we are predestined to express (Ch. 68 *ad fin.*).

But this return can be no simple ascent of unchecked progress. Redemption implies the restoration of something lost, the cure of an evil. Julian's intuitions of redemption presuppose, therefore, a doctrine of evil. When she saw God in all things "Sin was not showed and I saw verily that sin is no deed." Elsewhere "I saw not sin; for I believe it had no manner of substance, no part of being, and it might not be known but by the pain that it causes." In the shorter version she says: "Sin is neither deed nor liking." These words, omitted later no doubt owing to the danger of misunderstanding, mean I believe, that sin is no positive act or desire. For a sinful act is as a positive activity good.

5. Whether of belief or merely of expression I will not here attempt to determine.

6. Tauler is careful to distinguish between the created and uncreated ground.

Its sinfulness consists in its exclusion of other factors that ought to have been present. And a sinful desire is always for something possessed of a certain value without which it could be in no way desirable. Its sinfulness consists in the undue imperfection of that good. Thus the object of sin differs from the object of a good will by a defect of being, and the sinner is as such one who chooses nothingness.

Towards the end of the shorter version is an eloquent declamation against the "naught" of sin. But Julian does not therefore regard sin lightly, as in practice unreal and unimportant. "If it were laid before us all the pain that is in hell and in purgatory and in earth, to suffer it rather than sin, we should rather choose all that pain, than sin; for sin is so vile and so much for to hate, that it may be likened to no pain; which pain is not sin." Baron Von Hügel found these utterances inconsistent, ascribing the former to neo-platonic theory, the latter to Christian experience. There is no inconsistency. That which has no substantial existence may be in another sense very real. A famine is a terrible reality. Yet it is no positive thing—simply the undue absence of food. And if evil *had* a positive reality, there must either be an ultimate principle of evil, a bad God, or God must be partly evil.

Cold comfort before the hideous countenance of the world's sin and our own, this abstract consolation of its metaphysical nonentity! But it has its practical importance. For it proves that, despite appearances, the universe is ultimately and fundamentally good. Hence also wrongdoing cannot be truly profitable, or finally triumphant. But Julian has further comfort. She sees sin as God's scourge for our discipline. It humbles us and increases our knowledge of His love. For redeemed humanity, sin is also an occasion of greater good. "Sin is behovely," that is, has its part in the Divine economy of good. "Adam's sin," Julian insists, "was the most harmful that ever was done," but the satisfaction made for it by Christ "is more pleasing to the blessed Godhead and more worshipful for man's salvation without comparison, than ever was the sin of Adam's harmful." God will bestow on redeemed mankind a better gift than we should have enjoyed had man never fallen. And this is true also of the individual sinner. "God showed that sin shall be no shame but worship to man; for right as to every sin is answering a pain by truth, right so for every sin to the same soul is given a bliss by love. Right as diverse sins be punished with diverse pains after that they be grievous; right so shall they (sinners) be rewarded with diverse joys in heaven for their victories, after as the sin has been painful and sorrowful in earth." We are reminded of the bold words placed by Dante in the mouth of Folco in Paradise: "Here we do not repent, but rejoice, not in the sin which is forgotten, but in the Goodness that ordained and provided."

Like St. Catherine of Genoa, who saw no wrath "in tender love," Julian is insistent that there is no anger in God. Possibly she is thinking primarily of the saved, and means that God's continuous love towards them without anger for their sin is His prescience of their good end in His eternity. But the scope of her words is universal. "I saw verily that Our Lord was never wrathful, and never shall be: for He is God, He is good, He is truth, He is love, He is peace.... I saw truly that it is against the property of His might to be wrathful (anger is due to impotence temporary or final before an obstacle to the will); and against the property of His wisdom, and against the property of His goodness. God is that goodness that may not be wrath, for God is naught but goodness."

Of the origin of sin Julian says little. She regards the question as a waste of time and thought; for "it is a high marvelous secret hid in God: which secret shall be known to us in heaven. In which knowing we shall see the cause why He suffered sin to come." And "all that is beside our salvation...is our Lord's private counsel, and it belongs to the royal lordship of God to have his private counsel in peace." Her theology is always practical, directed to the achievement of our salvation. Of merely theoretical questions she is impatient.

Julian's doctrine of man's fall and redemption is condensed in her parable of the lord and the servant. Though stated to have been a direct "showing" and of cardinal importance, this parable is strangely absent from the shorter version. The reason is, perhaps, that, as she herself hints, she found it very difficult to understand, and that until she had satisfied herself of its interpretation she judged it better to omit it. It consists of a vision with an intellectual illumination which in part explains it; in its present state doubtless the product of subsequent contemplation. Julian saw a lord seated on the earth, clad in a blue cloak. His eyes were "black most fair and seemly, showing full of lovely pity." On his left hand stood a servant wearing a laborer's tunic, "white, single, old and all defaulted, dyed with the sweat of his body." The lord looked with love on his servant who "for love having no regard to himself nor to nothing that might befall him, hastily did start and run at the sending of his lord, to do that thing which was his will and his worship." "There was a treasure in the earth which the lord loved… a meat which is lovesome and pleasing unto the lord." As "the servant ran in great haste for love to do his lord's will, he fell into a ravine and took full great sorrow and then he groaned and moaned and wallowed and writhed; but he could not rise nor help himself in any way. And of all this the most mischief was failing of comfort; for he could not turn his face to look on his loving lord, which was to him full near, in whom is full comfort; but as a man that was full feeble and unwise for the time he attended to his feeling and enduring in woe." "And I beheld…if I could perceive in him" any default, or if the lord should assign him any manner of blame. And there was none seen, for only his good will and his great desire was the cause of his falling. And he was as loving and as good inwardly, as he was when he stood before his lord, ready to do his will." "Then said this courteous lord in his meaning, 'Lo my beloved servant, what harm and disease he has had and taken in my service for my love and for his good will! Is it not reason that I reward him, his trouble and his fear, his hurt and all his woe? And not only this, but it falls not to me to give him a gift, that be better to him and more worshipful than his own health should have been; or else I believe I did him no grace."

The lord is God, and his constant love for the servant is His eternal love-will that no temporary state of sin can change. He sits on the earth, Julian tells us, because His dwelling is in human souls. The complex figure of the parable is the servant. He is at once Adam in his fall, Jesus Christ in His incarnation and passion, and all souls that are finally saved. For they with their natural head Adam are the mystical body whose Head is Jesus Christ. Redemptive solidarity in the body of Christ, the cardinal doctrine of Christianity, is thus the key to this central parable of the Revelations, if not indeed to the entire book.[7] "The servant," Julian here explains, "I understood was showed for Adam; that is to say, one man was showed and his falling to make thereby to be understood how God beholds all man and his falling, for in the sight of God all man is one man, and one man is all man." But later, "When I say the servant, it means Christ's manhood which is rightful Adam.... When Adam fell, God's Son fell, for the union that was made in heaven: God's Son might not be separate from Adam for by Adam I understand all man." Again the double point of view. In present eternity as opposed to time Christ's Incarnation and Redemption are already effected in Adam's fall in virtue of the solidarity between them in the Divine decree. And through its solidarity with Christ, redeemed mankind shares in God's love for His Son (Ch. 35; cf. Ch. 51). This then is the treasure—the meat sought by the Servant—His own body natural and mystical in one—the worship rendered by it to God—His human glory. Finally in the risen and ascended Christ Julian sees the servant, mankind, crowned and robed in the heaven of transcendent Godhead. This is the return by grace to God of that which came forth from Him by nature (for Julian the entire creation is recapitulated in humanity): a return already effected in Christ the head—in process of accomplishment in His members.

7. Cf., "If I look singularly at myself, I am not right; but in (the) general (body) I am, I hope, in oneness of charity with all Christians. For in this oneness stands the life of all mankind that shall be saved."

Beneath the picture of the lord and servant might be written the text, true of the cosmic as of the individual Christ: "I came forth from the Father and came into the world; again I leave the world and go to the Father."

But after all, this servant whose fall never lost him the love of his lord, this servant destined to share the Divine life, this servant one with the Son of God, is not for Julian the entire human race. He is saved humanity, the elect. What then of the finally lost—the reprobate? How does his loss consist with a God who is Love? Here Julian stands out from her environment in a light peculiarly sympathetic to modern feeling. The doctrine of eternal damnation presented no difficulty to the medieval mind. On the contrary, medieval Catholics invested it with an imaginative garb of physical tortures and seemed almost to delight in their contemplation. For their feelings were those of schoolboys, during those years of a cruelty due to an undeveloped imagination, vigorous indeed, but of insufficient depth. On the left of the chancel arch were depicted the nude files of the damned dragged by demons to flames and boiling cauldrons, or devoured by the yawning mouth of a hideous monster, the symbol of hell. The number of the lost was universally believed to exceed enormously the number of the saved. Dante's hell is comparatively as crowded as a football match; his heaven as empty as a church. Almost alone Julian is afflicted by this triumph of evil. Despite a nightmare of the grinning fiend, her contemplations turn away from hell and its inhabitants. She would have us put them out of our mind as far as possible. "As long as we be in this life, what time that we *by our folly* turn us to the beholding of the damned tenderly Our Lord touches us and blissfully calls us, saying in our soul, 'Let me alone my dear-worthy child; intend to me, I am enough to you, and enjoy in your savior and in your salvation.'" And when she affirms vigorously a final damnation—partly perhaps in view of the misunderstanding that she disbelieved it—it is the negative aspect on which she insists, the exclusion of the devils and lost souls from the society of God and His saints. "I saw the devil is reproved of God and endlessly damned. In which sight I understood that all the creatures that be of the devil's condition in this life, and therein ending, there is no more mention made of them before God and all His holy ones, than of the devil; notwithstanding that they be of mankind; whether they have been christened or not." She finds it hard to conceive human wills of this final malice against her "dear-worthy" Lord. In the shorter version she appears momentarily at least to indulge the hope that no man will in fact make this entire choice of evil. "If such there be," she says. But this bold doubt which can scarcely have represented her more deliberate attitude is significantly absent from the longer version.

Nevertheless, the simple dismissal of the damned from the life and mind of God in which she loves and lives is not her last word. She has a further intuition of inexplicable hope. "Our good Lord answered to all the questions and doubts that I might make saying full comfortably, 'I may make all things well'; and I can make all things well; and I shall make all things well; and I will make all things well; and you shalt see yourself that all manner of things shall be well.... There is a deed, which the blessed Trinity shall do in the last day as to my sight: and what that deed shall be, and how it shall be done, it is unknown of all creatures which are beneath Christ and shall be until it shall be done." Julian objects in astonishment the doctrine of eternal punishment, the more difficult because she understood it to involve the innocent heathens. "Standing all this, I thought it was impossible that all manner of things should be well, as Our Lord showed in this time, and as to this, I had no other answer in showing of Our Lord but this: 'That, that is impossible to you, is not impossible to me; I shall save my word in all things and I shall make all things well (Ch. 32).[8] Assuredly no answer this to reason—for Dame Julian the final triumph of love is God's ultimate mystery—but an intuition of infinite hope. Eternity is on a different plane from time, and the truth of a

8. The entire chapter should be read.

lower plane may be somehow included yet transcended in the complete reality of a higher. It is unphilosophical to deny facts, be they physical or spiritual, because we cannot also see their harmony. The problem of evil is the riddle of the universe, whose solution is attainable only in the universal vision of Divine Wisdom.

Besides these theoretic intuitions of God and His redeeming work, Julian has much immediately practical instruction. She warns us, for example, against the thought of other people's sins, which makes as it were a thick mist before the eye of the soul, points out that the penance God sends is more salutary than any we can take on ourselves, that it is the service of youth when the world is still attractive that has special value in God's sight, that "there is no fear that fully pleases God in us, but reverent fear " "which is soft," and "the more it is had, the less it is felt for sweetness of Love."

But I can only discuss here her doctrine of the practical means of union with God—her doctrine of prayer. Like all mystics, she reduces prayer to something at once very simple and very profound—the adherence of the soul through the will to God, whether we are conscious of His Presence or apparent absence, whether we find delight or dryness in our devotion. Julian is no Quietist, rejecting "means," that is, special devotions. But she would have us regard them not as isolated and independent ways of prayer, but as manifestations, partial aspects of one Love-Will accepted by the soul, that Love being the Nature of God, Absolute Goodness, indwelling its secret depths, and at the same time enveloping it as our clothes our body.

Confidence in the Divine love, as the ultimate reality of the Universe and the key to its history, is the substance of Julian's prayer (Ch. 6 and Ch. 41). Later she returns to the subject of prayer with a Divine locution "brought suddenly" to her mind. "I am the ground of your seeking. First it is my will that you have it: and since I make you to will it, and since I make you to seek it, and you seek it, how should it then be: that you should not have your seeking?" In her explanation Julian again employs the double point of view—the eternal will of God, the successive series of human psychoses. She points out that though our prayer cannot alter the Eternal Will, that is no reason to abstain from praying, but the reverse. For that Will is to grant our prayer through the means of our prayer (Ch. 41). But this prayer whose answer is the Will of God is not any petition we may choose to make. For we may ask for the wrong thing, or in the wrong way, or at the wrong time. "Either we abide a better time, or more grace, or a better gift."

And in the last resort this better gift is nothing less than God Himself. The Infinite Love can be satisfied with no gift short of Itself. Nor can man's need be satisfied by anything less. "God of your goodness give me thyself, for you art enough to me; and if I ask anything that is less, even if I want it, only in you I have all." And this gift of God Himself is given to the entire body of saved humanity through that work of redemption and notification in whose consummation all our prayers will find their fulfilment. This work is already in process of accomplishment—but God wills to forward it through our prayer (Ch. 42).

Thus prayer is a participation by the human will in God's will to manifest Himself in redeemed humanity. And it is increasingly a direct grasp by the center of the soul of that Centre where all the lines of our partial desires and petitions converge: the Centre of the world process which is Its revelation.

As a fundamental will union this prayer is continual. But from time to time it becomes a conscious union with God, directly experienced. Though Julian gives no systematic account of the character and degrees of her prayer she speaks of these direct contacts. One form of this mystical experience is the apprehension of some truth about God and His Work—the revelation of a particular aspect of God. This purely intellectual apprehension of divine truth, the ghostly sight, is fuller, deeper, more valuable, she insists, than the apparently physical manifestations. But it is therefore impossible to translate it adequately into the terms of conceptual thought, "the ghostly sight I cannot show as openly and as fully as I would."

And above these ghostly sights is the direct but necessarily unintelligible touch of God Himself. For God is the end and perfection of prayer. Prayer, in its highest form the prayer of mystical experience, is thus a veiled foretaste of the perfect and unveiled possession of God in heaven. "Prayer is a right-wise understanding of that fullhead of joy that is for to come...searching and seeing our bliss, that we be ordained to." The contemplation of God's "deed" of universal love leads Julian to experience of the Doer. "And when our courteous Lord of His special grace shows Himself to our soul, we have that we desire; and then we see not for the time what we should more pray; but all our intent with all our might is set whole into the beholding of Him. And this is a high unperceivable prayer [our experience of the incomprehensible Godhead necessarily lacks a clear intelligible content, whether of sense perceptions or ideas], for all the cause wherefore we pray is to be joined into the sight and beholding of Him." And "In this contemplation [the veiled and dim, often almost imperceptible, dawn of heaven's noonday vision] we pray marvelously, enjoying with reverent dread and so great sweetness and delight in Him, that we cannot pray right except as He stirs us for the time."

But in this world the Divine light cannot shine steadily. It must fade again into that other light, by comparison darkness, of common day, as the vision faded from the Mount of Transfiguration, or that passing flash of God which crowns the *Divina Commedia*. For understanding and feeling the prayer even of the mystic must vary between knowledge and ignorance, delight and dryness. For Dante's "lofty sight power failed." "But my desire and will were being driven on, as a wheel is evenly turned, by the love that moves the sun and the other stars." What Dante relates, Julian commands. "He says thus, 'Pray interiorly, inwardly though you think it helps you naught, yet it is profitable enough...pray interiorly, inwardly though you feel naught, though you see naught: yea, though you think you might not; for in dryness and in barrenness, in sickness and in feebleness then is your prayer full pleasant to me, though you think it helps you not but little: and so is all your living prayer in my sight.'" For whether visible or invisible, felt or unfelt, love is that Divine Will which is the law of the universe and with which our union is prayer. This is the final text of Julian's gospel, the key to her Revelations. "From the time that it was showed, I desired oftentimes to understand Our Lord's meaning; and fifteen years after and more, I was answered in ghostly understanding...thus: 'Would you understand your Lord's meaning in this thing? Understand it well, love was His meaning. Who showed it to you? Love. Wherefore shows He it to you.' For love. Hold you therein, you shalt understand more in the end. But you shalt never wit therein other without end. Then was I learned that love is Our Lord's meaning. And I saw full surely in this and in all, that ere God made us, He loved us; which love was never slacked, and never shall. And in this love He has done all His works; and in this love He has made all things profitable to us; and in this love our life is everlasting. In our making we had beginning; but the love wherein He made us was in Him without beginning. In which love we have our beginning. And all this shall we see in God without end."

In face of all we know of the pain, cruelty and folly of mankind Julian's message of love may sound a mockery of human woe. She may appear the victim of a pitiful illusion for whose sake she has flung away even those few poor pleasures this wretched and fleeting life might have given. Then indeed is the world without God, its meaning not love, but the despair of an unheeding and unconscious silence, of a void in which re-echoes the cry of man's torment. But she comes to us with the credentials of a personal experience whose reality we cannot doubt. She comes to relate, though with a unique beauty of manner, an experience common in its fullness to a multitude scattered through diverse lands and epochs, and implicit, even partially manifest, in the religion of millions. Can illusion produce, not only a deep and lasting happiness, but a wisdom lofty indeed, but broad and sane, doctrine of so rich and so full a content, given in an experience of widespread occurrence and substantial identity? M. Henri

Barbusse, himself lacking all religious belief, says of its most evident obstacle, *La souffrance, c'est la profondeur même*. And *if* Julian's revelations be after all the truth; if, for all its ugliness and seeming power, evil be without ultimate and therefore without final reality; if human history, despite its piteous record of sin and suffering, be the course of a servant who came from God and is returning to Him again; if the soul can pass beyond the changes and disappointments of time to an eternal Goodness that dwells in its depths, wraps it about on all sides and comes down to the lowest part of its need, *if* love *is* His meaning.

Bibliographical Note

Four manuscripts of the *Revelations* exist.

Shorter Version:

(1) Brit. Mus. Addit. MS. 37.790. This is the earliest extant MS. seen by Blomefield and subsequently lost. It was recovered, however, in 1909. Its editor, the Rev. Dundas Harford, ascribes it to the middle of the fifteenth century. As, however, the copyist tells us that Julian "yet is in life anno domini MCCCCXIIII," it must surely be dated in that year.

Printed edition:

The Shewings of Lady Julian (originally *Comfortable Words for Christ's Lovers*). Rev. Dundas Harford, H. R. Allenson, 1911, 1912, 1925.

Longer Version:

(2) Brit. Mus. Sloane 2499 (late Seventeenth Century).

Printed editions:

Rev. P. H. Collins. Medieval Library of Mystical and Ascetical Works. Richardson, 1877.

Miss Grace Warrack, Methuen & Co. 1st ed. 1901.

(3) Brit. Mus. Sloane 3705 (Mid-Eighteenth Century). Not published. Is it a transcript of one of the other two?

(4) Paris Bibliothèque Nationale. Fonds anglais, 40. Sixteenth Century.

Printed edition:

Dom Serenus de Cressy, O.S.B., 1670. Re-edited from Cressy's printed text by:

(1) G. H. Parker, 1843.

(2) Father Tyrell with introduction. Kegan Paul, 1902. This is the text that I have employed.

The definitive edition is still an urgent desideratum. The shorter version printed by Mr. Harford contains textual corruptions easily corrected by comparison with the manuscripts of the longer version. The same is true of these manuscripts in relation to the shorter version and to one another. Both versions should be printed side by side.

WILLIAM LANGLAND (1333–1399)

by CHRISTOPHER DAWSON

IT WOULD BE STRANGE TO WRITE OF THE ENGLISH WAY without some mention of one who is perhaps the greatest of English religious poets, and whose whole life's work was devoted to the finding of that way. And yet for some reason William Langland has never received the attention that he deserves. He is little read, and those who read him seldom realize his true greatness. It is a reproach to modern England that when every minor poet has been edited and re-edited to satiety, and when the classics of foreign literature are to be found on every bookstall, this great classic, which is one of the landmarks of English literature and English religion, should be inaccessible to the ordinary man except in abridged or incomplete forms[1] and that the only standard work on the subject should have been written by a foreigner.[2] And this reproach ought to be felt by Catholics before all others, since for them Langland's poem is a part of their special heritage. Here is the Catholic Englishman par excellence, at once the most English of Catholic poets and the most Catholic of English poets: a man in whom Catholic faith and national feeling are fused in a single flame. He saw Christ walking in English fields in the dress of an English laborer, and to understand his work is to know English religion in its most autochthonous and yet most Catholic form.

It is true that there is much in Langland that is likely to prove shocking to Catholics who know their Middle Ages only in a modern bowdlerized form. His England is not the idealized Catholic England of the apologist, nor the Merry England of medievalist myth. It is a grim enough land where oppression and misgovernment are rife, and famine and pestilence are never far away. For Langland, with all his Christian idealism, is also a realist who does not shrink from describing in pitiless detail the corruptions of the Church, the wrongs of the poor and the vices of the rich. He belongs to his age—the fourteenth century—which, in spite of Boccaccio and Chaucer, was not a cheerful one, but which, nonetheless, was a time of immense spiritual vitality and of momentous consequences for the future of Western civilization.

The fourteenth century was an age of profound social and spiritual change: an age of ruin and rebirth, of apocalyptic fears and mystical hopes. It was the age of the Great Schism and the Black Death and the Hundred Years' War, but it was also the age of Dante and Petrarch, of St. Catherine and St. Bridget, of Tauler and Suso and Ruysbroeck, an age of poets and mystics and saints. It saw the breakdown of the universal theocratic order of medieval Christendom and the rise of political nationalism and religious division, and at the same time it witnessed the passing of the old agrarian feudal society and the rise of capitalism and urban industrialism. Western Europe was stirred from end to end by a wave of social unrest which showed itself in

1. The standard edition (Oxford, 1886, 2 vols., ed. Skeat) is too expensive to be in general use. Wright's edition is both out of date and out of print. Skeat's popular edition of the text (Oxford) and his modern version (Dent), both somewhat expurgated, only contain the Prologue and the first seven *passus* (out of twenty) of the B text. Perhaps the most handy and accessible version is that by Arthur Burrell in Everyman's Library, but this is both translated and abridged. An excellent school text of the Prologue and Passus V to VII of the B text, edited by G. D. Parnely, was published by Messrs. Sidgwick and Jackson in 1928. In this essay I have thought it best to give my own versions of the passages that I quote, though I do not pretend to have found a satisfactory *via media* between a literal translation and a modern paraphrase.

2. *L'épopée mystique de William Langland*, par J. J. Jusserand, 1893.

revolutionary movements and bitter class warfare. At no other time in European history has the common people asserted itself more vigorously or found more remarkable leaders. It was the age of the Jacquerie and the Peasants' Revolt, of the wars of the Swiss peasants and the German towns against the princes, and the still more heroic struggle of the Flemish proletariat against their own ruling classes and the power of the French monarchy.

It was in the midst of this turmoil of change that the English people first attained maturity and self-consciousness. Three centuries earlier it had been submerged by a wave of foreign invasion, and the Norman conquest had made England for a time a province of Continental culture. Its churchmen belonged to the international unity of Latin Christendom and its nobles to the hardly less international society of French chivalry. Latin was the language of learning, and French the language of society. English became the speech of peasants, the mark of the simple and the uneducated. As the first English chronicler, Robert of Gloucester, writes as late as the beginning of the fourteenth century: "If a man does not know French he is little esteemed, but low-born people hold still to English and their own tongue."

The fourteenth century changed all that, and before its close English was not only the language of the people but was making its way into Court and Parliament, until in the last year of the century the first English-speaking king opened his first Parliament in English words. Trevisa dates the change, at least in education, from the time of the Black Death, and no doubt the great pestilence and the great war with France mark a dividing line in the history of English culture. But the vital factor in the new development was not so much the decay of the artificial Norman-French culture as the spiritual rebirth of the national consciousness. The English genius found simultaneous expression in the work of Chaucer and Langland, the poet of the *Canterbury Tales* and the poet of *Piers Plowman*.

These two great voices of England expressed the two aspects of English character and English culture. Chaucer represents all that

England had learned from its three centuries of incorporation in Continental culture. He is a courtier and a scholar who looks at the English scene with the humorous detachment of a man of the great world. He clothed the courtly tradition in an English dress and gave the common Englishman a right of entry into the cultivated society which had hitherto been the monopoly of clerks and knights.

This achievement is reflected in his style, which is so characteristically English and his own, and yet owes so much to the cultivation and imitation of French and Italian models. It is essentially classical in spirit, far more classical indeed than that of his French masters, such as Guillaume Machaut, since it is the result of a long process of experiment and elaborate artifice, which bears fruit not in the wooden rhetoric of Lydgate and Occleve or the empty grace of fifteenth century French verse, but in a simplicity and strength that make it not incomparable with that of the great Italian classics of the Trecento.

Nothing could be more different from this than the other great work of the new age, for it is as formless and as lacking in conscious literary artifice as any great work can be. It is a voice from another world—the submerged world of the common English—a voice that is by turns harsh and pitiful and comic, but always the authentic voice of the English people. Where Chaucer took the world as he found it, and found it good, the author of *Piers Plowman* judged the world and found it wanting. He represents the English view of life as it had been formed by nearly a thousand years of Christian faith, not the official view of the theologian and the scholar, but the spiritual vision of a prophet chosen from among his fellows by his inspiration alone.

And this contrast is not simply a matter of temperament or class: it has its basis in a profound difference of cultural tradition. Chaucer belongs, as I have said, to the international tradition of the courtly culture, and already has his eyes open to the dawn of the Italian Renaissance; but Langland owes nothing to the courtly tradition with its gay rhymed measures and its cult of love and romance. He looks back to the forgotten Nordic world and to the grave Christian poetry of Saxon

England. He uses the old alliterative accentual measure which was the native speech of English and Teutonic poetry and which now suddenly arose, as it were from the dead, as a sign of the renaissance of the English spirit. This return to the old alliterative meter was not peculiar to Langland—we find it also in the work of Huchown of the Awle Ryale and of the poet of the *Pearl* and *Gawain*. But Langland inherited the spirit as well as the form of the old northern poetry. He has the same attitude to life—that profound and gloomy meditation on the world and the fate of man that distinguishes the old Teutonic poetry from the light-hearted courtly literature that had its origin in Provence.

There is a striking example of this in Langland's vision of "The Mountain called Middelerde":

> And I bowed my body • beholding all about,
> And saw the sun and the sea • and the sand after,
> Where that birds and beasts • wander with their mates,
> Wild worms in the woods • and wonderful fowls
> With flecked feathers • of full many a color.
>
> Man and his mate • both might I see,
> Poverty and plenty • peace and war,
> Bliss and bitter bale • both saw I at once;
> And how that men took meed • and mercy refused.
>
> In sooth I saw Reason • ruling all beasts
> Save man and his mate • and thereof I wondered.[3]

Poetry such as this stands entirely outside contemporary literary tradition. Nevertheless, it has its tradition, which is that of the old Teutonic literature. It has far more in common with the melancholy

3. Skeat, Text C, xiv, 134–143 and 153. Hereafter all citations to *Piers Plowman* are to this edition.

of Anglo-Saxon elegiac poetry or with the oracular solemnity of *Muspili* than with the smooth technical dexterity of Machaut or Froissart. And it is characteristic of the Nordic strain in Langland's poetry that his Christian epic should end, like the *Volospa* and the epics of the heathen North, on a note of defeat and despair—with the vision of a final battle for a lost cause against the unloosed hosts of hell.

On the other hand, Langland's style has none of the stately and artificial rhetoric of ancient Teutonic poetry. His language is the everyday speech of his time—at least of the friars and the popular preachers. It is full of racy vernacular ruins of expression, as well as of latinisms and gallicisms borrowed from the mixed language of lawyers and clerks. Moreover, he belongs to his own age—the century of Boccaccio and Chaucer—by his interest in the spectacle of human life and his keen eye for realistic detail. And this union of profound melancholy and vivid realism shows itself in all that he wrote and imparts an extremely personal character to his poetry. There are, I know, learned men who deny the traditional authorship and the unity of the poem, and would make it the work of a whole platoon of poets. But it would be little short of a miracle if a single age had produced a succession of poets, or even two of them, with the same general attitude to the social and spiritual problems of their age and the same highly individual blend of realism and mysticism. It is true that there are considerable differences between the successive versions of the poem that have been classified by Professor Skeat as the A, B, and C texts. But these are no greater than might be expected if the different versions reflect the changes of thirty years' experience; in fact, they seem to show a consistent development of thought and purpose which is entirely consistent with the author's character as he draws it himself.

Consequently I see no reason to doubt either the unity of authorship or the traditional ascription to William Langland. Langland was born about the year 1333 in the heart of that West Country that has been so rich in poets, either at Cleobury Mortimer, or, as has been recently suggested by Mr. A. H. Bright, at Longlands, near Ledbury, just beneath the Malvern Hills, the scene of the opening vision of his poem.[4] According to the tradition recorded in a fifteenth century manuscript of the poem, he was the son of one Stacy de Rokayle, of Shipton-under-Wychwood, a tenant of the Despensers who held the lordship of Malvern Chase at this period. But if so, it is probable that he was a bastard, for the circumstances of his life as recorded in the autobiographical passages that occur in the later versions of his poem are irreconcilable with his being the lawful son of a noble and wealthy house. It is very hard to reject the evidence of these passages, for they bear an unmistakable note of sincerity, and though medieval authors often put their views into the mouth of a fictitious or pseudonymous character, so far as I know, they never created a purely imaginary character of this type. Internal evidence shows that the second version of the poem—the B text—was written about the year 1377–78, when the author was forty-five years of age. The first version—the A text—has been assigned to the year 1362 on the strength of a reference to the great storm that occurred on January 15th of that year,[5] while the final version of the poem belongs to the last decade of the fourteenth century. It seems that Langland did not survive the year 1399, for a conclusion that has been added to one manuscript of the A text before the close of the reign of Richard II by a certain John But writes of him as already deceased. Consequently he cannot be the author of the poem on the fall of Richard II—*Richard the Redeless*—which was ascribed to him by Skeat, but which is a purely political poem that bears little or no trace of Langland's characteristic mentality.

The greater part of his life seems to have been spent in London, for the autobiographical passages of the poem describe the author as

4. *New Light on Piers Plowman*, by A. H. Bright, Oxford, 1928.

5. On the other hand, it is difficult not to see in the description of Lady Meed and her trial before the King an allusion to Alice Perrers, the mistress of Edward III, and to the events of 1376, when she was banished from Court at the instance of the Good Parliament. If this were so, however, it would make the first version almost contemporary with the second, which is difficult to believe.

living "in a cot on Corn-hill" with his wife and his daughter, a member of that proletariat of clerks in minor orders who earned a bare livelihood by singing office in the chantries and saying prayers for the souls of their well-to-do patrons.

> I live in London, and on London too
> The looms that I labor with • my livelihood to earn
> Are my paternoster and primer • *placebo* and *dirige*
> And my psalter sometimes • and my seven psalms.
>
> Thus I sing for the souls • of such as do me help,
> And those that find me my food • vouchsafe, I trow,
> To welcome me when I come • otherwhiles in a month,
> Now with him and now with her • and in this way I beg
> Without bag or bottle • but my belly only.[6]

He pictures himself as a long, lean, eccentric figure wandering through the streets of London, paying little heed to those about him, "loath to reverence lords or ladies" or to bow before men in fur coats and silver chains, and regarded by his neighbors as no better than a fool.[7] His married life seems to have been unhappy, and he was always pursued by poverty and ill-health. Thus he lived in bitterness of spirit, in failure and suffering, always feeling the contempt of men and the emptiness of his wasted life. And yet he was continually spurred on by his power of spiritual vision and by a sense that somewhere, just out of his reach, was the prize that would make up for everything, the Pearl for which a man will sell all he has. He saw himself as the unlucky speculator who has always lost but who, some day, somehow, will light on the bargain that will make him rich forever.

6. C, vi, 44–52.
7. B, xv, 1–11.

That is sooth I said • and so I beknow
That I have tynt [lost] time • and time mispended;
And yet I hope as he • that oft has chaffered,
That aye has lost and lost • and at last him happed
He bought such a bargain • he was ever the better,
And set his loss at a leaf • at the last end,
• •
So hope I to have • of Him that is almighty
A gobbet of his grace • and begin a time
That all times of my time • to profit shall turn.[8]

Thus his poem is not a work of art like the poems of Chaucer, it is the vessel into which the poet poured his doubts, his hopes, his criticism of life, and his prophetic message. There is no other work of medieval literature, not even the *Testaments* of Villon, which has such a direct contact with life and which gives us such an insight into the heart of medieval humanity. It is true that though his style owes nothing to the medieval romance tradition, he borrowed from that tradition the external machinery of vision and allegory. All these cumbrous personifications of virtues and vices are the lay figures that had been the stock-in-trade of medieval didactic literature for centuries. And yet nowhere is the irrepressible originality and realism of the English poet more apparent. These abstractions are apt suddenly to become more personal and nearer to life than even the human characters of a great poet like Chaucer. As Blake showed, the classicism of the latter makes the Canterbury Pilgrims themselves universal human types, while Langland's realism transforms his allegorical abstractions into individual men and women. Gluttony goes into the alehouse and sits on the bench with

8. C, Passus vi, 92–101. The autobiographical passage of which this is the conclusion is of itself, to my mind, a sufficient refutation of Professor Manly's view that the author of the C text was an unimaginative pedant, and that the picture of the poet himself is merely a rhetorical device.

Watt the warner • and his wife both,
Tim the tinker • and twain of his prentices,
Hick the hackneyman • and Hugh the needeler,
Clarice of Cockslane • and the clerk of the church,
Dawe the diker • and a dozen other;
A ribibor, a ratoner • a raker of Chepe,[9]
A roper, a retainer • and Rose the disher,
Godfrey of Garlickhythe • and Gryffin the Welsh,
And a heap of upholsterers.[10]

And he drinks with the best of them as though he were an honest drunkard instead of a moral abstraction.

In the same way Sloth appears as a lazy priest who knows the rhymes of Robin Hood better than his *Paternoster*, and who

can find in a field • or in a furrow a hare
Better than in *Beatus vir* • or *Beati omnes*
Construe one clause well • and ken it to my parishioners,

while Avarice is a merchant who recounts his rogueries with naive relish and apologizes for himself as a plain man who knows no French but that of the far end of Norfolk.

All this is characteristic of Langland's strength and weakness. He has no control over his pen. He is hardly launched on his sermon before reality bursts in tumultuously and turns his moral allegory into a vivid portrayal of the vulgar humanity of a fourteenth century English crowd.

Yet this realism is not always present. He is often content to leave his allegory on a plane of frigid abstraction, and there are occasions in which Langland surpasses the Puritans themselves in the

9. A musician (rebab-player), a rat-catcher, and a Cheapside scavenger.

10. B, v, 316–325.

grotesqueness of his nomenclature. He tells us of a croft called "Covet-not-men's-cattle-nor-wives-nor-none-of-their-servants-that-might-annoy-them," and the children of *Piers Plowman* have names that are longer and odder than those of the Barebones family. Nevertheless, at any moment the flame of pure poetry may blaze out and silence the creaking machinery of didactic allegorism, and the artificial vision of medieval tradition may pass into the spiritual vision of the seer. His art is more like that of the Hebrew prophets than that of the modern poet, since it is not literature but the utterance of the word that God has put into his mouth. It is the common speech, which human folly has spoiled, brought back to its true function. For speech, he says,

> is a shoot of grace,
> And God's gleeman • and a game of heaven.
> Would never the faithful Father • (that) his fiddle were untempered,
> Nor his gleeman a gadabout • a goer to taverns.[11]

The one poet with whom one may compare him is his greater predecessor, Dante, though they represent in many respects the opposite poles of fourteenth century literature. For Dante, no less than Langland, conceived his task in a prophetic spirit and used the convention of the vision to convey his criticism of life and his religious ideal. Both of them felt that the world had gone astray, and themselves with it. Both had an intense faith in the Catholic way and yet were profoundly dissatisfied with the state of the Church and convinced of the need for a drastic reform. Both looked for a deliverer who should set priests and people on the right way. But Dante brought to his task all the wisdom of the schools and the art of a highly conscious literary culture. His way was the highway of classical tradition—the royal road of imperial Rome—and he found his guide in Virgil and his savior in

11. B, ix, 100–103.

the Messianic Emperor, the *Messo di Dio*, who will slay the harlot and the giant with whom she sins.

Langland, on the other hand, had the scanty learning of a poor clerk, a knowledge of the liturgy and the Bible and the common faith of Christendom.[12] His way was the muddy highroad of common life, and he found his guide and savior in the common man, Piers Plowman, who is the type of Labor and Christian charity and at last of Christ Himself.

In *Piers Plowman* the social crisis of the age attains clear and direct expression. It is not only the first authentic voice of the English people, it is the first and almost the only utterance in literature of the cry of the poor:

> Old men and hoar • that be helpless and needy,
> And women with child • that cannot work,
> Blind men and bed ridden • and broken in their members,
> And all poor sufferers • patient under God's sending,
> As lepers and mendicants • men fallen into mischief,
> Prisoners and pilgrims • and men robbed perchance,
> Or brought low by liars • and their goods lost,
> Or through fire or through flood • fallen to poverty,
> That take their mischiefs meekly • and mildly at heart.[13]

With all its talk of class consciousness modern Socialism has failed to produce any work of "proletarian" literature that is comparable to this in depth and poignancy. The bitter cry of the socially disinherited against the injustice of their lot breaks out again and again in Langland's poem piercing through the cumbrous super-structure of theological exhortation and moral allegory:

---

12. The limitation of his learning is shown by the fact that on one occasion he translates *ne moechaberis* as "you shalt not kill"!

13. C, x, 175–183.

There the poor dare plead
To have allowance of his lord • by the law he it claims,
Joy that never Joy had • of rightful Judge he asketh
And saith 'Lo, birds and beasts • that no bliss knoweth,
And wild worms in the wood • through winter Thou grievest them
And makest them well-nigh meek • and mild for default,
But after You sendest them summer, that is their sovereign joy
And bliss to all that be • both wild and tame.
Then may beggars like beasts • ask after bliss
That all their life have lived • in languor and in dearth.'
But God send them some time • some manner joy,
Either here or elsewhere • else were it ruth,
For amiss he were made • who was made not for joy.[14]

Or again in a passage which I do not wish to weaken by translation:

Ac porepeple, thi prisoners • in the put of myschief,
Comforte tho creatures • that moche care suffren
Thorw derth, thorw drouth • alle her dayes here,
Wo in wynter tymes • for wantyng of clothes,
And in somer tyme selde • soupen to the fulle;
Comforte thi careful • Chryst, in thi ryche,
For how Thow comfortest alle creatures • clerkes bereth witnesse.[15]

But Langland is not merely alive to the sufferings of the poor, he is also intensely conscious of the social changes that accompanied the introduction of the new economic order and the evils that they brought in their wake. He was loyal to the old hierarchical ideal of a society based on custom and loyal service, and looked askance at the new power of money that was transforming the world. In his vision

14. C, xvi, 289–301 (B, xiv, 108–120).
15. B, xiv, 174–9.

of Lady Meed, which occupies the first part of his poem, he draws a picture of a society intoxicated by the power of wealth and governed by purely economic motives. The Lady Meed is nothing more or less than the power of the purse.

> Trust in her treasure • betrayeth full many,
> She has poisoned Popes • and impaired Holy Church.
> Monks and minstrels • are among her lovers,
> Both learned men • and lepers in hedges.
> Summoners and jurymen. • are such as prize her,
> She is with the sheriffs • who rule the shires;
> For she robs men of their lands • and their life as well,
> And giveth the gaoler • gold and silver
> To unfetter the false • to fly where he will.
> And taketh true men by the top • and tieth them fast,
> And hangeth them for hatred • that never did harm.
> To be cursed in consistory • she counteth not a straw;
> For she gives a cope to the commissioner • and coats to his clerks;
> She is assoiled of sin • as soon as she will.
> In a single month • she can do as much
> As the privy seal • can do in six score days,
> For she is privy with the Pope • provisors know it,
> Simony and she • seal their bulls.
> She blesseth these bishops • though they be unlearned,
> Promoteth parsons • and giveth protection to priests,
> To keep lemans and lotebies • all their life days,
> And to bring forth bairns • against the law's biddings.
> Where she is well with the king • woe is the realm.[16]

In reply to this arraignment, Lady Meed defends herself by an appeal to the universality and sovereignty of the economic motive:

16. B, iii, 123, 127, 132–152.

It becometh a king • that keepeth a realm,
To give Meed to men • who serve him meekly,
To aliens, and to all men • to honor them with gifts,
Meed maketh him beloved, • and esteemed as a man.
Emperors and earls • all manner of lords,
By Meed get yeomen • to run and ride.
The Pope and all prelates • take gifts and presents,
And give Meed to men • to maintain their laws.
Servants for their service • take Meed of their masters:
Beggars for their prayers • beg for Meed in return;
Minstrels for their mirth • Meed they ask.
The king has Meed of his men • to make peace in the land;
Men that teach children • crave of them Meed.
Priests that preach good words to the people
Ask Meed and mass pence • and their meat at meal times.
All kinds of craftsmen • crave Meed for their prentices;
Merchants and Meed • must needs go together,
No wight as I ween • without Meed may live.[17]

Against all this Langland sets his vision of a new age, when Truth shall return and "Love shall be leader in the land."

No more shall Meed • be the mistress as now,
But love and lowliness • and loyalty together,
These shall be lords in the land • truth to save.
• •
And kind-love shall come yet • and conscience together,
And make law a laborer • such love shall arise,
And such a peace among the people • and so perfect a truth,
That Jews shall ween in their wits • and wax wondrous glad,

17. B, iii, 208–226.

> That Moses or Messias • be come into this earth,
> And have wonder in their hearts • that men be so true.[18]

This apocalyptic hope of a spiritual renewal of Christendom was characteristic of the central Middle Ages. It attained peculiarly clear expression with Joachim of Flora and with the spiritual Franciscans, but it is also found in almost every quarter of the medieval world—among mystics like Mechtild of Magdeburg and Rulman Merswin and also among men of letters like Dante and Petrarch and even among politicians such as Cola di Rienzo, as well as among countless obscure visonaries and reformers, of whom Langland is the spokesman.

But Langland expresses this current of ideas in a new spirit of ethical realism that is characteristically English. His interests are more social than those of the mystics, while they are less political than those of Dante or Rienzo. He saw the need of his time primarily as a social need for a spiritual remedy. Society was diseased, and the only cure for its sickness was to be found in Christianity. The tragedy of the age was that although Christianity was nominally supreme and was surrounded by all the pomp and external recognition that society could give it, it seemed powerless to change human life. Christ had been proclaimed king, but He was king in name only; the real sovereign was Lady Meed, who was honored by clergy and nobles, while Christ stood without in the dress of the poor.

> And now is ruth to rede • how the red noble
> Is reverenced before the rood • and received for
> the worthier
> Than Christ's cross, that o'ercame • death and deadly sin.
> Both rich and religious • reverence that rood
> That is graven on groats • and on gold nobles.[19]

18. B, iii, 288–290, 297–302.
19. B, xv, 501–3, 506–508.

• •

It seemeth now soothly • to the world's sight
That God's word worketh not • on learned or on lewd
But in such manner as Mark • meaneth in the gospel:
"If the blind lead the blind • both shall fall into the ditch."[20]

That is why Langland's anger is so hot against the new Scribes and Pharisees, the men who sit in Moses's seat and bind burdens on the people that they will not touch themselves. He describes the fat theologian who has just preached before the Dean of St. Paul's on the sufferings of the apostle "*in fame et frigore* and flappe of scourges," sitting down himself at the high table and gorging on wild boar and tripe and pies and puddings, while the poor man sups below on a sour loaf.[21] He describes the rich men arguing on religious matters "at meat in their mirth when minstrels are still."

Thus they drivel on their dais • the Deity to know
And gnaw God in their gullet • when their guts are full.
But the careful may cry • and complain at the gate
Both a-hungered and athirst • quaking with cold
Is none to call him near • to help his need.
But they hue him away like a hound • and order him off.

• •

God is much in the mouths • of these great masters,
But among mean men • His mercy and works.[22]

In Langland's eyes, the only true religion is a religion of works, and the only works that avail are works of charity.

20. B, x, 274–76.
21. B, xiii, 60–110.
22. B, x, 51–70.

For though you be true of your tongue • and earn truly,
And as chaste as a child • that weepeth in church,
But save you love loyally • and lend to the poor,
And such goods as God sends you • give in goodly fashion.
You have no more merit • in Mass nor in Hours
Than has Malkyn of her maidenhood • that no man desireth.
For James the gentle • judged in his book
That Faith without Fact[23] • is right nothing worth
And as dead as a doornail • except deeds follow.
Therefore Chastity without charity • will be chained in Hell,
It is as lacking as a lamp • with no light in it.[24]

Langland's aim is to bring religion out of the palace and the pulpit into direct contact with common humanity. He wants to strip it of its rich vestments, its pious knick-knacks, and its load of useless learning, and set it to work in the slums and the highways, clearing up the mess that had been accumulated by generations of neglect. This ideal is embodied in the symbolic figure that has given its name to the whole poem. While Dante, a type of the political idealist, puts his faith in the coming of a prince,

Who may far off behold
Of the True City the eternal towers.

Langland finds the man who will put the world right in the shape of an English farmer, ploughing his half-acre by the wayside. Piers Plowman is at first simply the type of honest husbandry, a medieval John Bull who does his duty by Church and State and has no use for beggars or lazy workmen. But he is John Bull spiritualized, "Truth's pilgrim at the plough for poor men's sake," whose mission it is to

23. I.e., works, deeds.

24. B, i, 177–187.

bring Christendom back into the way of salvation.

Thus, the conception of Piers Plowman is a composite one which includes both a sociological and a theological element. Piers is primarily the peasant who works for all and toils to win the harvest that the idle waste. He is the true economic foundation of society, as opposed to Meed, which is the false economic motive. But also since the poor stand nearest to God:

> And in the apparel of a poor man • and a pilgrim's likeness
> Many times God has been met • among needy people.

Piers Plowman stands for none other than Christ Himself, the pattern of divine charity.

> Therefore not by looks nor by learning • shalt you know
> charity,
> Neither by words nor by works • but by one will only,
> And that knoweth no clerk • nor creature on earth,
> But Piers the Plowman • *Petrus, id est, Christus.*
> For he is not in lollers[25] • or land leaping hermits
> Nor at anchorholds with an alms box • all such are deceivers.
> For charity is God's champion • and gentle as a good child,
> And the merriest of mouth • where he sitteth at meat.
> The love that lieth in his heart • maketh him light of speech,
> And he is companiable and comfortable • as Christ Himself.
> I have seen him in silk • and sometime in russet,
> Both in gray and in fur • and in gilt armour,
> And gladly he gave • to all men that needed.
> Edmund and Edward • each was a king,
> And set as saints • for following of charity.
> I have seen charity also • singing and preaching,

25. Literally *idlers*, but also used as equivalent to the Latin "Lollardus."

Running and riding • in ragged weeds,
But bidding as a beggar • behold I him never,
But in rich robes • rather he walks,
Both capped and chrisomed • with shaven crown
And cleanly clothed • in cipress and silk.
And in a friar's frock • once was he found,
But it is far ago • in St. Francis' time.[26]

Here the conception definitely transcends all class limitations and becomes as wide and universal as charity itself. Nevertheless, Langland does not entirely abandon the sociological aspect of his figure. The last section of the poem, the vision of Dobest, opens with the passage in which he dreams

That Piers the Plowman • was painted all bloody,
And came in with a cross • before the common people,
Like in all limbs • to our Lord Jesus,

and goes on to treat of Piers as the symbol of St. Peter and the Church. But presently there is an approximation to the Piers Plowman of the earlier visions in the speech of the "ignorant curate" who wishes that conscience should be the keeper of the king's court and grace the guide of the clergy:

And Piers with his new plough • and eke with his old,
Emperor of all the world • so that all men should be Christian,
Imperfect is the Pope • that should help all people,
Yet sendeth men to slay • such as he should save.[27]

26. B, xv, 203–226.

27. This probably refers to "The "War of the Eight Saints" between Gregory XI and the Florentines in 1376–1378, especially to the massacre perpetrated at Cesena in 1377 by Cardinal Robert of Geneva, the future Pope Clement VII, in which the English mercenaries were concerned and which aroused much indignation at the time.

> But blessed be Piers Plowman, who toileth to till
> As well for the wastrel • and the wench of the stews,
> As for himself and his servants • save that he is first served.
> And travailleth and tilleth • for a traitor as sore
> As for a true tidy man. • all times alike.[28]

Thus the figure of Piers Plowman has both theological and economic implications and stands for an ideal of social and spiritual renewal—a drastic reformation of both Church and State. It is obvious that such an ideal is not devoid of revolutionary potentialities, and it seems at first sight easy enough to connect it with the two revolutionary movements that were making themselves felt in England in church and state at the very time when the poem was being written; I mean the Revolt of the Peasants and the Wycliffe movement.

Now there can be no question but that Langland's allegory made a strong appeal to the minds of the discontented peasants. Not only was the poem in itself an expression of the new social consciousness that also inspired the revolt, but we have direct evidence of its use for propagandist purposes by the leaders of the movement. The famous manifesto of John Ball to the commons of Essex calls on Piers Plowman to go to his work and chastise Hob the Robber, and it concludes with yet another reference to the poem:

> And *Do Well* and *Better* and flee sin
> And seek peace and hold therein.
> And so bid John Trueman and all his fellows.[29]

Nevertheless, there is no reason to suppose that Lang-land was himself a revolutionary or in sympathy with the aims of the insurgents. In the first version of the poem, written long before the rising,

28. C, xxii, 428–31, 436–441.
29. Thomas Walsingham, *Hist. Angl.*, ii, 33 (Rolls series).

there is a curious passage dealing with the exorbitant demands of the working classes:

> Laborers that have no land • to live on but their hands,
> Deign not to dine any day • on yesterday's cabbage.
> No penny-ale pleases him • nor no piece of bacon,
> But he must feed on fresh meat • or fish that is fried,
> Both *chaud* and *plus-chaud* • for the chill of his maw.
> Save he have high wages • else will he chide,
> Woe on the time • that he was born a workman,
> And curse against the king • and all his council,
> For allowing such laws • laborers to grieve.[30]

While in the later versions of the poem he writes against the propagation of communist ideas by the Friars, who

> Preach men of Plato • and prove it by Seneca
> That all things under heaven • ought to be in common.
> And yet he lieth, as I believe • that to the lewd so preacheth,
> For God made men a law • and Moses it taught:
> You shalt not covet your neighbor's goods.[31]

Langland is in fact thoroughly English in the way in which he combines an intense class-consciousness and a hatred of social injustice with a strong conservatism and a respect for the established order. He has the traditional conservative prejudice against the middle classes—against the lawyers and officials, above all, "who would do more for a dozen chickens or a sack of oats than for the love of Our Lord or all his dear saints,"[32] but also against the merchants, who get

30. A, vii, 295–303.
31. B, xx, 273–76.
32. A, iii, 71–75.

little pardon, and against the shopkeepers:

> The men who do most harm in the world
> To the poor people • who purchase piecemeal,
> For they grow rich by retail • and buy rents
> With that which the poor should put in their belly.[33]

On the other hand, he is no leveler. He holds kingship and knighthood in high honor, and accepts the traditional Christian ideal of society as a hierarchical order that has its pattern in heaven.

> When God began heaven • in that great bliss
> He made knights in His court • creatures ten
> Cherubim and seraphim • seven such and another.[34]

> Kings and knights • should keep the truth,
> Riding and roaming • the realm around,
> And take transgressors • and tie them fast,
> Till truth has determined • their trespass to the end.
> That is the proper profession • that pertaineth to knights,
> And not to fast on Fridays • for fivescore winters,
> But to help him and her • that hold by the truth
> And never leave them for love • or for lacking of silver.[35]

Such an ideal had indeed little in common with the practice of the fourteenth century, and Langland laments the degeneracy of his own post-war period, when gentle blood is of little account in comparison with money, when "Soapmakers and their sons are made knights for silver" and lord it over the sons of the old families that

33. C, ii, 104–106.
34. B, iv, 37–39.
35. B, i, 94–101 (C, ii, 90–101).

have mortgaged their estates in the national cause during the Great War in France.[36]

But though Langland is no democrat in the modern sense he remains a great exponent of the ideals of Christian democracy in the sense in which it has been defined by Leo XIII.[37] Indeed, nowhere else in English literature, nor even perhaps anywhere in the literature of Catholic Europe, do we find these ideals so clearly and passionately expressed. For Langland's social consciousness is rooted in his religious faith and finds its ultimate ground in the doctrine of Christian brotherhood:

> For all we are Christ's creatures • and of his coffers rich,
> And brethren as of one blood • as well beggars as earls,
> For on Calvary of Christ's blood • Christendom began spring,
> And blood brethren we became there • of one body won,
> As *quasimodo geniti* • and gentlemen each one,
> No beggar or serving-boy among us • save sin made us so.[38]

Thus Langland's social teaching is not based on revolutionary class hatred nor on a sentimental pity for the unfortunate. It transcends all purely social and economic categories, since it is nothing else but a logical development of the central doctrine of the Christian faith in its social implications. Langland's hope of salvation for society rests on his faith in the redemption of humanity in the Incarnation, and his work finds its true culmination in the great vision of the Harrowing of Hell, which is justly regarded as the finest passage in the whole poem:

36. C, vi, 72–75 (not in A and B).

37. In his Encyclical *Graves de Communi* (1901).

38. B, xi, 192–97; cf., B, xix, 38–40, "Those that became Christians—Are franklins and freemen • and gentlemen with Jesus."

For I that am Lord of life • love is my drink,
And for that drink to-day • I died upon earth;
But I will drink of no ditch • nor of no deep learning,
But of the common cup • of all Christian souls;
Though your drink was death • and Hell the deep bowl,
I fought so that yet I thirst • for man's soul's sake;
Sitio.[39]

Here Langland is at one with the great tradition of medieval mysticism and with the spirit of the universal Church. His social ideal is not limited to his own age and country: it is the same as that of the New Testament and that of the social encyclicals of Leo XIII and his successors—the realization of the Kingdom of God on earth and the restoration of all things in Christ.

But if his social teaching is thoroughly Catholic, what of his attitude to the Church and the Papacy? Are his bitter complaints against the corruption of the clergy and his demand for drastic reforms reconcilable with orthodoxy? Or should they be regarded as part of the same movement of religious disaffection and revolt which culminated in England during Langland's lifetime in the heresy of Wycliffe and the Lollards? It is easy enough to understand how later Protestant ages should have taken this view, as, for example, when Thomas Fuller hails the poet as the morning star of the Reformation, belonging rather to the day than to the night. Langland's criticism of the degeneracy of the religious orders is alone sufficient to explain this, above all the famous prophecy which enjoyed such popularity in Tudor times:

But yet shall come a king • and confess you all,
And beat you, as the Bible telleth • for breaking of your rule,
And amend you monks • moniales and canons,
And put you to your penance • *ad pristinum statum ire.*

39. C, xxi, 406–411; B, xviii, 363–66.

For the abbot of England • and the abbess his niece
Shall have a knock on their crowns • and incurable the wound,
But ere that king come • as chronicler me told,
Clerks and Holy Church • shall be clothed anew.[40]

But it is not difficult to find parallels to this passage in medieval writers of the most unblemished orthodoxy, notably in the no less famous prophecy of St. Hildegard two centuries before.[41]

But the resemblances between Langland and Wycliffe go much further than this. Not only do we find in both of them the same attitude of hostility to the religious orders, above all the Friars; the same contempt for pardoners and pilgrimages; the same attacks on the financial corruption of the Papacy and the Curia; and the same belief in the evil effects on the Church of excessive wealth and the desirability of a measure of disendowment by the secular power; but the resemblance often extends to matters of detail and turns of expression. For instance, Wycliffe's complaints of the bishops *in partibus* who, instead of going to their dioceses abroad and converting the heathen, carry on an easy and lucrative business as suffragan bishops in England, has its exact counterpart in Langland's lines about the need for preaching the faith to the Saracens, the neglect of which is:

A peril to the Pope • and the prelates that he maketh,
That bear bishops' names • of Bedlam and Babylon
Who hip about in England • to hallow men altars
And creep among curates • and confess against the law
"Put not your sickle into another man's harvest."[42]

40. C, vi, 169–172, 177–180 (B, x, 317–329).

41. I am inclined to think that this prophecy is the source of Langland's lines, as it was well known in the fourteenth century and is often referred to by Wycliffe.

42. B, xv, 537 seq.

Or again, Langland's description of the rich ecclesiastic riding through the land on a fine horse with his sword on his thigh and his hounds at his back, is repeated in Wycliffe's writings in almost identical terms.[43]

It is not, however, in passages like these that either the originality or the heresy of Wycliffe is to be found. The demand for reformation and the denunciation of ecclesiastical corruption were not peculiar to the Lollards; they are characteristic of the whole period. It was the custom of the Middle Ages to use strong language, and they had none of the modern prejudice against washing dirty linen in public. As Dr. Owst has pointed out,[44] many things that we regard as characteristic of Wycliffe or characteristic of Langland were the commonplaces of the contemporary pulpit, and it is easy to find similar views no less strongly expressed in the writings of champions of orthodoxy like Bishop Brunton and the Dominican John Bromyard, who took part in the Council at Blackfriars in 1382 that condemned Wycliffe's heresies. And it is here rather than in the writings of Wycliffe, which were posterior at least to the first version of *Piers Plowman*, that we should look for the source of Langland's views.

Where Langland agrees with Wycliffe is precisely where the latter was in agreement with English popular opinion. As we have seen, the second half of the fourteenth century saw the first complete emergence of the English national consciousness, which expressed itself in a widespread movement for reform in Church and State. This movement finds a clear expression in the proceedings of Parliament in the later years of Edward III and reached its climax in the Good

43. B, x, 306–316 and Wycliffe, *English Works*, ed. Matthew, 121, 149, 151, 212–13. 434; *de Blasphemia*, 188; *Select English Works*, ed. Arnold, III, 519. Other instances are their common views on marriage and the evil of marrying for money instead of for love (Wycliffe, "Of Wedded Men and Wives," *Select English Works*, III, 188–201; *Piers Plowman*, A, x, 106; B, ix, 150 seq.) and their criticism of the Pope levying war on Christians, etc.

44. G. R. Owst, *Preaching in Medieval England* (1926), pp. xii, 36, 131, and on Langland, 295–96.

Parliament of 1376, where for the first time the Commons took a leading part. Now, as Jusserand has pointed out, Langland's views reflect those of the Commons to such a degree that his poem often reads like a poetical commentary on the Rolls of Parliament.[45] "In religious, as in secular matters, Langland sides not with Wycliffe, but heart and soul with the Commons of England."

"Like the Commons, he recognizes the religious authority of the Pope, but protests against Papal encroachments and against the interference of the sovereign pontiff in temporal matters. The extension assumed by the Papal power in England appears to him excessive; like the Commons, he is in favor of the statutes of Provisors and Praemunire, and wishes to have them maintained and renewed.... In questions of this kind, Langland often agrees with Wycliffe; but it will usually be found that both share on these points the ideas of Parliament."[46]

One petition in particular which deals with the evil effects of simony and non-residence shows a remarkable similarity to the dominant theme of Langland's vision of Lady Meed. In the past, say the Commons, benefices were conferred on worthy men who stayed in their cures and spent the goods of Holy Church in works of charity. "And as long as these good customs were observed the kingdom was filled with all kinds of prosperity, such as good people and loyal clerks and clergy, knights and chivalry, which are things that always go together, peace and quiet, treasure, wheat, cattle and other riches. But since the good customs have been perverted into the sin of covetousness and simony, the kingdom has been full of diverse adversities, such as wars and pestilence, famine, murrain of cattle and other ills."[47]

And Langland expresses the same idea in poetical language:

45. J. Jusserand, *Piers Plowman* (Eng. trans., 1894), p. 112 and 71.

46. Ibid., p. 128, cf. pp. 129–136.

47. *Rot. Parl.*, ii, 337 in Jusserand, *Piers Plowman*, 133–34.

> Neither the sea nor the sand • nor the seed yieldeth
> As they were wont • in whom is the fault?
> Not in God nor in the ground • that they are good no longer;
> And the sea and the seed • the sun and the moon
> Do their duty day and night • and if we did also
> There should be plenty and peace • perpetual forever.

But:

> Now faileth the folk of the flood • and the folk of the land,
> Shepherd and shipmen • and so do the tillers,
> No more can they ken • the course of the seasons.[48]

Neither Langland nor the Commons desire revolutionary changes or the subversion of hierarchical authority, but a return to the sacred order on which society rested, according to medieval ideas. The Middle Ages were always striving towards this ideal and were never satisfied that they had attained it. And it was above all with regard to the reform of the Church that this tendency shows itself. The real Age of the Reformation was not the sixteenth century but the whole later medieval period from the eleventh century onwards. It was inevitable that such a movement should produce extremists and enthusiasts who intimately passed into schism or heresy, as was the case with Arnold of Brescia and Peter Waldo, and the Spiritual Franciscans and Ockham and Wycliffe. Nevertheless the movement as a whole was essentially Catholic and found its center and base in the reformed Papacy.

But in the fourteenth century this was no longer the case. The alliance between the Papacy and the reformers was temporarily broken and the disruptive element in the reforming movement got the upper hand. The Papacy ceased to be the center of unity and became itself the victim of schism.

48. C, xviii, 90–93; B, xv, 360–62 (C, xviii, 103–104).

It was not, however, the great schism so much as the translation of the Papacy to Avignon that marked the turning-point, by destroying the super-national prestige of the Holy See. It is true that the Popes of Avignon did not deserve the indiscriminate condemnation that was passed upon them by contemporary writers like Villani and Petrarch. They included men of high character and ability, such as Benedict XII and Urban V, who were not unmindful of their universal responsibilities. Nevertheless, the divorce of the Holy See from the sacred associations of the Holy City had a disastrous effect on public opinion. The charismatic aspect of the Papacy fell into the background, and Avignon came to be regarded simply as the center of a vast bureaucratic and fiscal organization which was governed by financial rather than spiritual motives. It was in the words of the Good Parliament, "*La peccherouse citè d'Avenon*," where "brokers of benefices" and worldly cardinals lived in shameful luxury on the exploitation of the faithful.

This state of things produced a situation in which it is far more difficult to draw a sharp line of division between the movement of Catholic reform and the heretical tendency to revolt than at any other period in the Church's history. This is seen, above all, in the Spiritual Franciscan movement, which embodied so much of the spiritual ideals of the age, while its extreme forms produced the most extravagant types of medieval unorthodoxy. But it is also characteristic in a greater or less degree of all the representatives of the religious thought of the age. A canonized saint like St. Bridget can denounce the Pope in unmeasured terms as "a murderer of souls, more unjust than Pilate and more cruel than Judas,"[49] while Dante can speak at times as if the Church had apostatized and had forfeited the divine guidance. On the other hand, some of the most characteristic doctrines of heretics, like Wycliffe's theory of dominion and grace, are borrowed almost without alteration from the writings of orthodox prelates, like Richard Fitzralph, the Archbishop of Armagh.

49. *Rev.* I, c. 41.

In these circumstances, it is not surprising that we should find many points of resemblance between the writings of Wycliffe and those of Langland. Both were children of the same age, who had grown up under the same spiritual influences and who reacted against the same abuses. Both, in spite of their hostility to the Friars, were strongly influenced by Franciscan ideas. And yet no two men could be more dissimilar in character and spirit. Wycliffe, the famous doctor, with his ponderous learning and his bitter tongue, has all the faults and virtues of the Puritan reformer—a narrow mind, harsh, unbending, arrogant, austere, which, in spite of its genuine religious earnestness, lacks human warmth and spiritual sympathy. Langland, the poor clerk, has none of Wycliffe's self-righteousness or his strength of purpose; he always pictures himself as a poor feckless creature laboring under a sense of inferiority and spiritual maladjustment.

> Woe-weary and wetshod • went I forth after,
> As a reckless wretch • that recks not of sorrow
> And fared forth like a losel • all my life-time
> Till I waxed weary of this world • and willed oft to sleep.[50]

Yet he has passion and pity and a profound sympathy for common humanity. He can see the squalor and absurdity of life without losing sight of the spiritual realities that lie behind the surface of existence. For all his bitterness of heart, he was a man of charity, and a man of faith in spite of his tendency to doubt and despair. And so, while Wycliffe became the harbinger of religious revolt, Langland embodies the spiritual unity of the English people at the very moment when religion in England stood at the parting of the ways.

For the English Church never really recovered from the crisis of the fourteenth century. The next age was an age of moral and spiritual decline. We had no San Bernardino to restore the old alliance between

50. C, xxi, 1–4.

the Papacy and the party of reform, and no St. Joan to rally the nation to unity in the name of God. Instead we had tough prelate-politicians like Beaufort and Morton and Wolsey and the men who helped to burn St. Joan and to pillory well-meaning reformers like Bishop Pecocke. Only in the following century did the movement of Catholic reform reappear with Colet and Fisher and More. But it was then too late to avert the crisis. The English way diverged from the Catholic way and ran astray into the waste lands of sectarianism. The spiritual successors of Langland are to be found not in the Catholic Church, nor even in the Church of England, but among the Puritans and the rebels, with Fox and Bunyan and Whitfield and Blake.

But this popular tradition of English religion which was divorced from Catholic unity and even from the national unity after the sixteenth century already exists in its purest and most unadulterated form in the work of Langland. He shows us what English religion might have been, if it had not been broken by schism and narrowed by sectarianism and heresy. Langland himself was not unconscious of the impending crisis. In the last pages of his poem he foretells the coming apostasy when the rich and the learned would follow the standard of Antichrist and only the fools would be left to stand by the unity of Holy Church. He pictures in prophetic words the new pagan pride of life that was to replace the old ideals of Christian chivalry:

> Loud laughed Life...
> And armed him in haste • with words of harlotry
> And held Holiness for a jest • and Courtesy for a waster,
> And Loyalty a churl • and liar a gentleman,
> Conscience and Counsel • he counted it a folly.[51]

And in despair Langland calls on his fellows, the common people, to make a last stand for the cause of Catholic unity:

51. C, xxiii, 143–147.

Come with me, ye fools,
Into Unity of Holy Church • and hold we us there,
And cry we to Nature • to come and defend
Us Fools from the fiend • for the love of Piers Plowman,
And call we to all the commons • that they come into Unity,
And there abide and do battle • against Belial's children.[52]

52. C, xxiii, 74–79.

SAINT JOHN FISHER (1459–1535)

by DAVID MATHEW

SINCE THE CHURCH HAS BEEN PROMISED PERSECUTION, the lines of the regional episcopates should in the ideal order lead to martyrdom. It is in this manner that the centuries of effort and the humdrum of laborious confessors receive their seal. Thus the spirituality of Catholic generations, long undisturbed, had gone to the molding of the mind and temper of John, Bishop of Rochester, who died in 1535 for Christian truth; in defense of the doctrine of Christ's foundation of an indefectible and visible Church.

Coming at the close of the medieval period and summing up in himself the theological inheritance of the Catholic Ages, it is difficult to reconstruct the picture of this man, the accidents of whose life seem so remote. Some impression of Bishop Fisher can be gained by a study of those Holbein drawings from which his tired, farseeing eyes gaze wearily on the great reign and its overblown splendor. Through his habits and his mode of life, tenacious and slow, the effects of temperament may be discerned; while each facet of his thought reflects the heavy and massed influence of tradition. Yet each reaction to the increasingly complex world by which he was surrounded only serves to emphasize his deep simplicity. The moment of his last arrest, which formed the prelude to his martyrdom, seems the converging point for all these forces. At this stage, too, a view can be gained from the State Papers of the domestic interior at Rochester, the minute detail of his poverty, the broken peace.

By the spring of 1534, Henry VIII's divorce case was over, the religious schism quite effective, the breach with Rome almost complete, and the bishop could gain but little consolation from the Easter festival. On the following sixteenth of April, his arrest, as the defender of the ancient discipline, seemed the mere final step, long since foreseen, in what was to the bishop's thought this tragic progress. The movement of men's minds appeared to him inscrutable, that rejection and questioning of the verities with which, since childhood, he had been familiar. For just thirty years he had ruled his see, riding on visitation through the Kentish country, with a period of preaching or confirming to vary the rhythm of his constant prayer. And now he was to leave the scene of his austere labors. Behind him lay the skeleton of works which an ardent faith had forced upon him, a declaration of Christ's presence in the Sacrament, a defense of chastity. The elaborate notes of sermons, the carefully piled crumples of erudition in which the formalism of his training stood revealed, belonged to that period of his life which was quite finished. With the order for his arrest, the sum of these active labors of mortification and study was complete. Henceforward he had merely to follow his own conscience and accept God's Mercy. The skepticism of the new age, the king with his carnality and self-communings, the sacrilege of heresy bore down on one whose life of prayer had led him far from worldly interests. Religion, in the sense of the practice of the Sacramental life and the absorption of the Testaments which the Church had guarded, alone seemed clear. It was the reality from which the world was moving. Serene amid this indifference, the bishop prayed with the forms that he had used in his distant boyhood as he had knelt by his father's grave beneath the rood in the minster at Beverley. He would always raise his heart to God in the same allegiance. The words of the Easter Sequence *Victimae paschali laudes* came with the memory of the voices of the clerks and the singing men of his cathedral. Here was the old medieval simplicity and the questioning to which his mind responded: "Tell us, Mary," so the words of the Sequence continued, "what you have seen in the way." Men spoke of the noisy Germans, disputers of a tavern theology, Magister Luther and Oecolampadius. The bishop retained the ancient questioning, *Dic nobis Maria, quid vidisti in via*?

This same Faith and the tranquility bred of an earlier and more peaceful time were alike implicit in every movement of the chaplains and the servants in that great ill-built house, the palace of Rochester. This had been the scene of his austerities and his quiet ruling. The bare untapestried walls of the sleeping chamber, with the green and white embroidered silk behind the altar in the corner and the rough blue sarcenet curtains by the window had that familiarity which can only come from a cell loved and well kept. Beside one wall there stood the bishop's bed with its counterpane of red linen sewn on the underside with canvas, which covered the hard straw mattress of his night's discomfort. Each detail of the room bore witness to a struggle for detachment from the things of sense and a determined following of the ancient ways. During thirty years, the bishop had looked out upon the view from these same windows, the flooding and unraveling of the tide banks, the gulls, the empty shore.

About him the worn equipment of the house and its empty spaces suggested that love of the poverty of the Gospel, which he followed without the constraint of vow; this desire which has so often marked those detached souls for whom the raised loneliness of the episcopate has something of the height of Calvary. The study place and the dining chamber both bore his austere impress, the table and the long forms and the bishop's chair with its black velvet. All here brought to the mind the withdrawn existence of one for whom the spiritual values would alone seem real. The grave and careful reading of a clerk moving through the Gregorian homilies would mark a fitting background to the scene, while the bishop sat alone in his dark moth-eaten tippet, his wide jaws moving slowly as he munched the bread in his thin pottage.

Upon the bare table stood a skull to keep him company, beyond the mazer bowl and the little silver cellars. Such silverware, small in quantity and in value, yet indicating that formality which his episcopal ranking still demanded, had come, as had so many of his possessions, from his patroness the Lady Margaret, the old king's mother. Personal acquisition did not square with his conception of the pastoral role.

Beneath him in the town the travelers from the Cinque Ports jostled, and in the Medway lay the Gravesend wherries. With the casual strangers he had little contact, but the innkeepers and the other townsmen and the close gathered households of that Kentish country were of his flock. He could not fail to remember that God would hold him as steward for their Faith and his own. And the emphasis on this fact stands out more clear, since his great age at length forbade him his cherished pastoral contact with the poor. Now as he stood, supporting himself with a stick on account of his weakness, it was clear that he would be called upon for his final duty to seal his testimony to the truth of Christ. Erect, with the hair shirt constantly grating on him, his emaciated figure only added to the impression of unexpected height. In his face, the blue veins showed more strongly now that his seventies were far advanced. The spare white-haired figure, with those eyes which mark his detachment from the world so clearly, suggests the last months of some early bishop, weakened in body, but strong willed to die. Bishop Fisher's thoughts upon this matter, his great sense of the duties of the pastoral office and of the feeding of the sheep, are presented in the sermon which he preached upon the books of Martin Luther. "And Peter," the bishop had declared, "was made by Christ, to whom he commissioned in his absence the cure of the Christian people saying: *pasce oves meas, pasce, pasce*."[1] One word sums up the Bishop of Rochester in life and death—*pasce, pasce*.

1. Feed my sheep, feed, feed.

The meaning of his arrest, the steps by which the king had separated from the Holy See, the casting off from the unity of Christian Faith were seen without illusion, events sharply defined and evil. It was not with the court that his own sympathies had ever lain, nor his career depended. The piety and old-fashioned scholarship, the careful fine calligraphy, the controlled appreciation of good letters, would all seem to have marked out Dr. Fisher for a life of learning and quiet pastoral care; the stole, the doctor's cap; hardly the mitre. The crucial accident which had uprooted him from his Cambridge life appeared before him, that choice as confessor to King Henry VII's mother, the Lady Margaret. How remote it now must seem, the cameo-like form of the Lady Margaret, the high coif and the folded linen beneath the chin, the mild wide eyes, the figure, prim and diminutive. He could see her still with her hands folded before her Book of Hours, while her quiet speech fell on matters of the spirit, as she told of the dream of Saint Nicholas before her marriage; a miniature from an older time. Hers was a figure staid and a little aloof, as she arranged her household and her bounties in the purposed and now withered chastity of her third espousals. It was upon these bounties that there had hinged the bishop's chief administrative labors, the founding of St. John's and Christ's Colleges at Cambridge and the Lady Margaret chairs of Divinity. But twenty-five years had passed since the Lady Margaret had died, and customs changed quickly. That reading of Hylton and the ghostly counsel, the filigree of her devotion, to Our Lady's Nativity for instance, the whole devout way of living had now vanished down the wind. Yet such a spirit had never been at ease in the court atmosphere, and in the new rather tasteless glitter, the king's gentlemen could develop freely, subject to the requirements of good breeding, a hearty and respectful avarice. The new strange world in which the bishop moved appeared in the light of his detachment with frosted clearness.

As to the king, it was not hard to judge him, the crude theological antitheses, the full-fleshed yet equivocal laughter, the mind clogged a little by the body, that Yorkist inheritance, large-boned and raw. To place Queen Catherine of Aragon would seem less easy. Her outward aspect, likewise, was so familiar, the long brown hair, once beautiful, now dulled, the wide and pleasant features, placid and dignified. She was devout in her own Spanish fashion, to Walsingham and the Franciscans; she used with persistent care the Latin Office. Yet it was difficult for the bishop, a Yorkshireman, direct and very humble, to fathom her reserved mind and its mainsprings, the heavily conscious royalty of the new Spanish kingdom, the barred, yet tremulous, Castilian pride. He was not her confessor and was only consulted upon occasion. On the other hand, he had formed a sharp impression of Mistress Boleyn. He knew her home at Hever, with its new terraces, and he had been the ordinary of that unsound knight, Sir Thomas Boleyn, the lover's father. Yet the personalities of this struggle seemed far away, like that garishness which had come in with Wolsey.

Even the bishops of the court party moved in circles, which his own orbit never touched, while day by day their contact with the king enmeshed them in those toils of the royal policy from which his own detached life kept him free. "Now be many chalices of gold," the Bishop of Rochester had written, "but almost no golden priests." Difficult as it is to indicate his own remoteness, some impression is conveyed by his biographer. "Truly," this Marian admirer wrote of Fisher, "of all the bishops that we have known or heard of in our days, it may best be said that this bishop has well lived and well and truly hidden: for who at any time has seen him idle walk or wander." Through the strange phrases, the special quality of his life comes clear.

As he moved on towards prison, the new court life was present to him, that magnificence, high colored, rather vulgar, which the late Cardinal Wolsey loved. Even now there remained a suggestion of that unseemly power in Master Cromwell, the king's new secretary, with his little eyes and quick, too pleasant speech. It was an unsavory remembrance that Master Cromwell had survived from the late cardinal's gaudy wreck. The bishop had no prejudice against new men, for he was one himself, a mercer's son from Beverley; but he could feel the loss of true religion. The politicians shared the courtiers' indifference, and there arose the image of the noisy, crafty Brandon, with slashed sleeves and ostrich feather and the groups in apple green and russet satin at the king's ponderous archery. Whatever the self-tortured king might do, the courtiers had calmed a facile conscience, and the appetites led them—and the bishop knew to his sorrow—to the riches of the Church. All finesse was abhorrent to his firm straightforward mind, and few signs of the new age seemed so repellent as this gambling upon religious truth. The courtiers possessed a prudent anticipation of prosperity as they maneuvered to obtain the weather gauge. The bishop could see them as they flocked around the uneasy Boleyn, the concubine with her dark eyes and her forced French ways and her virulent laughter. There was something of gambling fever in the life of these parasites, as they moved through the king's new palace of Placentia by the river. Placentia—the very name conveyed a flushed, false pleasure and the impermanence of that house of cards, the royal favor: Bishop Fisher passed on slowly to the calm peace of the Tower.

The bishop stood for the old ways and the heart of England. It was clear that he must now defend his flock, as they dug and ploughed and chaffered, faithful and simple. The literary and scholarly friendships of the past had worn thin in this testing time. Erasmus was now remote and his action doubtful. As the bishop remembered that great scholar, whom he had first befriended in Cambridge long ago, their conversations seemed so far away, faint like the smile which lit his guest's lined face, when his courteous fancy turned on learned matters. The detail of the visits seemed most distant; the heavy cloak and rich black fur from out of Germany showing dark against the poor wall hangings, as the scholar played with an ivory sand caster or other toy in his quiet talking. No man could be more pleasant to those whom he admired than Erasmus. The young painter from Basel whom he had sent—Hans Holbein, a mere name upon the memory—had spoken of him. But in this stress a certain triviality marked such scenes. The bishop was absorbed in his single duty to protect, as an *alter Christus*, the flock of Christ.

Behind him lay his own small diocese, and the experience of the German wars had shown the insecurity of religious practice, once the unity of Christian Faith was broken. He knew that he could count on Sir Thomas More's clear conscience, but the strength of the new monarchy, the pervading influence of the Tudor power and the well-executed maneuvers of the court had left them now in isolation. The vitiated atmosphere of the court, from which all his life he had kept free, would hinder most great men from that prayer for fortitude which martyrdom exacted. The king's counsellors were subtle, as had been proved in the case of the nun of St. Sepulchre's at Canterbury and her treasonable sayings, in which the bishop had so nearly been involved; but all that was required in these last stages was to go forward in the light of Faith.

In the churches, hospitals and chapels, the Holy Sacrifice of the Mass was offered and the shriving and receiving of the Sacrament renewed the life of Grace for the Christian people. The religious houses stood as firmly rooted in the countryside as the oak in which Saint Simon Stock found refuge; while the changing pattern of each shrine stood clear. An atmosphere of high spiritual doctrine marked Dartford, the bishop's sister's convent, Dominican, a school for manners and good letters, with its strict well-born community, whose diluted conservatism still showed through their courteous phrases. The calefactory at Greenwich brought back another scene: the form of Master Forest, keen and busy, and the tough, austere Franciscans; while at Aylesford in its quiet elms the shadow of Saint Simon lay upon the Carmelites in their simplicity. At Boxley, just beyond his borders, there stood the abbey of the Rood of Grace. Here was the ordered religion of the Christian centuries, now threatened. The light of the spring days fell upon these houses with the first apple blossom in their orchards in the calm weather. The bishop could not forget for an instant that God had raised him up as their protector. In this lull before the storm, there was no movement. The disturbances of the court found no reflection in the religious peace which lay unbroken on the See of Rochester. The freshening breeze from off the Channel slowly turned the sails of windmills.

The closely woven skein of town and country had led the bishop to that understanding of the rural life implicit in the outlook of that time. He had written long ago of the winter season and of "the trees when they withered and their leaves shaken from them and all the moisture shrunk in to the roots and no luster of greenness nor of life appears outwardly." When he put the worldly things behind him he had a sense of all that he was leaving, as he rode away and his old eyes slowly drained the Kentish fields.

In another region, also, the freshness and the limitations of the medieval knowledge defined his thought, while the restrained quality of his imagination kept the whole, as in a miniature, within due limits. The very restrictions of his knowledge had brought the Holy Land closer to him than to the later ages. "The blessed Martha," he had declared in one of his more carefully wrought out sermons, "was a woman of noble blood to whom by inheritance belonged the castle of Bethany." The Ancients, too, had come within his ken, and he was still sufficiently medieval in his concepts to realize spontaneously and humbly how closely he approached the sum of knowledge. "Where is now," the bishop had declaimed with his naive rhetoric, "the immemorable company and puissance of Xerxes and Caesar, where is now the great victories of Alexander and Pompey, where is now the great riches of Croesus and Crassus." "The great riches of Croesus and Crassus." How remarkably the phrase suggests the Elizabethans and their tall forests, but what unsympathetic hands have strewn these acorns?

The intermingling of these strands of thought, the curveting simplicity of the bishop's pastoral rhetoric, is seen in his sermon on Martin Luther. "Such a cloud," he wrote of the early heretics, "'was Arias, who stirred so great a tempest that many years after it vexed the church of Christ. And after him came many other like clouds as Macedonius, Nestorius, Eutices, Donatus, Iouinianus, Pelagius, and

Joannes Wycliffe... And now such another cloud is raised aloft: one Martin, hither a monk, who has stirred a mighty storm and tempest in the church and has shadowed the clear light of many scriptures of God." His following of the evangelical counsels is here reflected; that prayer and meditation which had armed him, the devotion to the scriptures of God. Thirty years of a tranquil episcopate and the slow maturing of religious experience, absorbed since childhood, had gradually prepared the bishop for his time of trial. An incessant search for God had left his spirit free and untrammeled, while from the moment when he yielded himself to his last captivity this freedom of the soul breaks through each word and movement.

It was on the Thursday after *Dominica in Albis*, in that Eastertide of 1534, that he was brought down to the Tower. Through this week in the liturgical calm of the Paschal Season, the Proper of the Mass had remained unchanging. "And there are three that give testimony on earth," the meaning would come to him as his filling eyes peered towards the missal with the Lady Margaret's portcullis on the cover, "the spirit and the water and the blood." How strongly the Epistle would sound forth as a demand and a warning. *Et tres sunt qui testimonium dant in terra: spiritus et aqua et sanguis*. It was a not unfitting prelude to the leadership of the white robed army, *te martyrum candidatus*. As the gates of the Tower of London closed behind him, the bishop had marked out his future. The imprisonment lasted for a year, and finally, on June 22, 1535, the Bishop of Rochester was put to death for his refusal to accept the Royal Supremacy and for his statement that "the king our sovereign lord is not supreme head in earth of the church of England." In the previous month he had received the title of Cardinal Priest of the Church of Saint Vitalis, so that Peter's approval sealed his action. He died that the English provinces might still remain within the unity of Catholic Faith.

It is well to consider now the final actions of this determined life, which bind together each divergent trait. Among the principal accounts of the actual martyrdom are the Rastell fragments, the work of an eye-witness, and the various manuscripts of the English Life, the earliest of which can be traced to the reign of Queen Mary. As a pendant to a description of his outlook, these papers make each salient feature clear. The details of his last hours show again the workings of a life's simplicity.

"The 22nd day of June next following," so runs the Rastell fragment, "about five o'clock in the morning, the Lieutenant of the Tower came to this holy man in his bed asleep and waked him and showed him…that the king's pleasure was that he should suffer in that forenoon.

"'Well," said the bishop, 'if this be your errand hither, it is no news to me; I have looked daily for it. I pray you what time is it?'

"'It is,' said the Lieutenant, 'about Five.'

"'What time,' asked the bishop, 'must be my hour to go out?'

"'About ten o'clock,' said the Lieutenant.

"'Well, then,' the bishop said, 'I pray you, let me sleep an hour or two. For I may say to you, I slept not much this night, not for fear of death, I tell you, but by reason of my great sickness and weakness!'

"With which answer the lieutenant departed from him until about nine o'clock, at which time he came again to the bishop's chamber, and found him, upward, putting on his clothes; and showed him that he was come for him.

"'Well,' said the bishop, 'I will make as convenient hast as my weak and sickly aged body will give me leave. And, I pray you, reach me there my furred collar to put about my neck.'

"'Oh, my Lord,' replied the Lieutenant to him, 'what need you be now so careful of your health? Your time is very short, little more than half an hour.'

"'I think none otherwise,' said the bishop; 'but, I pray you, yet give me leave to put on my furred collar, to keep me warm for the while until the very time of execution; for I tell you truth, though I have, I thank our Lord, a very good stomach and willing mind to die at this present, and I trust in his goodness and mercy; he will still continue it and increase it, yet will I not hinder my health in the meantime not a minute of an hour, but will preserve it in the mean season with all such discrete ways and means as almighty God of his gracious goodness has provided for me.'

"Then was he carried down out of his chamber between two in a chair and so to the Tower gate."

The next passage appears in the early English Life, attributed to Richard Hall, and therefore has only such authority as that work will carry. "But as he was mounting up the stairs," so runs this extract, "the southeast sun shined very bright in his face; whereupon he said to himself these words, lifting up his hands, *Accedite ad eum ei illuminamini et facies vestrae non confundentur.*" How significant are these words, "Come to him and be enlightened." But for the last words on the scaffold we have an eye-witness's authority: "Then spoke he in effect as follows," the Rastell fragment continues, "Christian people, I am come hither to die for the faith of Christ's Catholic church."

A carol, very familiar to the religious thought of Bishop Fisher's time, reflects in dawn-clear phrases the England and the cause for which he died. In the first reference to Our Lady, the intimate religion of the little shrines and churches lies revealed.

> For in this rose contained was
> Heaven and earth in little space,
> *Res Miranda.*

The miracle of the Incarnation is suggested, the nearness of Bethlehem, the lowing cattle, God's Presence in tranquility in the fields. And then the last couplet brings to mind the spirit of the bishop's martyrdom.

> Leave we all this worldly mirth,
> And follow we this joyful birth
> *Transeamus.*

SAINT THOMAS MORE (1477–1535)

by G. K. CHESTERTON

IF ANYONE HAD LOOKED FOR THE NAME OF THOMAS More in the century or so after his death he would probably have found first the isolated mention of a sort of legend: that he was the Man Who Died Laughing. He is mentioned in this manner in more than one of those quaint collections of freaks and monsters and old-world anecdotes such as were common in the whole period from Aubrey to Isaac Disraeli. The story is something of a simplification and an exaggeration; but it is not one which the admirers of Thomas More will in any sense desire to deny. There is no doubt that he died jesting; and that he would have been the first to see the fun of having his death commemorated in a jest-book. In other words, he was not only a humanist, but a humorist; a humorist both in the contemporary and the modern sense. Anyhow, most modern people know what they mean by a humorist; whereas, the more modern they are, the more they dispute about what is meant by being a humanist. And sometimes, I grieve to say, a humanist seems to mean a man who is not very human and not at all humorous.

If, on the other hand, anyone confine his curiosity about Thomas More to an inquiry about the popular notions surrounding the name in quite modern times, he would probably find that More has mostly been remembered as the author of *Utopia*; in some sense as the author of all the Utopias; even all the six or seven separate Utopias of Mr. H. G. Wells; a rather serious responsibility for Thomas More, if looked upon in that earnest light. And here again the impression is not false; and need not even be disproportionate, if it is stated in its proper proportion. Thomas More was most emphatically a man of the Renaissance; a man whose mind went outwards as well as inwards; and thought of the ends of the earth as well as of the end of the world. He was quite as much of a reformer and rational pioneer as Erasmus or Colet; though certainly more devout than the former, and probably more tactful than the latter. The two men were his friends; and the two friendships make up a great part of his life. Moreover, it is true that his life reaches its first natural turn or turning-point with the publication of *Utopia*; and that if we take that date with the subsequent date of his resignation of the Chancellorship, we shall have the two pivotal points of his general movement; before the last and finest passage of all.

Everyone knows that he was the son of a judge of Henry VII, Sir John More, and became the page of Archbishop Morton, who prophesied great things of him even in his childhood; that he became a typical Hellenist, learned especially in the New Learning; that his natural gaiety and good manners made him popular with everybody, and not least with Henry VIII, who sought his companionship, asked his advice and at length persuaded him to a reluctant acceptance of the dangerous dignity of Lord Chancellor. It is also well known that More was well aware of the danger of such dignities. Somebody congratulated him, after an interview in which Bluff King Hal had been slapping him on the back with uproarious amiability, and More answered grimly, "If my head would win him a castle in France, it should not fail to go." It was indeed destined to go, to be used in the storming of a larger and more ancient castle, which was also a cathedral.

But, as I have said, the modern instinct is so far right that if we wish for a moment that marks the morning of his career, with its widest liberty and liberality and even relative irresponsibility, we could not take a better one than that of the publication of *Utopia*, during one of his holidays abroad in 1516. It is undoubtedly full of all the ideas of his time, and many ideas of his own; artistically and imaginatively it responds to a real appetite for experiment and a gigantic gesture making for elbow-room; which were of the best promise at that time. We see something of the same thing later, in the Utopian speech made by one of Shakespeare's characters, on landing on the magic island of *The Tempest*. But when this is said, there is something else to he said, which for some reason or other very seldom is said, about the significance of *Utopia* in the life of Thomas More. It must be taken in conjunction with that other stray legend of the laughing man; and the knowledge that More was not the sort of humanist who sternly refuses to be a humorist.

Unfortunately many modern humanists, who know that he even jested in his death, cannot bring themselves to believe that he ever jested in his youth. The fact is that *Utopia* is one mass of the sort of questions which are asked by jesting youth, as by jesting Pilate, even if neither of them waits for an answer. Why should we have all this complicated botheration about private property; how about having property in common, like the monks? Why not assassinate the one foreign statesman who is certainly planning a world-war, instead of massacring millions of harmless people who never wanted any war? Are animals immortal; or why aren't they? Wouldn't it really be a jolly good thing for the country if all lawyers were kicked out of it? Would not divorce be a very comfortable solution of a lot of uncomfortable problems, if only it could be allowed? Might not Nudism be at least a temporary measure; as connected, for instance, with what is now called Companionate Marriage? Is it really possible for a man to think anything except what he does think; and in that case, can it be right to make him responsible even for fake doctrine or bad influence? Is it really impossible to have a simpler society, with all the Gordian knots of life cut with this sort of private pocket-knife of common sense?

Those are the sort of random rationalistic questions which filled his head, and his period, and his first fantastic book; and if Mr. Bernard Shaw had put them into the mouth of a highly Nonconformist African, many might now suppose that they were quite novel. But if it be asked how or why a Catholic, let alone a great and holy Catholic, even entertained such ideas, the answer is that a thinking Catholic always does entertain them—if only to reject them. Thomas More did primarily entertain them and did finally reject them. A Catholic is not a man who never thinks of such things. A Catholic is a man who really knows why he does not think they are true. But when people begin to think they are true, to think that far worse things are true, to force the worst things of all upon the world, the situation is entirely different; and cannot be related in any way to the jokes which a young Renaissance humorist put into a book like *Utopia*. This is the point of the supposed difference between More the author of *Utopia* and More the Chancellor of England. The difference is that England exists, unlike Utopia; and this somewhat eminent Englishman wanted England to continue to exist; and especially the England that he loved.

For this is the main moral charge against Thomas More; indeed, the only moral charge against Thomas More. The ordinary English authorities, in the Victorian tradition, pay a tribute to his virtues and talents, his charity and charming personality, but say that the great "stain" on his character is the fact that he did when chancellor the work that would have been done as a matter of course by any other chancellor; and that this work included the suppression of heretics. They are forced to admit that he only did what all the other people would have done; what all the heretics themselves would have done. He could not possibly have been a chancellor without doing the work of a chancellor, and he had long refused to be a chancellor, and was then much blamed for throwing up his chancellorship. But, though it is clear that More only did rather reluctantly what all his friends and foes would have done resolutely and ruthlessly, there is more in the matter than that; and there is a sense in which he really was resolute and might well force himself to be ruthless.

It was connected, not with any change in Thomas More, but with a change in the whole world around him. In the early days in which he wrote the *Utopia*, the new world was really expanding into wider horizons. As it expanded geographically to the discovery of America, so it expanded psychologically to the discovery of Utopia. It may be that even in that liberty there were the beginnings of the peril. But the liberty was liberty; it had not yet hardened into heresy. For a heresy is only a fossil liberty. The young Renaissance romancer was in a double sense free of his Utopia; he was free to enter it, but also free to leave it; he was free in it, and also free from it. He was not to be tied for life to the idle fantasies and hypotheses which he had thrown out in the daydreams of his youth, to be the laws of fairyland. In all that the new movement was an expansion; but there came a definite time when the new movement ceased to be an expansion, and the wise could see that it was already becoming a contraction. The Renaissance was an expansion; but the Reformation was a contraction. Even by the time of More, men as clear-sighted and sensitive as More could see that the coming of a new tyranny out of the North had altered all the conditions of liberty; and especially of the old liberties and levities of the South. It was no longer a question of the dubious broadening of the old broad philosophy; it was a question of a new and narrow religion. The author of Utopia had had his fancies; but the Chancellor of England realized that other fancies, far less humane than his fancies, were quite likely to become facts. The new men, the new reformers, were not men like his old cronies Colet or Erasmus, and they were meaning business. Nobody accused them of being jesters, and some of them never laughed in their lives, let alone in their death. And they were heartily and horribly in earnest. They really meant to drive out all the priests, as the author of Utopia had never really meant to drive out all the lawyers. The Calvinist was fanatical about the fixed predestined necessity of good men going to hell, as even Mr. Hythlodaye had never been fanatical about horses going to heaven. A new sect really began by going about naked, on ordinary occasions, whereas nobody supposes that More wanted people to do so, even on the very extraordinary occasions his romance describes. In other words, *Utopia* was written by a particular man, in a particular mood, at a particular moment, when he was light-hearted and full of levity because he believed that civilization was growing more civilized. At the later period, he definitely believed that civilization was in danger of going to the dogs; to all the mad dogs of religious melancholia and barbarian self-conceit. It measures the depth of his understanding of the real moral danger that he seems to have been especially indignant about the denial of free will. Everybody then alive thought that poisonous doctrines ought to be materially suppressed like poisonous drugs. He had no more doubt about these poisonous doctrines than about poisonous drugs. He felt as a man would feel struggling with the growing power of gangsters and gunmen in Chicago. That is the only change there was, and it was not a change in Thomas More or even in Thomas More's opinions. It was the change from liberty to martial law.

The change, such as it was, was masked for some time by a fact often forgotten: his essential agreement with the king. What then was the essential point of his disagreement with the king? The answer is the study of the two characters; and especially of More's character. For the king, let it be remembered was, or seemed to be, quite as much of an orthodox Catholic as More, and much more of a persecutor or crusader than More. Henry Tudor was rigid in every detail of Catholicism; perhaps too rigid to be a Catholic; to the very end he thought himself rather more Catholic than the Pope. In his hatred of the heresies, he was quite as decided as More and much more merciless. What was the matter with him was that he was the sort of rigid Churchman who always does, consciously or unconsciously, want to be head of the Church. There are High Church laymen, there are even Catholic laymen, in whom their respective priests will mournfully recognize the type. "Everything in the parish church must be absolutely Catholic or Anglo-Catholic; but as to what that is—why, I will decide."

Now Thomas More was a layman of exactly the opposite type. He was, indeed, in his interior life, intensely sacramental and even ascetic; and his real religion was of the sort that the saint possesses and the saint never parades. But, by the standard of a certain fussiness about ecclesiastical affairs, which sometimes marks the clerical layman, he might almost be called a lazy layman. He was the sort of Catholic who specially incurs contempt by "leaving everything to the priest." But, above all, there was at the back of his mind, a sort of grand humility and philosophic abnegation, which can never be understood by the clericalist who merely wishes to boss things. The issue between Henry Tudor and the friend whom he rather reluctantly murdered is really this: Henry was a strict Catholic, wishing to keep everything straight, but insisting that the man to keep them straight must be himself; while More was really a more liberal Catholic, admitting that things sometimes needed to be sharply put straight; admitting (above all) that he himself might need to be put straight; but insisting that the man who put things straight should not be himself, but another. Henry always wanted to be judge in his own cause; against his wives; against his friends; against the Head of his Church. But the link which really connects More with that Roman supremacy for which he died is this fact: that he would always have been large-minded enough to want a judge who was not merely himself.

Mr. Belloc has pointed out, in a brilliant and penetrating essay, that More died for the Papacy because it was a part of the truth; not because it was his favorite part, or to him and his friends a particularly sympathetic or popular part. And this, of course, is profoundly true; the need for the Papacy is far more obvious now than it was then. Nevertheless, there is this true relation between the martyr and the doctrine for which he died; that he died, not only defending the Pope, but defying the sort of man who wants to be Pope. There is no true Pope who wants to be Pope. More was the sort of man who would write a hundred wild satires or romances like *Utopia*, by way of a joke; but he was also the sort of man who would wish that a better man might judge whether the joke had gone too far. Therefore, when Henry and his hangers-on began at last to press him upon the supreme question of Henry's rightful supremacy, he knew that the claim was wrong in spirit and motive; and after an interlude of odd silence and reflection, suddenly rose up and defied it. He did not at all want to die; he was the kind of man to enjoy life to the last; but he did die, and having thus released his soul, he died laughing.

SAINT EDMUND CAMPION (1540–1581)

by C. C. MARTINDALE, S.J.

THESE FEW PAGES DO NOT PROPOSE TO BE A GLORIFICATION either of Campion or of his Englishism, but a very brief account of a man who undoubtedly was an Englishman, and lived most of his life and died in England, and was a real factor in her history, though less when he took on the color of his environment, than when he resisted it.

Campion's family was middle-class and commercial—his father, a "very honest bookseller." Enormously rich people then were such, on the whole, because royalty made them so, having looted the monasteries so as to bestow largesse upon those whom they feared or liked. Simpler folk were not then possessed by the desire to imitate, nor to use their sturdy ambitions merely to get rich quick. It was not from snobbishness that Edmund's father wanted to educate him well, but because a guild or company (probably the grocers') saw the boy's quick wits, sent him to a grammar school that the older man could not afford, and then to Christ's College in Newgate Street, which King Edward's "advisers" had made him found out of the relics of confiscated moneys. To my mind, it was here that Edmund Campion ran his first real perils. If there was not a social snobbery then as there is now, there was a far greater educational or literary snobbery. The idols of the New Learning were everywhere being worshipped. But Campion's cleverness must certainly have been notable, since, when Mary Tudor made her state entry into London and passed by St. Paul's School, they left that school aside and chose Campion, winner of all prizes, to be boy-declaimer at her welcome. She was "pleased," and this began a whole series of appearances before queens. Meanwhile, Sir Thomas White, founder of St. John's College, Oxford, had also liked him; and by grace of the Grocers' Company he was sent on there and became a Fellow at eighteen!

His oratorical gifts made him noticeable: in 1560, though a layman, he preached the panegyric over Amy Robsart, of whom people were saying that her husband, Lord Dudley, had murdered her to be more at his ease with Elizabeth; afterwards, he was to preach the funeral oration for Sir Thomas White also. Did he, in 1564, take the Oath of Supremacy? Seemingly he did, though helping others to escape it. Oxford had gone to his head. He was its idol. Students mobbed him; imitated his walk, his accent, his dress. He was temporizing, playing tricks with conscience, committing himself in neither direction. When in 1566 the queen herself came to Oxford, he greeted her in the name of the university; afterwards, he "disputed" in her presence, but on safer topics than the semi-political ones entrusted to others—whether rule by prince alone were not better than rule by law alone; whether princes did not rule better by succession than by election. Campion merely had to argue that the moon rules the tides, on which certainly he talked much nonsense and was in arrears upon Aquinas, but he made up for it by an adulation no less inevitable than disgusting both of the queen and of her lover Dudley, chancellor of the university. They fell into ecstasies over Campion; he was made to discourse extempore before the Spanish ambassador, and again before the queen at Woodstock. Cecil and Dudley took him up, and when Dudley had become Lord Leicester, Campion still was to pursue him with flatteries that we must condone because princes exacted them.

Nonetheless, Campion was sick at heart; he revolted against the inscriptions put up at Christ Church, as though Elizabeth's father, if not she herself, had created Wolsey's college. A brilliant Latinist, Hellenist, and Hebrew scholar, he now was studying the Fathers, and could see neither how not to be a Catholic, nor how to be one. He found that St. Peter Martyr had said that it was not absolutely prohibited for a Catholic to assist at profane and execrable rites, and, in a moment, I think, of nervous exasperation, took the enormous step of being ordained deacon in the queen's new church. At once his conscience started to torment him.

A downright sin may operate in two ways. A man may be so appalled at himself that he resolves: "Never again!" and adheres to his resolve. Or, horrified to see that he *can* do what he never expected of himself, desponds. Campion still temporized, but drew back. His "tone" in preaching was all too Catholic. Invited by the suspicious grocers to preach at Paul's Cross at Candlemas, he hesitated, and asked for a reprieve until Michaelmas. Then he met them and asked to be let off. They suggested somewhere less important—Walbrook. He resisted. They delivered an ultimatum. He refused it, resigned his exhibition, and, on the feast of St. Peter in Chains, 1569, resigned also his proctorial office and left Oxford.

In the midst of this brilliancy, or glitter, of this suspicion and adulation, Campion had genuinely loved education, had worked hard, and had hated unchastity. This, to my mind, is what really saved him. Off, now, he went to Ireland, where there was question of reviving the old Dublin university, dead because of the suppression of those monasteries without which there would have been no universities at all. Under Leicester's unfailing patronage, he seemed to have new scholastic glories ahead of him. He wrote a treatise on *The Academic Man* anticipating thus Newman's *Idea of a University*; and indeed how strange is the resemblance-in-contrast between these two men, not excluding the visit of each to Ireland and the respective causes of their going and leaving! Certainly, Campion's "Academic Youth" was to be equipped with qualities beyond any Crichton; still, his ideal young man was not only to be a scholar: "he must wash thoroughly and dress properly"; he must always stand to study; he must live not only among those corpses that books are. The intellectual vitality of Campion reveals itself.

But the Catholic hinterland of his mind also revealed itself. Almost at once they suspected him, though he had not been received back into the Church. One difference between him and Erasmus surely was that Erasmus was a humanist who could not help being a Catholic; Campion, irrevocably a Catholic with a convinced longing to be a humanist: and again, Campion urged positive ideals, and criticized others only in so far as they fell short of his standard; Erasmus really disliked men personally, and snarled and sneered.

Campion, hidden away from pursuit, put together a History of Ireland. For this he had really tried to make due researches; foiled in this, he wrote the least kindly book he ever did write, unredeemed, to my mind, by its glittering style, but acute, full of observation, of knowledge of human nature, and of gay vivacity. But as his presence was exposing his good hosts to too much danger, he resolved on flight. Campion always possessed a sort of sanctified impertinence. He enjoyed, I feel sure, dressing as the lackey of the Earl of Kildare's steward, who was crossing to England, and standing under the very nose of officers who boarded the ship to search for him, and who questioned every person save himself. He spent the time invoking St. Patrick in his mind, a new patron to whom, he was thenceforward ever true.

In England he not only missed the warm-hearted hospitality of the Irish, but found himself in a world of "fears, suspicions, arrestings, condemnations, torturings and executions." In the June of that year, 1571, the aged Dr. Storey was kidnapped by a base trick in the Lowlands and executed in a manner more revolting even than was usual. Campion, in Westminster Hall, attended his trial. I cannot but think this was a turning-point. Shocked beyond measure, he made an end of temporizing and took a boat for Douai. An English frigate stopped them in mid-channel, arrested Campion, brought him back; but, succumbing to a tip, the captain winked and let him go. The seaman walked west; Campion, east. In Kent, he found means to get across to France. Cecil said that England had lost one of her diamonds.

He went to the English seminary at Douai, founded by Doctor, afterwards Cardinal, Allen, and found himself in an all-but Oxford atmosphere once more. He throve, was ordained sub-deacon, delved into St. Thomas, and wrote boldly "martyrdom" against a passage dealing with "baptism of blood." He also taught eloquence, and wrote controversial letters; but I feel that, his conscience now being clear, there is already much more of his native sweetness and less artificiality in his style. He writes like a simple Englishman, not like a Ciceronian in disguise.

But suddenly he asked to go to Rome and become a Jesuit. His deepening piety may have made him desire the religious vows, and his adventurous spirit seek companionship with men who, they said, were the Church's skirmishers and light cavalry. But he could have got all that in the destiny that any English priest had to foresee. Possibly he did not feel quite in sympathy with Allen. Much had happened in England since Allen had left; Campion felt sure that Elizabeth had come to stay; Allen thought that Philip of Spain was rightful king there. But the generous-hearted Allen gave him leave; off he went, on foot, meeting on the way an Oxford friend who had last seen him "in great pomp," thought he must have been robbed, and offered him his purse. Campion answered in terms of self-sacrifice for Christ's sake, and plodded on.

In Rome, catechized about the effect of the Pope's Bull of Deposition, he said frankly that it had made things harder for Catholics, and begged for a "mitigation"; Elizabeth could not be unexcommunicated, but might not Catholics acknowledge her as queen without themselves incurring excommunication? Thus they could honestly say they were not traitors nor teachers of treachery. He was duly received into the Society as a novice. There was then no English Jesuit province; foreign provincials fought for him; Austria won, and he was sent to Prague, where he could contemplate the spiritual and moral decline due to Hussism. But he was soon shifted to Brünn, in Moravia, where things were still worse. He was put to teach the poorer people, which he did almost as a reparation, recalling that Hus derived some of his more anarchic ideas from Wycliffe. Brought back to Prague, every task in the house seemed placed on his not over-strong shoulders; he also taught rhetoric and afterwards Aristotelian philosophy.

You might have feared he would relapse into artificialities, especially as the only model allowed was Cicero. But no. His directions are definite. First think exactly what you want to say, and, then only, say it as well as you can. Thus, you will not be mimicking what Cicero said, but speaking as Cicero would have spoken. Meanwhile he wrote plays and dramatic dialogues with incredible fluency, and had much talk with his old and dear friend, Sir Philip Sidney, Elizabeth's envoy to the Emperor Rudolph II. Sidney professed himself convinced of the truth of the Faith, but alleged that he could not draw back from the brilliant career that already, at twenty-three, was his. Campion prayed that some missionary, home in England, could help this "poor wavering soul." (Not a phrase usually applied to the chivalrous poet!) Ordained in 1578, he was begged for by Allen as member of the English mission now to be developed, and, with Parsons, was allotted to it. Everyone realized what it held in store. One of his colleagues painted a wreath of lilies and roses over his bed; another wrote "Father Edmund Campion, Martyr" over his door. On March 25, 1580, he went to Rome, and learned that he would be starting for England somewhat after Easter.

Rome seems to me to have been filled with men as ignorant as possible of the real state of things or of feeling in England, yet extremely wise about the technique, so to say, of missionary work there. Indeed, the situation was everywhere confused. Henry VIII had really thought he could remain a devout Catholic while calling himself head of the Church in England; Elizabeth, the perfect cynic, yet imperious, was finding she had to play off king against king, parties and nobles one against the other, and really might have urged that she had been forced into anti-Catholicism by Rome itself. English Catholics did not at all want to apostatize, but by now, I think, did regard Elizabeth as their queen, and may have been almost proud of her. Campion left Rome with the "mitigation" he had asked for, and instructions to let laymen do all the spade-work of instruction—the priest was to arrive only to put the finishing touch to conversion; they must avoid sarcasm or the appearance of seeking alms or legacies; they must eschew politics, and not even write to Rome about them. Yet just at that moment, a papally-backed expedition sailed for Ireland to assist rebellion both by money and arms, so that there was not the least chance of the missionaries in England seeming anything but hostile intriguers, sent by a Pope who could not possibly be thought neutral, let alone friendly. Probably Pius V, holding that he had rights over every island, had felt he was no less able to take away Ireland from the English crown, just as his predecessor had "given" it, than to excommunicate and depose Elizabeth; nonetheless, and despite the affectionate farewell spoken to the missionaries by St. Philip Neri, not to insist on the fuss and notoriety that surrounded the departure, so that everyone in authority in England knew all about the expedition before it had got halfway, the enterprise was doomed from the outset.

They travelled by foot and on horseback, Campion in the poorest clothes, gaily alleging that a man enroute for martyrdom need not worry about the fashion. Morning and night he pushed on ahead for meditation and prayer; during the day his infectious high spirits encouraged the others, some of whom were old. At Milan, they met St. Charles Borromeo; and, having crossed by Mont Cenis, at last they reached Geneva. In Geneva, Beza was living, successor to Calvin. With almost school-boyish audacity five of them visited him. They definitely "cheeked" him, and when soon afterwards they challenged him and his fellows to a discussion—the vanquished to be burned at the stake—no wonder it was hinted that they had better leave Geneva quickly. I think that Campion felt that they had behaved rather excitedly; they did penance by tramping to a shrine.

In May 1580 they arrived at Rheims. Allen welcomed them, and a great tragedy occurred. Bishop Goldwell, who, with the Bishop of Lincoln now in prison, was sole survivor of the deposed Catholic hierarchy, fell ill and had to return. He implored that bishops might be created for England. They were not: no one at Rome imagined that Protestantism would survive there; mendicant bishops destined to the rack and the gallows did not appeal to the official mind; none were sent. When, long afterwards, bishops were given back to us a tradition had been irreparably snapped.

Next, on all sides the little band was being told that their mission was a hopeless one. Campion, sensitive to every mood, began to wonder if he had done right in abandoning the manifestly successful work in Bohemia for so forlorn a hope. Every detail, even the appearance of the missionaries, was known to Walsingham by means of his superb system of espionage. The Irish expedition made it inevitable that they should be regarded as political intriguers. But no. Allen said that Campion's Bohemian apostolate could be done by anyone equally qualified—or "at least by two or three such persons"; so let him persevere. They crossed therefore from Flanders by ones or twos—Parsons dressed as a soldier "such a peacock!—such a swaggerer!" Campion wrote to Rome. He himself went as "Mr. Edmunds," jewel-merchant, along with the little lay-brother, Ralph Emerson. The "searcher" of all such immigrants at Dover had been so perfectly taken in by Parsons that he actually helped him with a horse on his way to London. Reprimanded and bidden to be more careful, he arrested Campion and Emerson, thinking that Campion answered to the description of a brother of Allen's. Who knows why—they were freed, and finally reached London.

He was lodged in the very house of the chief pursuivant—was this another instance of his audacity, that he had found to pay so well, or had the man been bought over? Both explanations are offered. But, at any rate, the apostolate had now begun.

The stay in London was not a long one. The place was full of unconfessed Catholics, longing to meet the priests; but almost at once an apostate spy had caused the arrest of a Mr. Orton and of Fr. Johnson; and it was decided that both Parsons and Campion must go farther away from this storm-center. Before leaving, Campion, by request, wrote a rapid profession of his sincerity—politics were "strictly forbidden" to him; from them he "gladly estranged and sequestered his mind." His extreme simplicity of soul and candor are seen in his petition that he might be heard by three audiences—by the Lords in Council, on the relation of the Church to the English Government; by the heads of houses in both universities, on the proofs of the Catholic Faith; and, by the courts spiritual and temporal, to justify the Faith by "the common wisdom of the laws standing." He really did believe that men's heads and hearts were so essentially right, that he would but have to put the thing in a clear and charitable way before them, in order to bring them round. Begging, too, a special audience of the queen, he ended with often-quoted words; "Hearken unto those which spend the best blood in their bodies for your salvation. Many innocent hands are lifted up unto Heaven for you, daily and hourly, by those English students whose posterity shall not die, which, beyond the seas, gathering virtue and sufficient knowledge for the purpose, are determined never to give you over, but either to win you to heaven or to die upon your pikes. And touching our Society, be it known to you that we have made a league: cheerfully to carry the cross that you shall lay upon us, and never to despair of your recovery while we have a man left to enjoy your Tyburn, or to be racked with your torments, or to be consumed with your prisons. The expense is reckoned, the enterprise is begun; it is of God; it cannot be withstood. So the Faith was planted; so it must be restored."

He concludes by saying that if he be refused, and rewarded with rigor, he can add no more, but commends their cause, and his own, to

God, and prays that they may find themselves at accord at least on the Day of Payment, and at last "be friends in Heaven, where all injuries shall be forgiven."

This document at once became known, though it was meant to be kept private, save in case of his arrest, and was nicknamed "Campion's Brag and Challenge," though that was exactly what he had declared that it in no way was.

He then moved from house to house in the more southerly Midlands, finding everywhere hosts of Catholics, desperately grateful to receive at last their sacraments, instruction, and encouragement. This occupied the latter half of 1580 and most of the next year. He went, of course, further north, too, into Derbyshire and Nottingham, and finally to Lancashire. All, fascinated by his clear discourse and extreme personal charm, yet acknowledged that a certain "hidden infused power" gave him his efficacy. The saint was beginning to grow within him; and when sanctity had been achieved martyrdom was assured. He could not doubt of that. Five of the little band that had set out from Rheims were already in prison cells, broken by the rack. Yet in all this, his irrepressible vivacity kept breaking out. I can but recall the day when speaking to a village girl by a duck-pond covered with green scum, he saw the pursuivants turn the corner. He pretended to insult her; she pushed him into the pond; he emerged unrecognizable; the officers passed by laughing.

The "event" of this period was the writing, printing and publishing of his *Ten Reasons*. They were ten considerations put forward "on the side of the Faith." At first he wanted to call it "Heresy Hopeless"—*De Haeresi Desperata*. But no one could help smiling. Heresy, just then, and as it turned out justifiably, was so very sure of itself! At Campion's suggestion, Parsons set up a private printing press in the attics of Dame Cicely Stonor, near Henley. Some 400 copies were rushed through (not even being stitched); and on June 27 the church of St. Mary the Virgin, then used for the learned effervescences of commemoration, was snowed under with the pamphlet which undergraduates eagerly read while the solemn function was proceeding. The dons were furious. They, a second rate crew, imposed by Elizabeth, were trying to dragoon the intelligence of young men more alert than they, into thinking with the State. Somewhat so, in Soviet Russia, you must not tell the truth about Russia to the outside world, nor even the truth about the outside world within Russia. Opposition was mobilized. It was almost wholly abusive, not argument.

I am not fond of the *Decem Rationes*; but then, I detest the whole of this period; and it remains that despite the all-but total confiscation of the original edition (it is said that only two copies exist), nearly thirty Latin editions are said to have been demanded, and many translations into European languages were made. Anyway, in this shattering booklet there was some true "Campion" especially when he appeals to the queen herself, when he assures her that "one heaven cannot contain Calvin and these thine ancestors"—he had alluded to St. Edward, St. Louis, St. Henry of Saxony, St. Stephen of Hungary, and other sainted kings; and cries that the day will come that shall make it clear "which of the two did love you best: the company of Jesus or the brood of Luther." The book roused the authorities to fury, and Campion was warned to run back into Lancashire. But he received a letter from a Mr. Yate, in prison for the Catholic Faith, begging him to visit his house, Lyford Grange, in Berkshire, where his wife, his mother, and some Brigittine nuns were living. Parsons gave leave reluctantly. Campion was too "easygoing." "If they once get you there," he said, "you will never break away."

Campion went; he spent a night there, and was actually leaving when news came that a large number of Catholics had arrived, all longing to see him. Even Brother Ralph Emerson thought he should stay, and that it would be safer for the priest to be surrounded thus with friends. He himself went on alone towards Lancashire.

Among the crowd of sixty who heard Campion preach that Sunday was George Eliot, an apostate and a spy. Mrs. Yate's cook had known him in old days, let him in at once, and actually told him that

Campion (the warrant for whose arrest he had upon him) was in the house. Eliot sent to Abingdon for one hundred men to effect that arrest, went upstairs and heard Campion's Mass devoutly, and then left. After dinner a look-out man saw the armed force approaching, and Campion was hurried into a hiding-place, though he had begged them to let him try to escape alone, without involving them in his danger. The magistrate, who loathed Eliot, arrived, and at his bidding was forced to make his men ransack the house and then return to tear down the very paneling. Mrs. Yate raised an outcry; the magistrate apologized, and, seeing she was an invalid, said she might sleep where she pleased. She had a bed made up close to the hiding-place—thus, she hoped, to protect it. Late at night, having smashed all they could, and by now probably half drunk, the men went downstairs and slept. Mrs. Yate—fatuity surely unparalleled in history—thereupon collected her guests, caused Campion to get out of his hiding-place, and demanded just one more sermon. Campion spoke; as they tip-toed away, someone tripped; others fell over him; there was a clatter. The men awoke, and with lanterns and axes poured up the stairs. They could find nothing, and were for making Eliot pay for their interrupted sleep. Eliot felt sure that something had been implied by that midnight noise, and abruptly noticed the bit of paneling as yet unbroken. He demanded that it too should be pierced. A servant, who knew that the hiding-place was just behind it, protested that enough damage had been done, and then, catching Eliot's eye, could not prevent himself from turning white. That settled it Eliot, seizing a hammer, struck it into the woodwork and Campion was revealed. Two priests, seven gentlemen, and two yeomen were taken with him.

After four days, imprisonment orders came from London that they were to be removed thither, strongly guarded. The Berkshire sheriff did what he could to show respect to his prisoners, but could not prevent the indecent exultation of Eliot, at whom the people shouted "Judas" all the way. At Abingdon, men came across from Oxford to salute what they knew would be the last they saw of their scholastic glory, and the man whom still they loved. Eliot half apologized to Campion: "Mr. Campion, I know well you are angry with me for this work." "Nay; I forgive you, and in token thereof, I drink to you! And if you repent and come to Confession, I will absolve you...but large penance must you have!" At Henley, they passed close to Parsons, who was forbidden, most wisely, to show himself; but Campion recognized his servant and greeted him as best he could; and a young priest who tried to speak to him was at once arrested as a "comforter of Jesuits." At Colebrook, the sheriff received orders from London to treat with ignominy the men he had gladly hitherto respected: their elbows were tied behind, their wrists in front, their feet beneath their horses. On Campion's hat (Parsons' hat, really, for they had exchanged hats when last they parted) was fastened a placard: "Campion, the Seditious Jesuit." So was he exhibited through London. He was taken to the Tower and put at once into the "Little Ease," where he could neither stand nor lie down. There he was kept for four days, till his spirit should have been broken.

And then he was taken out by the Traitors' Gate. Whither? Surely to the most dramatic encounter ever staged by life. To the town house of the Earl of Leicester, who, with Lord Bedford and two secretaries of State, stood at the side of Elizabeth on a great chair. I cannot but think that the earl and the queen had not even now quite recovered from their long-ago fascination; perhaps they felt that if Campion could be won the Catholic game was up. They catechized him; they assured him there was nothing wrong with him save his papistry. "My greatest glory!" he answered. Elizabeth offered him liberty and honors, would he but recant; still smiling on him, she sent him back to the Tower; for three days promises and cajoleries were applied—even up to the offer of the Canterbury archbishopric, if no post at court could satisfy him. Word was sent round London that he was about to yield—soon he would be preaching at Paul's Cross, burn the *Ten Reasons* with his own hand, and be crowned with the Protestant mitre. On the third day of Campion's obstinacy these cynics, to whom caress and cruelty came with equal ease, sent Campion to the rack, and the hideous engine tugged his limbs apart. During the torture he was plied with questions; he was asked for his views of certain old political utterances of his friends; his own views as to the legitimacy of Elizabeth's position; whom he had met in England; who had welcomed him; whose confessions he had heard, and much more. Lord Burghley wrote to Lord Shrewsbury a letter, still existing, that proves he said nothing of moment. Still, he said something.... Exactly what? The world was informed that he had yielded to pain, acknowledged every detail; and a series of arrests, trials, and condemnations went forward on the strength of this. Campion was branded among all, Catholics included, as renegade and traitor. Exactly what Campion said may never now be known. I think, when names were mentioned to him as already known, he may have acknowledged them as Catholic, knowing they were known, and having—even so—exacted an oath that no additional harm would befall them owing to this corroboration. The first and only real informants had been, it seems probable, three panic-stricken servants. If, indeed, then, Campion, delirious with pain, did say anything, he made up for it amply afterwards, and immediately rose above it.

For Campion was an object of interest. He had often asked for a public discussion. This was when they chose to grant it, out of curiosity, and indeed forced it on him. Without warning or preparation he was suddenly taken to the Norman chapel, filled with personages—Deans of St. Paul's and Windsor, Regius Professors, Puritan preachers, and what not. They sat with books, paper and ink, before them; they could raise any objection they chose: he had nothing for reference, and had to answer without being allowed to offer his own objections, let alone to put forward any harmonious statement of the Catholic Faith. Sitting on his little stool, his body and nerves still desperately in anguish, he made the wicked absurdity of his position clear enough. Their "argument" was chiefly vituperation and jeering; he never lost his temper. They actually gave him a Greek Testament of such small print that in that gloomy place he could not read it, and then had the triple nerve to say he knew no Greek. No word, existing or yet to be coined, could serve us for the description of this ignoble episode. At least the laity were both shocked and impressed. Philip, Earl of Arundel, found in it the origin of what became a life and death of noble fidelity. In that same Tower, he was to die. Again racked, Campion was made similarly to answer questions before other assessors; his ease, charm, and learning brought it about that the Bishop of London decided that the system did more harm than good, broke the discussions off, and for the third time Campion was racked, so violently that he thought they meant to kill him. A cousin of the queen cried that it were easier to tear the heart from his breast than one word against his conscience from his lips. This time the pain had taken him beyond sensation itself. "How do you feel?" asked his gaoler, next day, who had been won by Campion's gentleness, "Not ill," he answered, "because not at all."

Other tactics were tried. Campion was accused of having been involved in the Roman-Spanish-Irish expedition and rising of a year ago. But they could find no evidence—naturally; there was none. He had not been involved in it. Then they invented, all of a piece, a "Rheims-Rome" Plot, and spent time briefing false witnesses as to what they should say. Then the Duc d'Alençon, whom Elizabeth had said that she would marry at last, arrived. Much younger than she, he was also brother-in-law to the Queen of Scots, a prisoner then in Sheffield. Did it look as if Elizabeth was parleying with Papists? Best make a counter-manifesto.

On November 14, nine men, of whom Campion was one, were arraigned in Westminster Hall on a charge of high treason and much more. They were told to plead guilty or not guilty. The men "who had travelled," said Campion, "only for souls," raised their right hand, to answer "Not guilty"—all save he. Racked and re-racked, he could not. From his swollen hands the very finger-nails had fallen. A comrade took off his fur cuff, and kissing it, lifted the poor hand that it too might attest the man's guiltlessness. Even had not Ralph Sherwin cried aloud: "The plain ground of our standing here is religion, not treason," all knew in their hearts that the men were innocent. The Chief Justice, a Catholic at heart, remembered evermore the disgraceful day with anguish.

It is impossible to relate the trial in detail. Campion, whose "sweetness of disposition." all men knew, had to say of the witnesses (amongst whom was Eliot) that "they have nothing left to swear by, neither religion nor honesty." It has to be confessed that Campion, when suitable, eluded, and when apt, demolished, the arguments of his accusers; so much so, that the queen's prosecutor, Anderson, lost his temper and exclaimed that, logic or none, "I will bring it to purpose anon." The men were foredoomed, even though Campion, questioned about his allegiance, was able to rehearse by heart what he had said to Elizabeth in Leicester's house, and how he had satisfied her with his words...and he reminded the jury that again and again he and his comrades had been promised that if they would but become Anglicans all would be well. "So great are the treasons" that he and they were, in honesty, believed to have wrought! Public opinion was wholly on their side; but "the poor twelve" came back from their consultation; the accused were guilty on all points; yet again Caesar had conquered Christ. When asked what "Campion and the rest had to say why they should not die"—this was his answer:

"It was not our death that ever we feared! But we knew that we were not lords of our own lives, and therefore for want of answer would not be guilty of our own deaths. The only thing we have now to say is, that if our religion do make us traitors, we are worthy to be condemned; but otherwise we are and have been as true subjects as ever the Queen has had. In condemning us, you condemn all your own ancestors, Bishops and Kings: all that was once the glory of England, the Island of Saints, and the most devoted child of the See of Peter. For what have we taught (however you may qualify it with the odious name of treason), that they did not uniformly teach?

To be condemned with these old lights, not of England only but the world, by their degenerate descendants, is both gladness and glory to us! God lives. Posterity will live. Their judgment is not so liable to corruption as that of those who are now going to sentence us to death."

They were condemned and sentenced. A cry of protest echoed in the very hall; but above it could be heard Campion's voice: "We praise You, O God!"; and Sherwin's: "This is the day that the Lord has made, let us rejoice and be glad in it!" Protest was hushed in astonishment, and then the cries of exultation were taken up, and it seemed to be already the martyrs' Easter Day.

Elizabeth did not at all believe the charges of treason, and continued to send offers of Church preferment to Campion, would he but apostatize. Campion's own sister was one of those chosen to make this offer. And as though no act of melodrama, even, were to be omitted in that strange world, Eliot too arrived, trembling for his safety, sure that the Catholics would take vengeance on him, and begging Campion to protect him. Campion, without one word of rebuke, sweet and attentive as ever, promised him a letter of recommendation to a German duke, who would accept his service. The gaoler, present at this conversation, was overwhelmed; he never forgot the talk, and it became the beginning of his conversion to the Faith. Authority deemed it wise to hasten the date of execution, lest petitions addressed to the queen might occasion a reprieve. One pitiable incident occurred. The Duc d'Alençon, still present in England, had promised to intercede for Campion. As the days went by and he seemed to be doing nothing, his confessor actually went into the tennis-court where d'Alençon was playing. He said that France's royal blood would be forever disgraced were so foul a judicial murder not prevented. The duke stood still for a minute, stroked his face with his left hand, and then said: "Play!" and the game proceeded. Along with Sherwin, Campion endured another long argument, and as ever, had the best of it. But that would not help. "Soon I shall be above yon fellow!" said Sherwin gallantly, looking at the sun as they passed through an open court, on their way back to their all but lightless, airless confinement. But they could not quite always keep their spirits high, as the days dragged; just how to kill them had not been settled. "Delay of our death does somewhat dull me," Sherwin wrote. But finally December 1st was chosen. Campion represented the Society of Jesus; Sherwin, the college at Rheims; Alexander Briant, the English college at Rome.

The day dawned cold and raining. "God save you all, gentlemen!" cried Campion as they left the Tower; "God bless you all and make you all good Catholics!" Then he was thrown down and tied to his hurdle; the two younger men shared another. Each hurdle was tied to the tails of two horses, and then dragged at full speed down Cheapside, under the New Gate, and then Holborn. After this came a mile of open country, and then Tyburn. As they went under Newgate, Campion struggled to raise himself a little, in order to salute the statue of Our Lady over the arch. Now and again the pitiful procession halted its pace; then the martyrs spoke cheerily to the horrified crowds; and once a gentleman leaned down and gently wiped the mud from Campion's face. So anxious was officialdom, that no less than 3,000 horsemen had been gathered round the gallows; and "an infinite number of souls." Just as the hurdles reached the place, the sun shone out. Campion was the first to mount the cart and to put the noose round his own neck. He began to speak—it was his right. "We are made a spectacle unto the world, to angels and to men—we are fools for Christ's sake." But they prevented him, and kept arguing about "treason." "If you esteem my religion treason, then am I guilty. As for any other treason, I never committed any—God is my judge." But a proclamation was read out in the queen's name—a plan unparalleled before or after—stating that it *was* for treason, not religion, that these three men were being killed. Again and again he was questioned, and had to repeat the wearisome denials, and then tried to pray. He used liturgical words, in Latin. Someone shouted to him to pray in English: "I will pray to God," said he, "in a language we both well understand!" Still once more they harried him, and told him to pray for Elizabeth.

"Yes," he replied, "I do pray for Elizabeth, your queen and my queen, unto whom I wish a long quiet reign with all prosperity." At these words they drew the cart away. An official, touched with mercy, had ordered that he should remain hanging till he was quite dead. He was not therefore, according to the directions of the sentence, conscious when his limbs were placed upon the quartering-block to be hacked asunder. But as the executioner tossed them into a cauldron for boiling before they were exhibited on spikes, some of his blood fell on the sleeve of a young and brilliant writer, Henry Walpole. The lad had not been pious, but had felt indignation at the treatment given to men like Campion, and had already befriended him; this blood turned him into the hero and martyr that he afterwards became, and was but a symbol of the wave of conversion which all over England swept men anew into the Church. And all Europe rang with the news; so much so that the English government had to send out its *apologias* on all sides. But not a soul believed them. Campion died a martyr, and as such we venerate him.

We have, then, outlined the story of a man whose character was such that no one could fail to love him, and whose innocence of the crime for which he was allegedly put to death so horribly was manifest. I cannot think of a trial or execution that approach more closely to Our Lord's, from that specific point of view, than Campion's. No one believed him guilty—neither the Caesar of the hour, nor her ministers, nor his judges, nor the crowd.

But in a book called *The English Way*, which I presume does not merely mean the path that English history has followed, but the sort of "way" in which Englishmen do things, Campion has not to be seen only as an individual, but somehow as a type, and so must his murderers be. Neither he nor they contain in themselves all the characteristics of their race—in any national history, national characteristics will be found parceled out: *non omnia provehunt omnes*.

My personal conviction is that all nations are worth one another. But it would take long to elucidate that. I think that the Zulu "way," the Boer way, the French and German ways, the Irish and English ways, are in the long run equivalents. That may not be a popular view; still, it is mine. Practically everyone has in him the elements of the gentleman and the cad. Sometimes one set of elements rises uppermost and subordinates the rest. Very seldom, but also sometimes, a sort of electrolysis occurs, and all one sort of element goes to one side, the other to the other. In Elizabeth's time, the State became the cad as such. The queen herself was a dislocated woman, who ended by existing altogether on one side, though most of her life she had succeeded in diffusing herself towards both sides, and not even caring much about her ignominious position. She finished up by a furious, miserable, and very ugly death, from whose consequences perhaps the prayers of her martyrs may have rescued her. We, too, pray that they may have. We, too, like Campion, might have prayed that her reign might have been truly prosperous, though, perhaps also like him, we do not see how it could have been. She had absorbed the cad-element in her advisers; out of Campion had been strained any such infection—he became and remained the ideal gentleman—English or any other sort. The perfect purity—undilutedness—that sexually had always been his and spiritually became his; the high-heartedness; the cheery audacity; the deep inwardness; the supreme forgivingness; the inability even to believe in dishonesty—not to insist on stupidity; the humility and the pride—these are proper to the gentleman, duke or docker, whenever to the glory of God he appears. Alas, that none of this can we perceive in those who—knowing what they did, as the government's subordinates did not—destroyed so precious a life from out of humankind.

MARY WARD (1585–1645)

by MAISIE WARD

I

"IT THEN OCCURRED, AND SO CONTINUES IN MY MIND," wrote Mary Ward, after long meditation on the Institute she was founding, "that those in Paradise, before the first fall, were in this estate. It seemed to me then, and that hope remains still, that our Lord let me see it, to invite me that way, and because He would give me grace in time to arrive to such an estate, at least in some degree...That word justice, things done in innocence, and that we be such as we appear and appear such as we are—those things often since occurred to my mind with a liking of them...I have moreover thought upon this occasion that perhaps this course of ours would continue till the end of the world because it came to that in which we first began." But Paradise is not easily won back.

The surroundings of Mary Ward's childhood are a curious mixture special to the country and period. Marmaduke Ward, Mary's father, was a man of substance and position, related to most of the historic families of the north. One seems at first to see the child living the life of any little Catholic girl in a country house, taught her faith and her letters, needlework and the other accomplishments which even so late as our grandmothers were still learned, hearing Mass, playing with her sisters and cousins, walking round the farm, visiting the neighboring families. Yet in and out of this simple pattern of life runs the thread of something utterly strange to us today—persecution. It is not wonderful perhaps that with this scarlet line woven into their lives their level of piety and earnestness was higher than ours.

They had already held on a long time when Mary was born, three years before the Armada. They held on steadily through what was left of Elizabeth's life. The bitter disappointment of James I's accession passed into the heartbreak of his reign, and his death was to bring no improvement. All this was in the unforeseeable future. But even so, early weariness was upon them, hope fading. Mary's grandmother had already endured for many years when she received the five-year old Mary at Ploughland, having indeed "in her younger years suffered imprisonment for the space of fourteen years together." With her, Mary stayed for the best part of five years. At ten, she was betrothed to a youth who died within a few months.

Marmaduke Ward tried again, but Mary, with that relentless honesty and clear-sightedness to be seen whenever she writes of herself, thus describes the issue and analyzes her own feelings: "Nor after twelve years old did I ever see any that I did, or, for aught I knew, could affect even, in way of marriage; for it was ordinary with me to hate the party or parties in such extremity (especially when the marriage was offered to myself), as could not stand with Christian charity, and this towards several and for many years together...(though I refused not those they offered forth of any desires to be religious, nor other reason, but because I could not affect them)... I had during those years burning desires to be a martyr, and my mind was for a long time together fixed upon that happy course; the sufferings of the martyrs appeared to me delightful for attaining to so great a good, and my favorite thoughts were how and when?" Between fifteen and sixteen, she first realized that she had a vocation to the religious life, but it was not until she was twenty-one—this was in 1606—that she won her father's consent to go overseas. Her confessor still opposed the design: but when, on the occasion of a mysterious and most moving incident at Mass, he not only withdrew his opposition but declared her resolution "holy," she was free to carry out her vocation—had she been sure of its nature. But in fact her preparation was not yet complete. "This affection to the religious life," she writes, "was in general, for I had no inclination to any Order in particular, only I was resolved within myself to take the most strict and secluded, thinking and often saying, that as women did not know how to do good except to themselves (a penuriousness which I resented enough even then) I would do in earnest what I did...."

II

This choosing of "the most strict and secluded" was for her bound up with a "penuriousness" in the activity held good for women which she resented....How strangely interesting is the working out of human vocation. Even in the natural order, few people find quickly the path that is to be theirs. There are gropings in the dark, tentative efforts, apparent failures. In the spiritual life it seems the same. The Curé d'Ars tried again and again to abandon his unique and stupendous work for souls and become a contemplative. Therese of Lisieux had to push aside the *Annals of the Propagation of the Faith*, for they were for her a "temptation." God had called her to a life of contemplation. For her, "penuriousness" lay in external activity; for Mary, in a life from which such activity was excluded.

Mary, on arriving at St. Omer, went straight to the Jesuit college with her letter of introduction. "Immediately came to me one called Father George Keynes, who told me that I was and had been for some time expected at a monastery of Poor Clares in that town, wherein were and had lived for many years several gentlewomen of our nation...that my place was already granted amongst the lay-sisters.... That the state of lay-sisters was indeed held amongst worldlings more abject, and of less renown.... And verily, quoth he, 'I judge it the Will of God you should be there and enter as lay-sister.'

"I remained silent," she says, "for a time feeling an extreme repugnance to accept their offers. But arguing interiorly with myself, it appeared to me that the repugnance and aversion which I felt could spring from nothing but pride. Those words, 'the Will of God,' so pierced my heart, that I did not dare to speak or think otherwise....

"Turning myself therefore to God, I applied myself to prayer with extreme diligence, entreating that the Divine will might be done, whatever it should be, without regard to my content or consolation, present or future, and then, with all sincerity, I declared, both to my confessor and to the superiors of the monastery, the internal suffering which I felt, and the exceeding difficulty which I found in embracing that vocation, throwing myself for the rest upon the providence of God, to follow whose holy will, I resolved to do whatever should be ordered me by them."

For a year Mary, as a lay-sister, begged from door to door, carrying a heavy basket, having far less leisure for prayer and contemplation than in her father's house, suffering for many months with an "impostume" in her knee. Protests began to pour in from the people of St. Omer, which were apparently more effective than Mary's own quiet statement of her conviction. After two months in the Convent, Fr. Keynes told her it was God's will she should come out. She answered, however, that "before she entered she had no guide but her confessor, now the superiors of the Order were hers and were to dispose of her, accept, or send her away as seemed good to them."

At the end of a year her novice mistress told her as definitely that it was God's will she should come out, as before she had told her it was God's will she should enter.

Much amazed was Mary at this sudden change in both her confessor and novice mistress. She had been pressed to be a lay-sister, as she could not but clearly see, for the convenience of the convent, and the change seemed effected rather by the opinions of the General of the Order and the leading layfolk of St. Omer than by a real conviction of God's will for her who had put herself so fully and unreservedly into their hands.

Mary suffered severely from bad direction, and the topic of souls crippled and injured by foolish and presumptuous guides is today a favorite one. Yet there must be another side. "Be you subject to every human creature, for Christ's sake," said St. Peter. Human nature is always pretty much the same, and such a course must have presented grave inconveniences—outweighed, the Apostle seems to say, by the positive value of obedience. We have lost that passion for obedience and subjection which possessed not only the early Christians, but those of many succeeding generations. Mary Ward was among them. Even after this terrible experience she felt still that through confessors and superiors could and would come to her the knowledge of God's will.

Mary, having left the convent, could probably never have carried out the next work God asked of her, had she not been convinced that it was the entry into the longed-for haven of complete tranquility. She realized that she must try to have a convent of Poor Clares founded for the English. The customs, the language, all made it extraordinarily difficult for English girls to join the existing convents, even as choir-nuns. The General of the Order approving, Mary threw into this task all her energies and the greater part of the fortune her father had given her. The convent was established at Gravelines, with the English Jesuits as confessors, and her old novice mistress, M.M. Stephana Gough, as abbess. The bishop wished that Mary, in consideration of her year in the St. Omer convent and all her efforts in bringing about this foundation, should be professed before the other novices, but the abbess opposed this suggestion. Mary was perfectly happy to wait: she had found peace, although the Rule was so severe: the fasting in particular was such that she said later she had never slept more than two hours from hunger.

For four or five months she remained in tranquility, and then came a fresh blow in a sudden intellectual vision of overwhelming clearness: "It was shown to me that I was not to be of the Order of St. Clare; some other thing I was to do, what or of what nature I did not see, nor could I guess, only that it was to be a good thing, and what God willed." Intense reluctance internally—to leave her peace, to have the approval of the world turned into contempt, to go out in utter uncertainty of what she was to do. And externally? Fr. Roger Lee, now her confessor, expressed complete disbelief and disapproval; the abbess ordered her to "reject this thought or imagination, and as often as it came to her mind she should leave what she was about and go make a discipline, be it never so often in the day."

Seven months more—three years in all from her entry into religion—and Mary was out in the world again, her body "more like a dried up corpse than a living being," her fortune spent, her conduct criticized on all sides, her future dark. Yet "she found," says Winefride Wigmore, "a special and fatherly assistance from God, so as not to be the least discouraged...ever serene, peaceful and judiciously present to herself in all occasions."

She set out for England.

III

On this visit to England began gropingly, tentatively the new Institute. Mary went home, stayed in various friends' houses, where she worked for souls, wearing sometimes the rich dress of a lady of rank, sometimes a serving maid's garments. During these six or seven months, winning souls from sin or heresy, helping the dying, securing religious vocations, Mary collected a group of some half-dozen friends. With them she returned, in that same year 1609, to St. Omer, and there opened a school where they taught the children of the town gratis, and also children sent from England "to be brought up as Catholics under the care of the said ladies, in the Faith and good manners, in order that they may either be religious in these parts, or, returning to marry in England, may there maintain what here they have learned."

For five years the one house of the Institute was in St. Omer, but in the years that followed it spread over Europe amazingly. In 1614 they took a house in London, which instantly became a center of missionary activity. Then came foundations in Liége, Cologne, and Treves. By 1621, the Institute was in Flanders, Bavaria, Austria, and Italy. In that year, she first applied to Rome for approval of the Rule. But the Rule was a storm center.

From the very beginning, she and her companions had continued with incessant prayer and most penitential life to seek light on the shaping of their society. It came to Mary suddenly, in the second year of the St. Omer foundation, after a severe illness and a pilgrimage to a shrine of Our Lady: "I heard distinctly, not by sound of voice, but intellectually understood, these words: '*Take the same of the society!*' So understood that we were to take the same both in matter and manner, that only excepted which God by diversity of sex has prohibited. These few words gave so great a measure of light in that particular institute, comfort and strength, and changed so the whole soul, as that impossible for me to doubt but they came from Him, whose words are works."

In this now explicit design of enabling women to do for the Church what men were doing in the Society of Jesus, Mary Ward was attempting something of stupendous difficulty. The human mind tends to form conventions, and any society that has gone on long without upheaval is set about with much framework of law and custom. By the end of the Middle Ages, social life was highly elaborate. So, too, were all the externals of religious life. Divine though the Church be, she is also a society of humans who are liable to behave as such. "Novelty is often error," says Cardinal Newman, "for those who are unprepared for it," and the average mind usually is unprepared for it. At that date, ladies went about attended by maids and lackeys, they drove in carriages, they were guarded and protected. The rules for enclosure of nuns had been reinforced by the Council of Trent; woman's answer to the menace of the Reformation had been, above all, in the person of St. Teresa, an increase of solitude, of penance, of contemplation. In England itself the religious life could not be lived, but most families who held to the faith sent one or more daughters abroad to become Benedictines, Clarisses (Poor Clares) or Teresians (Carmelites). Mary was born in the darkest days of the persecution—darkest because the Catholics themselves were no longer a homogeneous body, but split by dissensions. By taking the Jesuit Rule, she infallibly awakened the opposition of their opponents. But neither did she secure the support of the Jesuits. A few of them stood by her through thick and thin—Fr. Lee, Fr. Gerard and others. But most of them thought the "Jesuitresses" a tiresome and useless addition to their own difficulties and were eager to disown them.

This hostility—often enough sneering hostility—was not a matter of a year or two only. How strong it was in England a dozen years later, both in Jesuits and opponents of Jesuits, is illustrated by a couple of incidents in the narrative of a lay-sister—Sister Dorothea—who worked for a long time in English villages: "Mr. Palmer, the Benedictine, and others being much pleased to see my manner of living and the good success that God has given unto my poor endeavors, fell many times into speech of our Mother and Company, and said they would see Mrs. Mary Ward send some of hers to live and labor in the manner I do, then they should like well of them, etc., but they live in great houses for their own ends only, and by their means to draw the Society hither.... Another time there came to my lady's a priest who was to enter the Society; he spoke bitterly against our Mother and the Company, calling them notable Goshops (sic), etc.... I say little to them, but see much. Upon April 2, 1622, Mr. Palmer again disputed against our Company, and in jesting manner asked me if I would be 'a galloping nun' or 'a preacher,' etc. I answered I was content with my present state."

Years later, and in more peaceful times, St. Francis de Sales and St. Vincent de Paul both failed to do what Mary was now attempting—to found an Order of nuns without enclosure. St. Francis accepted enclosure, St. Vincent denied that his sisters were religious, made their vows only yearly ones, calling them not an Order but a Congregation. Mary Ward had not the episcopal prestige of St. Francis or the powerful court influences which stood behind St. Vincent, yet she was determined to press the request for this complete novelty—a religious order of nuns really ranking as such yet without so much as "two stakes put in cross in form of enclosure."

Children going to convent schools had by the Church laws of that date to be temporarily enclosed. They lived in the convent inside the enclosure for the period of their school life. Mary started public day schools. "I fear these subtle wenches," she wrote once to Winefride, "have some help at home to make their themes, but you will look to them for that."

She went herself and sent her companions to England disguised sometimes as poor women, sometimes as ladies of quality. They wore, it was said, "yellow ruffs, very phantastical." In such a guise they could penetrate even into the prisons, and the "golden angels" they spent on tipping the warders brought on them accusations of wild extravagance.

Mary herself was imprisoned several times, and so were more than one of her companions. Once she "was guarded so strongly as not able to be private in her own bedchamber, but her presence had such authority as seemed to command her own freedom, and the guards' power was no more than to make apparent the limit God had given them." Once she was condemned to death, but for some reason reprieved. Her activities were so annoying to the Archbishop of Canterbury that he said she did more harm than six Jesuits. One day, hearing his great wish to see her, and being "importuned to take some recreation," Mary walked along the river to Lambeth; finding His Grace had gone out, she wrote her name with a diamond on one of his window panes, to the terror of her companions.

Once, being brought before the justices in Guildhall, Mary showed openly a rosary or some token of Our Lady, which caused one of the justices to utter a blasphemy. "What," exclaimed Mary, "a miserable man, a good for nothing wretch, is to blaspheme and revile the most holy and Divine Mother, the Queen and Lady of all creatures." It is hardly surprising after this remark (even if the biographer has slightly improved on the phrasing) that Mary was committed. "She aloud, with a courageous and heavenly voice, said Our Blessed Lady her litanies, as she passed in coach from the place of judgment to the prison, where arrived she knelt down and kissed the threshold of the gate, as a place sanctified by the cause for which she entered there; and this publicly before them all in the presence of the officers who conducted her, which humanly was to incense their rage and fury against her." But "contrariwise, they seemed all her slaves. It was without doubt, that He, whose honor she sought, undertook her defense."

In country places, the chief business of the Institute was to instruct, to prepare lapsed Catholics to be reconciled, and then (hardest of all) to find a priest to reconcile them. Sister Dorothea—whose work is clearly typical, for it is headed "a relation of one of ours, a lay-sister, one of those that live in villages in England"—would walk twelve miles or more to fetch one, and then "bring one of them into a byfield" or others "to the poor house where, under pretense of gathering herbs to make salves with, I had called them together some days before.... I cannot keep schools publicly as we do beyond the seas, but I teach or instruct children in the houses of parents.... I endeavor to instruct the simple or vulgar sort. I teach them their Pater, Ave, Creed, Commandments, etc."

Mary said herself that those to be sent on the English mission must be "of well-tried piety and without the smallest fault or defect." The work in London was perhaps more important, certainly more perilous than that in the villages, for many had to be reconciled in the prisons themselves; the hunt for priests was fiercer, the disguises had to be more various, more subtlety was needed in escaping. Mary toiled on, now in prison, now at liberty, and "God so blessed these her endeavors, as many and persons of note, both for the quality of their birth and malice and perverseness of their heresy, were converted."

Magnanimity was in Mary almost a natural quality. Risking her life was easy "which merely in nature she esteemed a slavery to be too much in love withal." "I cannot think it is a great matter," she once said, "to speak with princes or to whomsoever, to effect or bring to pass whatever is necessary...indeed in that I am unsatisfied, because I know not from whence that proceeds though I hope well." Meditating on venial sin, she notes as a motive to avoid it, that it makes "our mind abject and disposition servile." "Verity" is a word she loves, and "liberty."

Constantly she made retreats to seek into her own heart, to learn to cling more closely to God's will; daily she meditated and examined the springs of her actions. "Because I am inclined," she notes, "to affect and undergo more willingly such things as has the title or outward appearance of excellency and greatness, I will henceforth endeavor to embrace and execute more simpler things with a particular love, devotion and diligence...."

"When any lights or other motions occur unto me about the institute, I will still commend the same unto the Sacred Wounds of Christ, and make acts of resignation."

"Novelty is often error," and perhaps it was not surprising that the devil was successful in interfering with the good being done by the Institute. It was reported of Mary Ward that she assumed the office of priest and "preached publicly" (a thing at least a little difficult in England at that date, had she wanted to ever so much). The disguises worn by the little party were so effective that their character was sometimes mistaken. An admirer on one occasion sent Mary "an elegant collation," which she sent back, afterwards spending the night in prayer and penance. Her enemies related how "at Knightsbridge, an infamous place, Mrs. Ward and her company lived with no less vanity than before at Hungerford House, and the waites, I mean the musicians, came from London to salute her night by night, and received the reward of two shillings every time."

Again, "she came like a duchess to visit the Ignatian prisoners at Wisbeach, in coach, attended with pages riding with her in said coach, and two or three attendants of her own sex, and was so bountiful or rather prodigal, that she gave each keeper (who wished more such guests) an angel apiece."

Protestants had often criticized disguised Jesuits for the dress that had long kept them safe ("the one, a flaunting fellow, used to wear a scarlet cloak over a crimson satin suit"), but poor Mary was attacked by Catholics for the same reason. Women should not behave thus: it was a risk to modesty, it was a defiance of authority. To the title "galloping girls" was added that of "Apostolicae Viragines"—Apostolic Viragoes—and all these attacks were piling up, to reach Rome in due course.

It was a bad moment for women. Earlier in Church history they had held great positions—St. Hilda and St. Radegonde were not the only abbesses who ruled men as well as women. St. Jerome, dedicating his scriptural treatises to Paula and Eustochium, would hardly have agreed with St. Teresa that learning was not for "simple women." It remained for the seventeenth century to efface the dedications on St. Jerome's manuscripts and substitute the heading "Venerable Brethren." Mary Ward has been called ahead of her time in her claims for her sex, but she was in fact going back to an older tradition—that of the early Church.

Returning from one of her visits to England, she found the community at St. Omer much upset because the priest temporarily hearing confessions had spoken slightingly of the Community as being "but women." This occasioned one of Mary's rare outbursts of feeling:

"If women were made so inferior to men in all things, why were they not exempted in all things, as they are in some? I confess wives are to be subject to their husbands, men are head of the Church, women are not to administer sacraments, nor preach in public churches, but in all other things, wherein are we so inferior to other creatures that they should term us 'but women'? For what think you of this word, 'but women'? but as if we were in all things inferior to some other creature, which I suppose to be man! Which I dare to be bold to say is a lie; and with respect to the good Father, may say it is an error.

"I would to God that all men understood this verity, that women if they will be perfect, and if they would not make us believe we can do nothing, and that we are but women, we might do great matters."

The reasons for Mary's success and her failure all seem to me to be present in this speech. She had immense strength of character and great personal charm, giving her "authority" over her very jailers. On one occasion, crossing to England, she quelled, to her amazement, a mutiny among the sailors. She had that perfect submission to authority always to be found in the lives of the saints. But she could not compromise—she could not yield on a minor point for the sake of securing something greater, she could not temporize. Probably she also lacked judgment. Once certainly, a letter of Father Gerard gives what seems now obviously sound advice, which was disregarded by the growing institute—that they should make very few foundations and consolidate those instead of trying to spread too rapidly.

The temptations to rapid growth were great. At first, the difficulties in England did not touch the foundations abroad, and invitations came on all sides to multiply these. It was later said that Mary had acted without ecclesiastical sanction, but in fact it was with the approval, usually at the request, of the local authorities that she opened her houses—the Bishop of St. Omer, the Prince Bishop of Liége, Cardinal Pazmanny; St. Omer, Liége, Naples, Perugia, Munich, Vienna, Presburg, Prague, Rome itself; no wonder that the success of her work in all these places confirmed Mary in the belief that the Institute was needed, "Because experience and the great mutation of manners in the world, in all sorts of people, does show it to be so because we have proved now these twelve years, that the practice of the same Rule does much conduce to our own profit in perfection, and no less to the help of our neighbor."

So she phrased it in an appeal to Rome for the confirmation of the Institute which had been tried so successfully under the watchful eye of so many bishops. She adds a pathetic note on the nature of their vocation. "And if it were wrong to force any private man to marry a wife whom he cannot affect, much more must the selection of every one's vocation in this kind be free; which is not only more sure to last all the term of our life (since the other party never dies) but it is forever to endure and does determine our place with Christ for all eternity...."

IV

So it seemed to Mary Ward. And so it seems to the Church now, when what she fought for has at last passed into the normal life of Catholicism, and unenclosed orders of women are everywhere taken for granted. But confirmation of such a rule at such a time would have been revolutionary, and Rome does not like revolutions. She presented her first petition in 1622. From then until 1629 the issue remained uncertain, but on the whole it was moving against her. In Rome itself, that the highest authority might see the Institute in actual operation, she set up a school for the poor, unique in the Rome of its day; for it was an industrial school, it was for girls, and there was no payment. There were various meetings of cardinals and much papal interest; but there were too many things against her.

Mary was English, and a document embodying the gravest charges against her had reached Rome from England, signed by the archpriest and all his assistants. Mary did not lack friends in Rome, but they were not English: not one voice from her own people was raised in her support.

She wanted the Jesuit Rule; and the Jesuit authorities would have none of her.

She asked for—and would have absolutely nothing less than—an utterly novel sort of Order: religious women, but not "so much as two stakes put in cross in form of enclosure." And from a Judas in her own company, Mary Alcock, "Mother Minister" at Liége, had come circumstantial accounts of the disorders resulting from this freedom. "When she travels, she is extraordinarily jovial, and (to the Mother Minister's grief) most lavish in expenses...at her return from England...her manner was to be feasted for three days successively, the first night an extraordinary great banquet."

In 1625, her school in Rome was closed. Then three years later a special Congregation of Cardinals decided that measures should be taken, through the legate in each country, to break up all the houses of the Institute. Mary thereupon returned to Rome for one final effort.

She obtained an audience with the Pope, who was deeply impressed with her. He appointed men he believed friendly to deliberate on the Institute, including "the general of a certain Order" who was in reality exceedingly unfriendly—again poor Mary's fate in the dealings between her and the Jesuits, which always made so twisted a pattern. Upon receiving an adverse report from them, the Pope appointed a further committee of four cardinals, who were to hear Mary in person and decide on her cause. It is to be noted that she pleaded before them without the aid of a theologian as advocate. Could she have had one? Opinion was divided even among the greatest, Suarez taking one view, Lessius another; but no one in Rome seemed willing to come forward personally in her defense. "There were," she writes, "hot businesses betwixt the good cardinals and us"; and again: "the cardinals mean to do the worst...who can do no more than God will suffer them."

When Mary had done all that in her lay to press for confirmation she left Rome—probably an unwise proceeding. She was at Munich when the blow fell, and it came in a form so severe as to be overwhelming. All her convents were to be closed, the nuns scattered among other Orders or sent back to life in the world; Mary herself was to be imprisoned in the Poor Clare convent as disobedient and a heretic.

V

"This glory is to all His saints that they buy not cheap in this market..." Mary had always known it. Many years earlier she had written: "Presented that perchance there was some great trouble to happen about the confirmation of our course...I offered myself willingly to this difficulty, and besought Our Lord with tears that He would give me grace to bear it, and that no contradiction might hinder His will...I saw there was no help nor comfort for me but to cleave fast to Him, and so I did, for He was there to help me. I besought Him that the love I felt to this course now might stead me then, when that trouble should happen, because perhaps I should not then have means or force or time to dispose myself, or to call so particularly upon Him. I left with a solid contentment, and, as I think, desirous to serve and suffer for God; but I thought such a thing would certainly happen."

This paper was headed "The Loneliness"; and shortly before her imprisonment, Mary wrote to Winefride: "*Soli*. I think, dear child, the trouble and long loneliness you heard me speak of is not far from me, which whensoever it is, happy success will follow. You are the first I have uttered this conceit so plainly to; pray for me and for the work."

She was not in the least degree shaken in her conviction that God had really moved her, was still upholding her in the "course" which seemed to stand condemned. "Happy success would follow." But neither does she seem to have found any difficulty in what was grievously difficult to some of her children.

"I confess my wickedness," says poor Mary Poyntz; "it has grown a horror to me to see priest or friar, but at the altar and in the confession seat, which that blessed servant of God did sharply reprehend, seeking to imprint in us all that treasure which she herself possessed in an inexpressible degree, of loving enemies."

Mary found a nickname for her enemies, for whom she prayed daily—"Jerusalem." Quite simply she looked on them as the means supplied by God to win Heaven for her, the means even for the perfect working out of His will on earth. "The pain," she had said earlier of her difficulty in discovering God's will, "was great, but very endurable, because He who laid on the burden also carried it…I would not have attained the knowledge of it at a less price, nor can I be surprised at the imperfections of those who acquire it cheaply."

Mary with one companion was imprisoned in a tiny room from which a dying consumptive had been hastily removed. The room had not been cleaned, although, in Mary's own graphic phrase, "she has spit up all her lungs." She goes on: "Where sometimes we fry and sometimes we freeze, and there do all that we have to do, two little windows close walled up, our door chained and double locked and never opened but at the only entrance and departure of our two keepers and the lady abbess who is our chief guardian."

The orders given to the Poor Clares had led them to expect something in the nature of a dangerous lunatic, and the nun most reputed for sanctity, after seeing Mary, exclaimed: "My Mother, how have we been misinformed. This is a great servant of God whom we have received, and our house is happy in her setting foot in it." They had been forbidden to speak to her, but this nun begged permission to go to the door, and kneeling there, gazed at Mary for some minutes with deep reverence. She does not seem, however, to have thought of cleaning out the room or improving the ventilation.

Mary entered her prison hoping that she was now to have a time of respite from effort, "in which she had nothing to do but to think of God, love Him, and depend upon Him, with all confidence in His Fatherly protection with regard to hers." But it would not do. She knew that first night that God was telling her: "It was not enough to content herself with passive suffering and give up labor and action."

The resolve once taken—with effort and reluctance—to labor to effect her deliverance and prove her innocence, in spite of the foul and deathlike atmosphere of her room, Mary fell peacefully asleep.

An art learned in English prisons served the little group in the efforts which followed. They were allowed to send in to Mary food and clothing. Daily the rough paper which wrapped their parcels went in and out, carrying Mary's directions written in lemon juice, bringing in her companions' reports of how they were progressing. Many of these notes are dated "From my palace, not my prison, for truly so I find it."

But the foul atmosphere was too much for Mary's health, which was rapidly failing. The doctors said she could not survive, and she begged to be allowed to receive the Last Sacraments. The dean imposed the condition that Mary should sign a paper saying that "if she had ever said or done anything contrary to faith or Holy Church, she repented her and was sorry for it." Mary, who appeared to be on the point of her death agony, asked if His Holiness or the Holy Office required this. Finding they did not, she said: "God forbid that I, to cancel venial sins, which, through God's mercies, are all I have to accuse myself of, should commit a mortal, and cast so great a blot upon so many innocent and deserving persons, by saying '*If* I have done or said anything against Holy Church.' My 'if' with what is already acted by my adversaries, would give just cause to the world to believe that I suffer justly. No, no. I will cast myself rather on the mercy of Jesus Christ and die without the Sacraments."

Then taking pen and ink, she wrote in Italian her apologia for her life and work. This was sent to the dean with a statement that she would sign naught beside, and if that was not satisfactory, she would die without the Last Sacraments. The dean held it to be satisfactory.

VI

After receiving the Last Sacraments, Mary, still in the horrible little cell which had brought her to death's door, made a swift and almost miraculous recovery; and now came the news that the Pope had not ordered her imprisonment and was much displeased thereat.

The Institute had fared badly, the houses in Flanders being closed, the revenues confiscated, and the subjects scattered. But in this, too, the orders of the Bull, crushing as it was, had been exceeded. The Institute was indeed officially broken up, but certain loopholes were left. The members were not actually forbidden to take private vows, nor was the work of religious education forbidden in so many words. Mary saw still the possibility—she believed in the certainty—of a revival. But the Pope alone could authorize their living together, the Pope alone could get them some redress for the wholesale confiscation. To Rome Mary determined to go.

Kneeling at Urban's feet, she said: "Holy Father, I neither am nor ever have been a heretic." The Pope broke in "*Lo credemo, lo credemo*" She had been tested and tried, as had so many servants of God, and he himself and the cardinals were satisfied, even edified, by her behavior. When she begged permission to bring to Rome those of her scattered children, especially the very young ones, who did not wish to return to the world or to enter religious Orders, he said: "We are glad that they should come, and we will take them under our protection."

A letter, too, was sent from the Holy Office to the Nuncio at Cologne, exculpating the English Ladies from the charge of heresy and urging that their revenues should be returned to them, while at Munich they were still allowed to live together at the Paradeiser Haus. When Mary's enemies protested to the Pope that the Bull was nullified by their being allowed to live together in Rome itself he answered: "Where should they live, or where can they live so well."

Much was lost, but not all. They were in terrible poverty; most of the revenues were gone beyond recall; the schools being closed, no fees were coming in; often the ladies went short of food. They had been forbidden to wear religious dress, but money was wanting to buy any other. Going out one day for confession, a lady dressed in the old habit was struck in the face by the sacristan and driven from the church. Constantly they met with insults and accusations of heresy. It is hardly surprising that very few of Mary's children persevered. The vast majority entered various Orders or returned to their families.

But one thing remained quite undiminished—Mary's courage. Within the bounds of obedience, she was irrepressible. The cause for which she fought might be condemned: so be it. But the work in which it was to bear fruit must go on.

The poverty she met with a smile. "Good Winn be careful and merry…God is rich enough for us all." She used to say of poverty "that it was to be entertained not like a beggar, but like a queen." "Which," says Mary Poyntz, "God did so bless in her person, that although what she wore was of mean price and worn so long, as it was not possible to hang longer on one's back, yet had such a grace on her, that others have wondered what rarity and curiosity she had in her dressings, some saying she went above her degree, till viewing and examining found all old and poor and mean and well patched."

The calumnies she met by instant application to the Pope. "Holy Father, what more can poor Mary Ward do to prove her fidelity and loyalty towards your Holiness?" "Be satisfied, my daughter," he answered; "none shall be able to wrong you with us henceforth in the least. It is true that in the process of information given we found both malice and folly."

No wonder that Mary's enemies were still spiteful, for they were still afraid. There remained of the Institute only two groups of ladies (most definitely not religious) impoverished and discredited. But they knew well enough that Mary was not likely to have abandoned a work she believed divinely inspired—and they were perfectly right!

In her guarded correspondence with the Munich house Mary speaks of asking the Pope "for a letter-patent to set up her loom." She seems, in fact, to have begun in Rome itself to take young ladies, especially English, *en pension*. At Munich, schools were again opened, including a poor school. "Jesus forbid," writes Mary to Winefride, in the depth of their own poverty, "you should make such children as you teach to pay one penny for windows, wood, or anything else. For God's love, if you do that work of charity, do it like yourself, not mercenarily."

Next, to England again—as soon as she felt that all was safe in Rome and Munich. Always failing in health, she had been so ill as to receive the Pope's last blessing. Yet she crossed the Alps in a snowstorm, pausing in Liége in hopes of restarting the work there, and finally reached England, where a small number of her companions had been working in a scattered fashion through all these years.

Mary never failed certainly for want of bold ideas. The Civil Wars had begun, the persecution no wise diminished. Yet "my meaning is," she wrote calmly, between daily visits of pursuivants, "to endeavor by prayer and private negotiation that we may have common schools in the great city of London, which will never be without a miracle, but all else will be to little purpose, the ungrateful nature of this people considered."

But her time was growing short, and it was not in London, but in her own county of Yorkshire, that Mary was to die. Three coach-loads of ladies and the children entrusted to them journeyed north in the wake of King Charles—for London had become too perilous alike for royalists and for Catholics. At Hutton Rudby, the ladies and their little school had a chapel, the Blessed Sacrament, and daily Mass. But it was too remote: they moved thence to Hewarth, to York, back again to Hewarth. Besieged by the Roundheads, Mary urged on all confidence in God and in His saints and angels. "Fear not," she said, "we will place St. Michael at one end of the village and St. Joseph at the other, and put the power of the great cannon and pieces on the Sacred Name of Jesus which will keep them from hurting."

It was at Hewarth that she died. Before she sailed for England she had been seen weeping much—a thing in her most unusual. As she lay dying, one of her companions said: "If you die, we will take pack in lap and away to the heathens." Mary answered: "If I thought so, it would break my heart."

Her whole life had been given for England. Her first light on the Institute had been that it was to be "very much to God's honor, and for the good of others, particularly England."

She had hoped later to die a martyr, but God showed her that it was in another way she was to help her country, and one so greatly to God's glory that she "remained for a great space without feeling or hearing anything but the sound 'glory, glory, glory.'"

Her death was shadowed like the life of her country. No priest was near her when she died, but her faith still saw the glory. "Most honored," wrote Mary Poyntz to the Munich house, in the figurative language that they fancied safer, "on the 20th of January, 1645... our dearest my father departed this toilsome life, at the age of sixty years and eight days. Said: 'God will assist and help you, it is no matter the who but the what; and, when God shall enable me to be in place, I will serve you.' Then with greatest love and embracing each, seemed to mind us no more, but with eyes and hands gave signs of sweet intrinsical entire acts...never sighed, groaned, nor rattled, only inclined his head."

RICHARD CRASHAW (1612–1649)

by E. I. WATKIN

THE LIFE OF THE POET RICHARD CRASHAW MAY PERhaps be thought to embody something of the paradox so dear to the *Seicento* culture of which his poetry is, as we shall see, so perfect an expression. For the singer of Catholic devotion in its most exotic and Latin form, was the son of a minister of North Country birth, remarkable for his virulent hatred of popery—a hatred which, not satisfied with pouring out a flood of controversial abuse, found final utterance in William Crashaw's will, in which he writes: "I account popery (as now it is) the heap and chaos of all heresies. I believe the Pope's seat and power to be the power of the great Antichrist and the doctrine of the Pope to be the doctrine of Antichrist."

But we must not think of Richard Crashaw's work as simply a reaction to his father's. The author of a *Manual of Devotion* and the translator of hymns did not confine his religion to the hatred of Rome. However loud the "no popery" bee buzzed in his bonnet, his heart was filled by a strong and, one would gather, a tender love for God and Christ.

Indeed, we must never forget that the Puritan movement was not purely negative, mere hatred of the Pope, the Mass, and ecclesiastical art and ritual. It possessed a positive aspect, an interior and sometimes even mystical, religion, such as appears in Goodwin's tender devotion to the Sacred Heart, in Rous's bridal devotion with its use of the *Song of Songs*, in the mysticism of a Sterry.

Moreover, as Ritschl has proved in his monumental *History of Pietism*, the devotion of Puritanism, as opposed to its theology, was not a genuine Protestant development, but an influx of direct or indirect borrowings from Catholic spirituality. Richard Crashaw must have inherited from his father his devotional temper, his bent towards religious poetry, and his aptitude for learning. William Crashaw was twice married, but both wives died shortly after marriage—so that Crashaw, son of the first marriage and the only child, was brought up almost entirely without a mother. To this Dr. Praz ascribes the craving for a mother's love, which for its satisfaction attracted the poet to his "mother" Mary Collett, to Madre Santa Teresa, to Our Lady, and finally to Mother Church.[1] That the poet did feel this strong longing for a mother's care and love is shown, I think, by the peculiar fondness which he displays for such images as "nest," "breast," and "bosom." Professor Martin even finds in the use of "nest" a sign-manual of Crashaw's authorship, and points out how he employs it as a rhyme-word no less than five times in his hymn to the Name of Jesus.[2] But with his tender half-feminine nature, he would probably have felt and expressed the same longing had his mother lived till her son's maturity. The boy was given a place as foundation scholar at Charterhouse, then in its infancy, where, however Spartan the life, his headmaster, Dr. Brook, seems to have reserved his rod for young Roundheads, his favor for young Royalists. Since Crashaw, so far back as we can trace his writing, probably to scholastic exercises in Latin and English verse, was a fervent Royalist, and since he addressed a Latin poem of obviously sincere gratitude to his former master, we may conclude that if his father's theology was Puritan, his sympathies were with

1. *Secentismo & Marinismo in Inghilterra*, pp. 152, 188.
2. *Crashaw's Poetical Works*, p. 463.

the King.[3] In 1632, at the age of eighteen, he went up to Pembroke College, Cambridge, to be elected three years later to a fellowship at Peterhouse. He was probably ordained to serve Little St. Mary's, a church attached to the college. At that time Peterhouse was a center of Laudian high churchmanship—not the Anglo-Catholicism of today, Catholic in everything but membership of the Catholic Church—but a deliberate compromise between Catholicism and Geneva. Cultured, devout, liturgical, in intention and in some respects actually primitive and patristic, Laudianism possessed an undeniable charm for Crashaw's studious and poetic piety. Its fundamental lack of logic troubled very little a temper more artistic than logical; but its cautious moderation, whose perfect representative in poetry was George Herbert, must, we should imagine, have conflicted with the ardor and abandon of Crashaw's devotion. But until 1644, we have no glimpse of his interior life, and even then it is only an obscure and passing glimpse. Whatever he thought of its position as against Rome, in its opposition to Geneva, its insistence on a dignified worship, and its rejection of the fundamental Protestant doctrine of justification by faith, Laudianism had his hearty support. We find him taking an active part in the adornment of the new Peterhouse chapel—a center of laudian worship. To aid the appeal for funds he composed two Latin poems, published only in 1648.

During these Cambridge years of study, poetry and prayer—"the little contentful kingdom" of his Peterhouse fellowship—he was in close contact with a unique and certainly the most gracious manifestation of Anglican religion, the community—a blend of family and religious house—directed by Nicholas Ferrar, at Little Gidding in

3. Again one wonders whether the elder Crashaw's Puritanism has not been exaggerated. However he hated Popery—and such a Laudian as Nicholas Ferrar hated it no less—it does not follow that he preferred the Presbyterian discipline and service to the Anglican hierarchy and liturgy. Nothing points to a reaction against his father's religion on the part of the youthful Crashaw, but rather to a gradual evolution from the starting point of its positive content.

Huntingdonshire. Though the type of devotion there practiced was of the more temperate type represented by Ferrar's friend George Herbert, rather than the ecstatic fervor which inspired Crashaw's poetry, the little Gidding community must have played a very important part in his development. It consisted of Nicholas Ferrar, a London merchant, who had retired from the world to devote himself to the service of God, his aged mother, his brother John with his wife and family, and his sister with her husband, Mr. Collett, and their family. Assisted no doubt by the masterful personality which he shared with his mother, Ferrar had fashioned the life of his relatives on the model of a strict religious house. Yet it was no servile copy, but an individual creation with a beauty all its own. There was service thrice daily in the little church outside the manor house, an hourly office throughout the day divided among the members of the community, and every night a watch from nine till one, during which two men or women recited the entire Psalter on their knees. These watches were relieved from time to time by singing or soft music on the organ. Ferrar himself watched two nights a week, and when he did not watch rose at one to spend the remaining hours of the night in prayer and meditation. To prayer was added a full round of study and work. Three schoolmasters were kept to teach the children. There was an almshouse for poor widows, surgical dressing by the ladies, exquisite bookbinding, the compilation of biblical concordances illustrated by the best engravings of the period, and from 1631 a little academy based on an Italian model, for Ferrar had studied in Italy, to which the various members of the household each taking a particular name, e.g., the Guardian, the Visitor, the Humble, the Affectionate, the Submiss, contributed a hymn or edifying story, told in the forcible and flavored idiom of contemporary English. A charming picture of the Gidding life, though inaccurate even in important details, is to be found in Shorthouse's once celebrated novel *John Inglesant*.

Crashaw was one of a little band of friends who from time to time rode over from Cambridge to spend a few days at Gidding. There, we are told, he took part in the night watches—congenial to one who, as the notice prefixed to his poems informs us, "like a primitive saint, offered more prayers in the night than others usually offer in the day." But we may be inclined to agree with Dr. Praz when he says, "Perhaps the feature (of the Gidding life) which attracted him most was the presence felt everywhere at Little Gidding of womanhood, in its most lofty and consoling aspect." Mary Collett, brought up from infancy with her Ferrar grandmother, had determined like her younger sister Anna to live a life of perpetual virginity. Indeed, she would have taken a vow of virginity had not Bishop Williams, her diocesan, dissuaded her from so "Popish" a step. On her grandmother's death she became, officially, the "Mother" of the community, as such presiding over the meetings of the Academy. In a letter of which we shall have to speak later—the only piece of prose by Crashaw which has survived—he calls Mary Collet his "Mother," his "good and gracious Mother." "He too had accepted the rule of the congregation, had found the tender mother which his earliest years lacked, in this devout young woman who, when she first met the poet, then aged nineteen, was thirty-two years old. The difference of age and the type of office with which she had been charged contributed no doubt to make Crashaw's relationship with her a homage and service of spirit in which the affection and respect due to a mother were blended with the tenderness inspired by a sister and the knight's devotion to his lady."[4]

The mutual fulfillment of the two sexes transcends the physical sphere, and neither poet nor saint has been molded without the aid of a woman's hand. The day indeed must come when Crashaw's path will diverge far from Mary Collett's. But she is not to let him go until he will leave her for an even more spiritual mother.

What poetry Crashaw wrote during these years, we can only in part determine. Elegies, all skillful and more or less inspired by genuine feeling on Cambridge dignitaries or friends—paraphrases

4. Praz, *Secentismo & Marinismo*, p. 188.

of two psalms—a host of Latin epigrams published in 1634, English translations of many of these—other Latin poems, including a Sapphic hymn to Venus never published—and the charming *jeu d'esprit* on a bubble to which Dr. Praz has called attention—also no doubt the famous *Wishes to his Supposed Mistress*, may with certainty be attributed to this period. There are also the verses prefixed to Nicholas Ferrar's translation of Lessius' book on temperance—the jibe at the "oraculous doctor's mystic bills" has lost nothing of its point in the intervening three centuries—and the verses prefixed to Shelford's *Five Discourses*. The conclusion of the latter, a caustic fling at the great negative dogma of Protestantism that the Pope is Antichrist, could not be printed. Unfortunately his friend Ferrar believed it. But it points to a significant divergence existing between Crashaw and many at least of his Laudian friends. To these years also we must ascribe his Ode Prefixed to a "Little Prayer-Book Given to a Young Gentlewoman" and its "Companion To the Same Party concerning her Choice." Here we are in the full flood of Crashaw's mature style, and that note of ecstatic mystical devotion is struck which will re-echo throughout his later religious poetry.[5]

But the storm fell in the shape of Dowsing and his iconoclasts, who visited Cambridge during the winter of 1643 and broke down, as Dowsing's diary gleefully records, a host of "superstitious" Cherubim, Crucifixes and Popes in Crashaw's homes of prayer, Peterhouse Chapel and Little St. Mary's. It drove Crashaw from his "contentful kingdom" into lonely wanderings which we cannot even trace. A letter written on February 20th, 1644 to one of his Gidding friends—probably John Ferrar or Mr. Collett, Mary's father—a solitary lightning flash in the midst of darkness, discovers him at Leyden. He had accompanied his beloved "Mother" on a visit to some Dutch relatives. For some

5. The anonymous authoress of the *Life of Nicholas Ferrar* published in 1892 argues very plausibly from an allusion to bookbinding, suppressed in the first edition, that the "M. R." to whom these two poems are addressed, was one of the Gidding family, and suggests *Margaret* Collett or *Mary* Mapletoft.

reason not specified—presumably his Catholic sympathies—they had closed their house to the poet and left him solitary and poor in the uncongenial atmosphere of a Calvinist city. In the principal church, he remarks bitterly, no figure of a saint—but "the plain Pagan Pallas Cap-a-pee with spear and helmet and Owl and all—so that I am either not scholar enough or not Pagan enough for this place." The object of this rambling letter, clumsily constructed and deliberately obscure, is an attempt to salvage part of his Peterhouse fellowship by resigning it to his old pupil, Ferrar Collett, who could in turn pass on a portion of the emoluments to his tutor.

Shortly afterwards, however, Crashaw was formally deprived of the fellowship for non-attendance to subscribe the Covenant. It is probable, but not certain, that he returned to England, joined the Royalists at Oxford, and was admitted to membership of the university. The reasons advanced by Mr. Martin seem convincing.[6] If so, he would there have met Queen Henrietta Maria and the patroness to whom he later addressed his moving appeal to join the Catholic Church, Susan Countess of Denbigh.

When he himself became a Catholic we do not know. Obscure hints in the letter of 1644 indicate that he was contemplating the step—but shrinking back on the brink. A reference in the Queen's letter recommending him to the Pope shows that his conversion cannot have been later than 1645. Not to speak of the ill-natured sneers of contemporaries at the toadying client of pious Catholic ladies, a more reputable criticism has regarded the step as due to despair at the collapse of Laudian Anglicanism. Shorthouse, in his hauntingly beautiful but subtly misleading romance, represents Crashaw as remarking to the hero "that he feared the English Church had not sufficient authority to resist the spread of Presbyterianism, in which case he saw no safety except in returning to the communion of Rome." "He lacked the courage and patience to wait for better days," writes the

6. *The Poems of Richard Crashaw*, 1927. Introduction.

anonymous authoress of the *Life of Nicholas Ferrar*. But for the debacle, Crashaw's conversion might well have been delayed; but had he lived long enough, there could surely have been but one goal to a predetermined development. The devotion which inspires his poems is not the moderate and cautious piety of Anglicanism. It is the flaming passion, the mystic fervor, of counter-reformation Catholicism. "His faith," writes Dr. Praz, "is utterly different to that of the Protestants. Entirely made up of contemplation and exultant awe in the presence of divine marvels, it does not delay over sermons and pedestrian discourse. It is faith of a southern and Latin type, the faith of an *anima naturaliter catholica*.[7] Apart from the misuse of the term faith to signify what would be more correctly denominated a type of devotion, spirituality, or spiritual life, we may agree with Dr. Praz.

It would be interesting if we could determine exactly what poems were written before and after conversion. For this, however, the data are insufficient. The hymn on the Assumption, which *a priori* we should certainly ascribe to the Catholic period, was, as is certain from manuscript evidence, written before his conversion. But we must not forget that the Laudian divine Stafford, in his famous book in honor of Our Lady, *The Female Glory*, taught the doctrine. Car, in his posthumous edition of Crashaw's sacred poetry, adds to the title of the Apology for the Hymn on St. Teresa "as having been written when the author was yet among the Protestants."[8] But the poem thus labelled has no reference to the writer's Protestantism. What is surprising is the open publication in England during the Puritan regime in 1646 and again in 1648 of poems so plainly Catholic—many of them paraphrases of Catholic hymns. One cannot conceive the publication of Protestant poetry in Spain. Another proof that English devotional

7. Praz, *Secentismo & Marinismo*, p. 273.

8. Professor Martin, who in his critical notes to the text points out that these words were first added in 1652, assumes in his biography that they appeared in the first edition of 1646—unlikely indeed in an edition published by Protestants.

life, even when Catholicism was most hated, was being fed from Catholic sources.

Whatever his movements, whatever the date of his conversion, our next certain information finds Crashaw in the autumn of 1646 among the English exiles in Paris—in touch with his old friend Cowley and under the patronage, for what it was worth, of the Countess of Denbigh and the impoverished Queen. His patronesses would seem to have made a collection to defray the cost of his journey to Rome furnished with a letter of recommendation from the Queen to the Pope. Unfortunately for the poet, the papacy had no interest in conciliating the wife of a fallen monarch, and nothing or nothing of any consequence was done to assist him. Though in such ecstasy of spirit that in the words of his friend Car he "had wholly called his thoughts from earth, to live above in the air a very bird of Paradise," he could not dispense with a minimum of subsistence—though it were only "what might suffice to fit his soul to heavenly exercise." A story was told years later to Sir Robert Southwell, that on receiving from Pope Innocent the paltry sum of twenty pistoles, Crashaw remarked to a friend "that if the Roman Church be not founded upon a rock, it is at least founded upon something which is as hard as a rock." Gossip no doubt, but quite possibly enshrining a genuine reminiscence.

After a long period of poverty and illness he was taken into the service of Cardinal Palotta, who finally in 1649 gave him a subordinate canonry in his gift at the Cathedral of Loretto. According to Dr. John Bargrave, the Cardinal was compelled to send Crashaw away from Rome to protect him from the hostility of the fellow members of his suite whose misconduct he had denounced. Of the truth of this report we have no means of judging. From the Cardinal's Letter of Appointment "*Crusio sacerdoti Anglo*" it would seem clear that Crashaw was now in priest's orders—but the date and place of his ordination are unknown. Already in ill-health, a frame never very robust worn by years of privation, the journey through the heat of an Italian summer proved too much for his strength. Shortly after his arrival at Loretto he died and was buried beside the Holy House, the concrete symbol of a Divine Infancy, and fit resting-place for a soul of childlike purity and simplicity.

> How well (blest Swan) did Fate contrive your death
> And make you render up your tuneful breath.
> In your great Mistress' arms, you most divine
> And richest offering of Loretto's shrine!
> Angels (they say) brought the famed Chapel there,
> And bore the sacred Load in triumph through the air.
> 'Tis surer much they brought *you* there, and they
> And you, their charge, went singing all the way.[9]

Dr. Praz introduces what is, perhaps, the best study of Crashaw yet written, by an illustrated description of Bernini's celebrated sculpture in Santa Maria della Vittoria, representing the transverberation of St. Teresa's heart. He writes:

> In Rome, there is a work of art which may be regarded as the epitome of the religious spirit of the *Seicento*. The angel, whose visage glows with the radiance of a triumphant smile, launches his gilded dart at the heart of the saint, stretched in languorous abandonment on a pillow of cloud. The alluring violence of the seraph's gracious and cruel gesture, the voluptuous bliss in which the saint's entire body is dissolved from a countenance inebriated with heavenly delight to the heel of the naked foot, soft and flaccid like a flower whose strength has been sapped by the sun, suggest a blend of the human and the divine, possibly best defined in a Shakespearian phrase dear to Swinburne, spirit of sense.... There is, a refined and Alexandrine quality in this Christian Love who displays, not the savage violence of a

9. Cowley, *Ode on the Death of Mr. Crashaw.*

> conflagration, but the lambent caress of flame, so tender and so feminine is his nature. The angel's gesture is graceful, gallant, his violence adorable as the wrath of a youthful cherub, he seems to be engaged in a delicate and cruel game with the saint and twists his dart as though he were playing a madrigal. And his victim surrenders herself with a consuming pleasure to the inebriating martyrdom; transformed by her ecstasy into a weary Maenad, not visited by a fury, but caressed by the grace of God.[10]

The literary counterpart of this typical baroque masterpiece he rightly finds in Crashaw, the perfect poetic expression of this baroque culture, the baroque poet *par excellence*, who celebrated St. Teresa and her ecstasy in verse, as Bernini in stone.

It is unfashionable to defend the sensuous and passionate religion that inspired baroque art, and, since a religion is the form of every genuine culture, constituted its form, the form therefore which its art must apprehend and express. First the Victorians, "those virgins queer with garments grimed and lamps all gone to snuff; who," continues Patmore, "tear their clothes and bawl out blasphemy" if their God is called Bridegroom, then from the opposite camp the psycho-analysts who for all their talk of sublimation, value what is sublimated solely in terms of its material, have made us ashamed and frightened of sense and sex in religion. A Belgian Jesuit can even denounce Bernini's statue as indecent! And the late Canon Beeching "can imagine," not unsympathetically, "a police magistrate characterizing the poems" of ecstatic devotion addressed by Crashaw to the young gentlewoman at Gidding "as poems that no gentleman should have written."[11]

If we have no sympathy or understanding for such devotion we shall never understand Crashaw. *Deliciae sapientiae de amore*,

10. Praz, *Secentismo & Marinismo*, pp. 145–46.
11. Introduction to M. R. Tutin's Edition of *Crashaw* (The Muses Library), p. xxxiv.

"wisdom's delight of love" is indeed the burden of his song, as of no other English sacred poetry, till Patmore recaptured once more this new religion of mystical passion. The directly sexual does not, indeed, play so important a part in Crashaw's poetry as in Patmore's; and compared with St. John of the Cross he makes very little use of the Song of Songs. Yet Patmore's use of the language of nuptial love is more external and theoretical—a faith defended with passionate conviction rather than lived with passionate experience. The passion of the much married poet was perhaps too preoccupied with an earlier love. The lesser flame can scarcely burn side by side with the greater; the sun quenches the starlight. But the unwedded Crashaw, whose sole Love was the God to whom he so readily surrendered all, put into his devotion and into the poetry which enshrines it, the entire ardor of a flaming heart. His prayer is passion, and his passion prayer. Prayer, passion, poetry—their unison is the formula of Crashaw's religious art. His entire writing is steeped in a spiritualized sensuousness, that "spirit of sense" of which Dr. Praz speaks, and in a diffused passion, ardent, tender and delicate, an indefinable all-pervading atmosphere of fragrance and sweetness. If spirit is simply the negation of sense, we must of course condemn baroque art, condemn Bernini, condemn Crashaw. But this is a false philosophy, doubly condemned by the doctrine of Creation and its fulfilment, the Incarnation. And if God is indeed closer to the soul than one human being to another, and united with her in the supreme mystic union more intimately than soul with body, religion must be essentially nuptial—the physical nuptials of earth its least inadequate reflection and image.

Nor shall we understand the baroque culture if we oppose it to the medieval, or its art to Gothic art. In all its manifestations, Catholic culture has always been of necessity an incarnation of spirit in sense and has made full use of the old pre-Christian culture. Roughly speaking, Christian art has hitherto been classical art—literary and plastic—informed by the Christian faith. The literature of Christian antiquity before the barbarian conquest of the West, for example, the prose and verse of a Sidonius Apollinaris—was curiously baroque in quality. Later, these conquests considerably reduced the classical ingredients of Western culture, though they never ceased to be present and active.

The Renaissance brought a further supply of classical material which for a short time in Italy threatened to stifle the Christian form and become a neo-paganism. But that was a passing and superficial phase, and with baroque the Christian form re-establishes an unquestioned supremacy. There is simply a larger proportion of classical elements in the edifice than in the Middle Ages. Not even the sensuousness is new. The Cistercian sermons on the Canticles, begun by St. Bernard, are as erotic as anything in St. John of the Cross, primitive Franciscan devotion as passionate, tender and personal as Crashaw's. To reject, minimize or apologize for baroque devotion is logically to reject, minimize or apologize for the entire devotion and culture of Catholicism. But "the feelings, the senses are dangerous—religion should be of the mind and will alone." Away then with liturgy, ritual, churches, sacraments. Be as Puritans—nay, more Puritan than they—for the Puritan sermon and devotion were far from dispensing with the emotions or even—witness Rous and Goodwin—with the sexual. But the senses, the emotions, the affections will turn against such a religion. The entire man must live with that intense life and concentrated experience that we call ecstatic. If religion is too "pure" to afford this ecstasy, man will turn elsewhere. But since religion is the highest value, the supreme truth and most abundant life, it has always produced this ecstatic living.

Such "a sweet inebriated ecstasy" was pre-eminently Crashaw's religion. He does not preach; he does not torment himself over his sins; he does not worry about the prospects of salvation; he simply adores—adoration is the quintessence of religion—contemplates, exults, dances, fiddles, plays. He can carry off the most preposterous conceits—yes, even the notorious "walking baths" and "voluntary mint" of *The Weeper*—for they are not frigid exhibitions of ingenuity, but the toys with which he plays before the shrine. "They came to him naturally," writes Mr. Shepherd, "these teeming multitudes of figures and fancies. They crowded upon him and would not be denied. So he gathered them up in armfuls and shed them upon his pages as a child does rose leaves on anything it loves. He brought them with him, like little crowding brownies, to surround the manger where Jesus lies. They surged with him in sorrowing fearful confusion up the hill of Calvary."[12] And he could toy with these conceits the more lightly because they refer to a body of knowledge—literary, theological, historical, legendary, or pseudo-scientific—common to all educated readers. Today one reader will have specialized in one department of science or literature, another in another. In the *Seicento*, knowledge could still be universal. A poet's allusions, therefore, would be dark only to ignorance, his most far-fetched similes within the compass of his reader's knowledge. Indeed, of all Crashaw's more important poems only one can fairly be called frigid—The Epiphany Hymn—not for its conceits, but because adoration is, quite exceptionally, replaced by a long-drawn comparison between the false cult of the sun and the true religion of the Sun of Justice now dawning on the world. Not even such lines as,

> O prize of the rich spirit! with what fierce chase
> Of his strong soul, shall he
> Leap at your lofty Face,

can reconcile us to the legend of the Areopagite told by the kings before the crib. But the rest are on fire!

If Bernini is Crashaw's counterpart in sculpture, assuredly St. Philip Neri was his prototype among the canonized saints. St. Philip passes long hours in his private oratory sipping the consecrated chalice, the Blood-Wine of Love—with such fervor and sweetness that his teeth have left their impress on the metal lip. So Crashaw:

12. Introduction to *Crashaw's Religious Poems* (Manresa Press).

O! let me suck the wine
So long of this chaste vine
Till *drunk of the dear wounds*, I be
A lost Thing to the world, as it to me.

Even in the sorrowful things of religion—Our Lord's wounds and death, the tears of Magdalen's penitence and Mary's desolation—his contemplation finds nothing but joy. For he sees in them only the love they express. It is the same with death. The shadow of death lies over the literature, the art, and the devotion of the seventeenth century. The death bell often tolls in the very measure of its verse, as in Bishop King's *Exequy* on his deceased wife. The elegy is a conventional form of poetry. Everywhere death's heads, skeletons, a dwelling upon the accidents of death and the tomb, even such macabre foretaste of corruption as the famous statue of Donne for which he dressed in his grave-clothes. Austin must needs compose his own funeral sermon,[13] and in the Epicedium attached to it—a poem not wanting in somber and quaint beauty—he finds the grave everywhere.

The womb was (first) my grave: Whence since I rose
My body (grave-like) does my soul enclose:
That body like a corpse with sheets are spread
Dying each night lies buried in my bed.
My close low-builded chamber to mine eye
Shows like a little chapel where I lie:
While at my window pretty birds do ring
My knell and with their notes, my obits sing.

Vaughan's thought is constantly returning to the tomb, and the meditation upon death is a recurrent theme in the conversations of that Gidding Academy of which we have already spoken. Not so

13. Austin's *Devotions*, 1635: *The Author's own Funeral made upon Himself.*

Crashaw. At Cambridge indeed, he composes elegies. It is expected of him as a budding poet. But even in these he dwells rather on the gifts, real or imagined, of the deceased than on death itself. For to his ardent devotion, death is already swallowed up in the victorious love-life of eternity.[14] The death which he celebrates is the mystic death "of love," ever renewed as a renewed life, the death—

> in which who dies
> Loves his death, and dies again...
> And lives, and dies; and knows not why
> To live, But that he thus may never leave to die.

It is "the wine of youth, life and the sweet deaths of Love": Wine

> That can exalt weak Earth; and so refine
> Our dust, that at one draught, mortality,
> May drink itself up, and forget to die.

Spinoza, reacting against his century's preoccupation with death, would banish it from the thought of the sage. Of this reaction and the universal *memento mori*, Crashaw's attitude is the higher synthesis. He will think of death, but only in terms of life. And Our Lord's death he will envisage only as the source of this new deathless life:

> So from His living and life-giving death,
> My dying life may draw a new and never fleeting breath.

14. One poem, it is true, *Death's Lecture at the Funeral of a Young Gentleman*, contemplates death from the conventional seventeenth century standpoint. But it is quite exceptional and belongs to Crashaw's early period before he had completely found himself. It contains, however, splendid lines worthy of their author.

And the deaths of martyrs—as Dr. Praz points out, their cultus was a favorite topic of *Seicento* devotion, though in truth it is well-nigh as old as Christianity itself—are but fresh victories of life and love.

> What did their weapons but with wider pores
> Enlarge your flaming-breasted Lovers
> More freely to transpire,
> That impatient fire
> The heart that hides you hardly covers
> What did their weapons but set wide the doors
> For you: Fair, purple doors, of love's devising;
> The ruby windows which enriched the East
> Of your so oft-repeated rising.

Sorrow, suffering, death are but expressions, occasions and victories of love. Even a cursory glance at Crashaw's favorite phrases is revealing. Wounds, blood, weapons are recurrent themes. Here too he is baroque. *Seicento* devotion loved to dwell on blood and wounds and darts, but the blood and wounds that attest love and the weapons wielded or vanquished by love. The preoccupation may be profane, a dwelling on the archery of Cupid, of a woman's eyes, or on the wounds of fleshly passion, even at times perverted and decadent, but it may also be sublimated into a contemplation of Divine Love wounded and bleeding and its human return in bodily or spiritual martyrdom. Blood, wounds, weapons—all are love's. The most obvious symbol of passionate love, indeed more than a symbol, its physical reflection and counterpart—fire or flame recurs abundantly in Crashaw's vocabulary. And as we already know, wine. The apology for the hymn on St. Teresa is chiefly a panegyric of this inebriating wine—"The king has brought me into his wine cellar." Crashaw's muse is seldom sober. "Let my soul swell," quotes Dr. Praz,[15] "with

15. Praz, *Secentismo & Marinismo*, p. 273.

the strong wine of love." "The images of blood, wine and fire," he continues, "recur in our poet with a frequency which seems extraordinary even in a Catholic accustomed to meditate on the mystery of the Eucharist, a frequency which he has in common with the poet whose inspiration seems so akin in temper to his, namely Swinburne. Images which serve as devices or emblems of the inflamed imagination of these poets, in the one associated with profane objects, in the other with sacred. Blood of love's martyrdom, wine which is the intoxication of sense, fire of dionysiac frenzy in the singer of Anactoria, blood of religious martyrdom, wine of heavenly vintage, fire of ecstatic ardor in the singer of Saint Teresa." As common, however, as fire and flames are images of the opposite element water, floods, showers, and the like. It is as though the heat of Crashaw's heart and imagination sought by a subconscious psychological necessity the cooling of water. This surely is the psycho-physical background of such a verse as this.

> Can these fair floods be
> Friends with the bosom fires that fill you!
> Can so great flames agree
> Eternal tears should thus distill you!
> O floods; O fires! O suns! O showers!
> Mixed and made friends by love's sweet powers.

And of all forms of water his favorite is the tear. Thirty-one melodious stanzas of *The Weeper* compose a rosary, whose beads are a series of images and conceits—quaint, charming, often lovely—told in honor of the Magdalen's tears. Vaughan, it is true, a poet of very different inspiration, recurs with equal frequency to the thought of tears. But they are the bitter tears of personal penitence or sorrow for the overthrow of the Anglican Church. For Crashaw, as we have seen, tears—even the tears shed at the foot of the Cross—are sweet, even happy, but another expression of all-triumphant love. The Magdalen is "a flaming fountain, a weeping fire"—her tears jewels of love's adornment, wine for the Beloved.

Another quality of Crashaw's apprehension is his sense of space. As his fire demanded water, his ardor, like the fire in St. Philip's breast, which to find scope for itself forced out a rib above his heart, demands room. Weapons "enlarge God's flaming breasted lovers *more freely* to transpire their *impatient* fire." He dwells on St. Teresa's "*large* draughts of intellectual day" and "*larger* draughts of love." "Glory flames in her own *free* sphere." "The song of praise is '*spacious*,' '*unbounded*,' and 'all *embracing*,'" and the martyrs' "*spacious* bosoms spread a throne for love *at large* to fill."

We should also notice Crashaw's predilection for the east and the dawn. Vaughan indeed also loved it and paid his tribute in an exquisite poem. But whereas he loves the dawn for its fresh purity and clear light, Crashaw dwells on the rich coloring, the pomp of sunrise. His dawn, I fancy, is later than Vaughan's. He contemplates "the rosy windows," "the ruby portals of the east," "the purple east," "the purple pride" that "laces the crimson curtains" of morning's bed. Always, as Dr. Praz has also remarked comparing in this respect his poetry with Rubens' painting, an opulence of brilliant color—purple, red, ruby, rose, crimson—ruby of dawn, purple of blood. Vaughan's favorite color, on the other hand, is not red but white, and for him day and the sun mean primarily light not heat. White light—or if gold at all, the sober gold of "calm golden evenings," red fire—in this contrast we have in a nutshell the difference between Vaughan's devotion and Crashaw's. Vaughan is pure because he loves purity and has achieved it, apparently, by a struggle. Crashaw is consumed by a fire so intense that the conflagration has extinguished earthlier flames. Mr. Aldous Huxley has analyzed earthly love into *tendresse* and *passion*.[16] Its spiritual prototype also comprises these two ingredients. And, if Crashaw's love is spiritual passion, expressed by the wine and the fire,

16. *Point Counterpoint*.

the blood, the purple and the red—it is also *tendresse*. If he thinks of God as the lover or bridegroom of other souls—of the martyrs, St. Teresa, or the anonymous gentlewoman—to himself Divine Love is primarily perhaps maternal.

Nor is this surprising. The love of a man for a woman when richest and most complete contains this element of filial love, and she is a mother to her lover. It may be that Dr. Praz is right when he ascribes, as we have seen, the predominance of this element in Crashaw's devotion—how little of it by comparison there is in Thompson or Patmore—to his lack of a mother's love. Whatever the cause, it runs a powerful current through his verse. It finds verbal expression in his fondness for breast or bosom—not only as the source of food but as a warm place in which to nestle and find shelter. And we have already noticed another favorite image, akin in feeling to the breast with which it is frequently rhymed—the nest. A place of shelter and warmth beneath the wing of maternal affection. This, no doubt, is the underlying motive of his choice. The tenderness thus expressed is not, however, in any bad sense effeminacy—for it goes hand in hand with the strength of a mighty passion of spirit. The reader of St. Teresa's works—

> feels his warm heart hatch'd into a nest
> Of little eagles and young loves, whose high
> Flights scorn the lazy dust and things that die.

If this is not, perhaps, Crashaw's finest poetry, it is the quintessence of his religion.

This love for nest and breast suggests Keats and the two are, I think, akin. Both are richly sensuous.

In his lectures on Keats, Professor Garrod points out that he is a poet who used all the five senses. This is equally true of Crashaw. His employment of imagery "practically never fails to justify itself by a genuinely sensuous quality favorable to strong contrasts of light and shade and color and appealing almost as much to the faculties of smell and touch as to the faculty of vision."[17] Sight plays indeed the least important part. As we have seen, Crashaw prefers heat and color to light, and his sense of form is so inferior to his sense of color that his poems possess little structure. As though conscious of this defect, he likes to find his structure ready-made and to get under way by the paraphrase or, as in the opening of his Hymn to St. Teresa, at least by the suggestion, of some existing poem or hymn.[18] But there is the sight of color. And all the other senses. Sound: his poems are full of music. Witness *Music's Duel*—a veritable *tour de force* in the verbal transcription of musical effects. "All things that are Or *what's the same* are musical." Smell: perfume and incense are favorite images. Touch: in the Christmas hymn you feel the texture of the Seraphs' fiery down—the softness of the snowflakes. Taste: sweets, nests of sweets for taste and scent combined—and for taste alone—the wine

17. Professor Martin, *Crashaw's Poetical Works.*, Introduction, p. lxvii.

18. The opening stanzas of the Hymn to St. Teresa are based on the Office hymn for the Vespers of her feast.

 Terris Teresa barbaris
 Christum datura aut sanguinem…
 So shall she leave amongst them sown
 Her Lord's blood or at least her own.
 Sed te manet suavior
 Mors, poena poscit dulcior
 Divini amoris cuspide
 In vulnus icta concides.
 O caritatis victima.

 Hence, with a slight transposition, Crashaw's:

 Sweet, not so fast! lo your fair Spouse
 Whom you seekest with so swift vows,
 Calls you back, and bids you come
 T'embrace a milder martyrdom…
 You art love's victim: and must die
 A death more mystical and high.
 Into love's arms you shall let fall
 A still-surviving funeral
 His is the dart must make the Death
 Whose stroke shall taste your hallow'd breath.

of which we have already spoken. And we taste the cream, the breakfast of Magdalen's tears. This sensuousness is Keatsian and in places the very rhythm anticipates Keats.

> The sweet-lip't sisters musically frighted,
> Singing their fears are fearfully delighted.
> Trembling as when *Apollo's* golden hairs
> Are fan'd and frizled in the wanton airs
> Of his own breath....
> Those parts of sweetnesse which with *Nectar* drop,
> Softer then that which pants in *Hebe's* cup....
> *Enthusiastic* flames, such as can give
> Marrow to my plump *Genius*, make it live
> Dressed in the glorious madnesse of a Muse,
> Whose feet can walk the Milky Way, and choose
> Her starry Throne; whose [holy heats can warm
> The grave,] and hold up an exalted arm
> To lift me from my lazy urn, to climb
> Upon the stooping shoulders of old Time,
> And trace Eternity.

With the exception of the few words I have bracketed these lines might well have come from Keats' pen—extravagances and all, they are his vein. If the resemblance is most striking in Crashaw's secular verse it is because the pagan Keats could never clearly distinguish the delights and apprehensions of sense from the spiritual apprehensions and joys which transcend them. Sensation and intuition are never adequately distinguished. Rightly dissatisfied with the former, Keats can find no alternative except thought or ethical endeavor. But these are alien to his genius. Hence mistakes and disappointments, frustrations and gropings. Crashaw, inferior in poetic genius, escaped this error. As sensuous as Keats, as little a thinker or preacher, he is free of that higher realm of mystical intuition which fulfils the promise of sense, a joy "whose hand is" not "on his lips bidding adieu," a beauty as immortal as the loveliness of art celebrated in the Ode to a Grecian Urn but living and personal.

> More happy love, more happy happy love.
> Forever young and still to be enjoyed.
> All breathing human passion far above.

But the picture of love is not love. Hence the melancholy almost disillusioned tone of the last stanza on which Professor Garrod remarks. The love which Crashaw sings, "young loves" which "scorn the things that die", is above all merely human passion. It possesses the eternity of Keats' Urn, is as timeless and deathless as the frozen immortality of art. But it is warm and living. It breathes the life breath of the Spirit and burns with the fire of Love Itself. Crashaw thus fulfills Keats, achieving the goal he sought in vain. I am not claiming for Crashaw a place in the first rank of poets. For that his fire lacked the necessary light, his color the indispensable mastery of architectonic form. Only the clear conceptual background furnished by Catholic theology and philosophy—assisted further by the borrowed form of the hymns and poems on which he embroidered—saved him, as indeed it saved the baroque devotion and culture of which he is the typical poetic exponent, from that deliquescence which is the malady of feeling as aridity is the malady of thought.[19]

Still less was Crashaw among those artists of sovereign genius who mount upon and above the common form of their culture to apprehend a more universal yet more individual form of beauty. Such was Milton among his contemporaries and Shakespeare in the age before him. But in virtue of a perfect adaptation of temperament and

19. Intuition the more concrete and obscure it is, is the more liable to the danger which attends the emotion that invests it; the more abstract and clear, the more liable to the danger attendant upon conceptual thought.

genius to contemporary culture, he was enabled to voice it as perhaps no other—certainly no other Englishman. In so doing he was compelled to pass beyond the provincial and incomplete religion of his country to the complete religion and culture of western Christendom. His bodily departure to Italy was but a symbol of this inner pilgrimage. Whether with better health and kinder treatment he would have produced lovelier and more perfect art than in those years before his arrival in Italy is a question more painful than profitable. He seems to have produced nothing, or almost nothing, during the last two or three years. Perhaps he was too ill; perhaps he wrote, but if so his poems have perished. Certainly what would seem to be his final surviving utterances are the magnificent conclusion added to his lines on St. Teresa and another splendid passage inserted into his appeal to the Countess of Denbigh—the latter saved only by the chance of a single copy, show a simplicity, directness, and force beyond his earlier scope. Life was now perhaps too stern even for the holy play of his earlier poetry. But love is as ever the sole theme of his singing. The austerity which has dispensed with love's trappings has only emphasized love.

O you undaunted daughter of desires!
By all your dower of lights and fires;
By all the eagle in you, all the dove;
By all your lives and deaths of love;
By your large draughts of intellectual day,
And by your thirsts of love more large then they...

When love of Us called Him to see
If we'd vouchsafe His company
He left His Father's Court and came
Lightly as a Lambent Flame
Leaping upon the hills to be
The humble King of You and Me.

When Dame Julian pondered the rich obscurity of her revelations, it was to learn that love was God's meaning in all. Crashaw's message is no other. In the teeth of a world full of hate and folly, of cruelty and death, the *Seicento* artist and the medieval anchoress proclaim the same simple but inexhaustible message—the omnipotence of Love.

> "Love was His meaning."
> "Love you art Absolute sole lord
> Of Life and Death."

This, the heart of religion, is the sole burden of Crashaw's religious poetry. What is religion? Ask Crashaw. What is mysticism? Ask Crashaw. What is love—the love which is religion and mysticism religion's crown? Ask Crashaw. His answer will not be a theological disquisition, but the music of a soul drunken with the ecstasy of God.

Bibliographical Note

The Poems English Latin and Greek of Richard Crashaw. Edited by L. C. Martin. Oxford: The Clarendon Press, 1927. The only adequate critical edition—also containing the most complete biography available. But Professor Martin need not search the collections of Mone and Daniel for a hymn contained in the Little Office of Our Lady.

The Poems of Richard Crashaw. Ed., J. R. Tutin. Introduction by Canon (later Dean) Beeching. The Muses Library. A fairly sufficient edition for slenderer purses and more portable use. Beeching's introduction is on the whole sympathetic and understanding—though Crashaw's Catholic and baroque devotion proves at times too strong meat for this Anglican and Victorian Dean.

The Religious Poems of Richard Crashaw. With an Introductory Study by R. A. Eric Shepherd. Manresa Press, 1914. Mr. Shepherd's introduction is certainly the best critical appreciation of Crashaw in English, besides being a fine piece of English prose—in fact a little masterpiece. But we must agree with Dr. Praz's criticism that Crashaw's enthusiasm was not simply, as Mr. Shepherd suggests, the enthusiasm of the convert, but the natural quality of his temperament and devotion.

Secentismo è Marinismo in Inghilterra: John Donne, Richard Crashaw. Dr. Mario Praz. Florence, 1925. If Mr. Shepherd's introduction is the best English study of Crashaw, the far longer study which forms the second half of Dr. Praz's book is to my knowledge absolutely the best. I have been indebted to it at every turn. Dr. Praz places Crashaw in his cultural and religious environment. Particularly valuable is his lengthy comparison between Crashaw's paraphrase of Marino's *Sospeto d' Herode* and the Italian original. He shows how the English poet fills in Marino's too rigidly classical outline with a baroque luxuriance of fantastic imagery which the Italians never achieved in poetry and whose parallel must be sought in their contemporary architecture. I would also call attention to a charming sketch of the community of Little Gidding.

See also for the Anglican period of Crashaw's Life: *Nicholas Ferrar, His Household and Friends*. Anonymous.

Ed. Rev. T. T. Carter, 1892.

Also for background only: *The Story Books of Little Gidding*. 1631, 1632. Ed. E. Cruwys Sharland, 1899.

Contemporary Editions.

Epigrammata Sacra. Cambridge University Press, 1634.

Steps to the Temple with Delights of the Muses. London, H. Moseley, 1646. Anonymous preface probably by one of the poet's Gidding friends.

Slightly enlarged, but less accurate re-edition. Same publisher, 1648.

Carmen Deo Nostro. Paris, Peter Targa, 1652. Ed. by Crashaw's friend, T. Car. Crashaw's religious poems omitting, however, the translation of Marino. New pieces added and many enlarged or remodelled. The text is illustrated by engravings (reproduced in Professor Martin's edition) which, if not (as Car claims) wholly of Crashaw's designing, are in part his work. (See Martin, p. xlviii-ix.)

Expanded version of the *Address to the Countess of Denbigh.* Ascribed in MS. to 1653. London, N.D. Only one copy known. B.M.

BISHOP CHALLONER (1691–1781)

by MICHAEL TRAPPES-LOMAX

I tell you naught for your comfort,
Yea, naught for your desire,
Save that the sky grows darker yet
And the sea rises higher.
Night shall be thrice night over you,
And heaven an iron cope.
Do you have joy without a cause,
Yea, faith without a hope?

~*The Ballad of the White Horse*

WHEN, IN DECEMBER 1688, KING JAMES II WAS FORCED to leave his country as the result of the treachery of English noblemen, helped by forgery and the capacity for lying of a Dutch prince, he took with him the last hopes of the English Catholics. They had survived the storm of Elizabethan persecution; they had survived nearly a century of the milder oppression of the Stuarts, though still in the face of martyrdom; they had seen toleration almost within their reach. And then, suddenly, everything was changed. To the accompaniment of incendiarism and looting—grim foretaste of the Gordon

Riots—Catholicism became once more a hunted thing. Thenceforward, for a hundred years, their ministers outlawed and themselves debarred from any normal participation in their country's life, the Catholics of England were to carry out the duties of religion in secrecy and fear, and generally, too, in places of such squalor "that the Catacombs where the ancient Christians held their assemblies in times of persecution, were elegant and commodious compared with them.[1]

Less than three years after that inglorious Revolution, on 29th September, 1691, there was born, at Lewes in Sussex, to Richard Challoner, "a rigid Dissenter" and wine-cooper of that place, a son, Richard, who was destined to lead the Catholics of England "over the dreary desert that lay between the Red Sea of martyrdom and the Promised Land of Toleration."

It seems probable that the future bishop's mother, Grace Willard, may have been, at any rate by birth, a Catholic; for, being left a widow in the early infancy of her son, she found domestic service in the household of Sir John Gage, fourth Baronet, of Firle, near Lewes, the head of a family distinguished alike for its faithfulness and sufferings in the cause of the Catholic Church and the House of Stuart. After a short stay at Firle, Mrs. Challoner and her son transferred to Warkworth, in Northamptonshire, another of those houses in which, in the face of ruinous penal laws and social ostracism and grave dangers, Catholicism was upheld to the solace of surrounding districts. But Warkworth had more to offer even than the generality of such houses; for about it hung the savor of martyrdom—its mistress was the widowed Lady Anastasia Holman, daughter of the Blessed William Howard—and its chaplain was the saintly John Gother, one of the foremost priests of his time, formerly a zealous missionary in London under the name of Lovell, and an outstanding apologist: a worthy tutor for a future bishop. It was probably at Warkworth that Richard

1. Except where otherwise clear, quotations in the text are from, or quoted in, Dr. Edwin H. Burton's admirable *The Life and Times of Bishop Challoner*, 1909.

Challoner was received into the Catholic Church, when about thirteen years of age. Shortly afterwards, in 1705, he entered the English college at Douay.

In these days, when the Victorian public school tends to be considered as one of the highest flights of the national genius, an essential point about such a place as the English college at Douay is in danger of being overlooked; and this is that the place was English; and not only so, but English to a peculiar and intense degree. Its denizens were exiles, and cherished the heightened patriotism of their kind. More, they cherished and transmitted (and were in exile for that reason) the tradition of an earlier time. The people of England as a whole, betrayed by their natural leaders, might acquiesce in turn in a change of Faith and in the successive enthronements of Batavian and German princes. But the men of the English colleges did not change. It is not without symbolic significance that the presidents of Douay at Challoner's entry and at his ordination, Dr. Edward Paston and Dr. Robert Witham, belonged to families long established before either Tudors or Cecils were first known in England.

Less than a hundred and fifty miles away—nearer than London is to Crewe—lay the friendly hills of Sussex; but thirteen years were to pass before Challoner should cross the narrow seas that lay between, and then only on a two months' visit. His youth and early manhood were to pass in that little English colony inside the walls of a small town in the flat lands of Flanders.

After finishing the ordinary school course, Challoner entered immediately upon his studies for the priesthood, during which time he also taught a class in the school and was appointed professor of philosophy, and Douay itself twice suffered siege and capture. On 28th March, 1716, he was ordained. Breaking through the usual form for entering such events, Dr. Witham described him in the college diary: "notable for learning and piety if ever man was."

This notability increased as the years passed, and the post of prefect of studies was added to that of professor of philosophy. A disgruntled priest named Breers, vivid in imagination but weak in intellect, saw fit to slander the college; and to Challoner, against whom even Breers could bring no charge, was deputed the task of defense. The Abbé Strickland saw fit to accuse the president of libel, and Challoner was again put forward. In 1720, the onerous posts of professor of theology and vice-president of the college fell vacant; and Challoner, then but four years ordained, was appointed to them. Two statements throw light on the personality which had emerged: that "This Office of Vice-President could not fail of being, at least in some degree, contrary to Mr. Challoner's inclinations, and afford him some distractions with regard to that internal recollection of soul which he always endeavored to cultivate and preserve"; and that, "To these Irish soldiers [then in the garrison of Douay] he devoted the time which would otherwise have been spent in recreation, and when he needed exercise he obtained it by walking to their quarters, where he went in and out among them, visiting those in hospital, and helping all so far as he was able."

In the following year, craving a life of uninterrupted prayer, and assuming additional work in lieu of his scant recreation from the onerous duties of his office, Challoner was once more put forward as champion. The right of the professors of the English college to present themselves as candidates for chairs in the University of Douay was in danger of lapsing through desuetude. A theological professorship, known as *la chaire royals du catéchisme*, fell vacant; and Challoner, in the face of unscrupulous judges, obvious chicanery, and even personal insult, asserted on behalf of the college his right to candidature. He failed to do more, for, in spite of being plainly the better theologian, he was not given the professorship. However, the right to sit had been asserted; and Challoner had shown that he could bear "great indignities...with uncommon meekness and patience." Six years later the university made some slight amends by conferring on him the doctorate of theology. But Challoner was desirous of a very different honor. He wished to return to England as a missionary priest.

Dr. Witham naturally demurred. He had been placed in charge of the English college in a period of considerable difficulty, and he did not wish to lose the services of so efficient a subordinate. Challoner, bound by the college oath, had perforce to obey. Galling as the delay must have been, it enabled him to write his first book, a small volume of meditations called *Think Well On't*, which proved of the greatest value to people of his own and a later time, and which throws a strong light on the personality of the man who should wish to exchange the life of the honored vice-president of a great college for that of an outlawed priest in the foul slums of eighteenth-century London.

In this little book, forerunner of his own more extensive *Meditations*, the mainspring of Challoner's life is made clear. On no occasion did he ever discuss his own spiritual life, but when trying to help others sincerity compelled him to speak from his own experience; and that experience was one of hidden intercourse with God, an almost incessant union in prayer. "With desolation is all the land made desolate," he wrote quoting Jeremiah, "because there is no one that considers in the heart," and by such consideration we realize that "We have within us the eternal, immense, omnipotent, infinite Lord and Maker of all things; and we are within this infinite being; wherever we are we have him with us." That was the only thing that really mattered, and at its consideration his straightforward prose turned lyrical: "We have this loving and most lovely God always with us; and always in us; why do we not run to His embraces? He is a fire that ever burns; this fire is in the very center of our souls; how is it that we feel so little of its flames? It is because we will not stand by it. It is because we will not keep our souls at home, attentive to that great guest who resides within us, but let them continually wander abroad upon vain created amusements." Always, and in the midst of whatsoever activities, Challoner "kept his soul at home" with God, the method which he practiced and advocated being systematic and regular mental prayer.

It was no new discovery. In fact, it was as old as sanctity. But in none of his books did Challoner strive for novelty. By nature and by training the old ways were to him the best. All he would ever try to do would be to give the old message in language which the new generation might understand; but in giving the old message he could not but expose the secret of his own heart, quiet, and traditional, and burning.

Somehow, in the summer of 1730, Dr. Witham was induced to yield. It was a grim situation to which Challoner returned. The forces of social oppression and grinding financial exaction were doing their work. During the fourteen years of his priesthood, Challoner had taken his turn with the other priests of the English college to offer Mass a week at a time for the conversion of England. But now there was no visible hope of that conversion. The number of Catholics was dwindling. Three years before his return, Sir William Gage, seventh Baronet, of Firle, youngest son of Challoner's old patron, had received the reward of apostasy in the parliamentary representation of Seaford. He was not alone. The tide of Catholicity was on the ebb.

Of the details of Challoner's pastoral work at that time, little is known but that it lay chiefly in the London slums that Hogarth satirized and in loathsome prisons as yet untouched by the zeal of John Howard. After two years Challoner was elected to the English chapter, a body analogous to a sort of self-elected privy council in English ecclesiastical affairs, and after five years (if not earlier) he was appointed vicar-general by Bishop Petre, vicar apostolic of the London District. But these testimonies were to be eclipsed by those which followed upon his controversy with Dr. Conyers Middleton, an energetic and litigious clergyman who, while giving good reason to suppose that he had "suspended his belief" in revelation, yet successfully retained a couple of small livings.

Challoner had begun his series of controversial writings two years after his return to England, and in 1736 he had been appointed "controversial writer" to the chapter. The recent excursion of Fr. Ronald Knox among the newspaper religious symposiasts has been aptly compared to "a champion shooting pigeons at Monte Carlo." Challoner's appearance, armed with extensive erudition and logical and theological training, among the common anti-Catholic slanders of the day was somewhat similar. Like Fr. Knox, Challoner did not satisfy himself with bald argument. Someone once remarked of the nineteenth century "scientific" onslaught on Christianity that, until the arrival of Mr. Chesterton, the jokes had all been on the other side. In the face of the ignorance, bitterness, and slander of the Protestant polemics of his day, Challoner made use of a similar method. The framework of logic and erudition was there, but over it was cast a strange atmosphere of gaiety. Hidden in his secret lodging in the slums of Holborn, fighting a losing battle and himself an outlaw, Challoner made fun—very courteous fun—of Dr. Conyers Middleton's *Letter from Rome showing an exact conformity between Popery and Paganism: or the Religion of the present Romans derived from that of their heathen ancestors.*

Dr. Middleton was not amused. He invoked the penal laws. "In short," as Milner afterwards wrote, "the situation of Dr. Challoner... became so much exposed to danger, which others shared with him, that he was advised to retire out of the kingdom for a certain space of time."

Dr. Witham, then far advanced in years, and worn by his long and arduous presidency, was delighted at the return of his former vice-president to Douay, and immediately began to work for Challoner's appointment as his successor. Bishop Petre, whose piety was only equaled by his diffidence as a ruler, was horrified at the prospect of losing permanently so capable a subordinate, and started counter-propaganda, urgently pressing his need for a coadjutor, and adding in the process one more to his own many unaccepted tenders of resignation.

For a time it looked as though he had failed, and Challoner was actually appointed president of Douay on the death of Dr. Witham. But his tenure was to be very brief. Bishop Petre's appeal was successful. Six months later, Challoner was appointed Titular Bishop of Debra *in partibus infidelium* and Coadjutor, with right of succession, to Bishop Petre.

In the interval, while opposing parties strove for the privilege of having his services, Challoner had not been idle. In 1740, he published *The Garden of the Soul: A Manual of Spiritual Exercises and Instructions for Christians who, Living in the World, Aspire to Devotion*.

This book, now almost universally known by name though edited almost out of all recognition, illustrates Challoner's mind to a peculiar degree. The old ways were to him the best. But at the same time, with that grasp of practical needs which people commonly discover with surprise in saints, he realized that something more was wanted and how that lack could be supplied. The English Catholics had two standard prayer-books, *The Primer*, with its medieval lineage, and *The Manual*. They also had various books of spiritual instruction. But in general they were too poor to buy many books; and in any case such dissemination was difficult. The need was for a small and inexpensive work, which would serve the purposes both of a book of devotions and a treatise on the spiritual life. In his *Garden of the Soul*, Challoner produced it.

The popularity of this book may be gauged from the fact that Challoner himself brought out seven editions in seventeen years; its influence, from the fact that a hundred years afterwards a large part of the Catholics of England was known by its name, the expression "Garden-of-the-Soul Catholics" being used to distinguish the hereditary Catholics, with their undemonstrative piety, from later converts with a tendency towards imported flamboyance in devotions.

On the other hand, it cannot too strongly be emphasized that Challoner neither was trying to supersede the old nor was the originator of that form of piety later to be described as "Garden-of-the-Soul." His purpose was to produce a useful supplement to the books already in existence, and in doing so he drew on earlier sources wherever they were suited to that purpose—they included *Ten Meditations out of the first part of St. Francis de Sales's Introduction to a Devout Life*, and *A Prayer taken out of Mr. Gother's Works, for obtaining Contrition*. And "Garden-of-the-Soul Piety" itself was no new thing. He had learned its elements from Mr. Gother, and it had upheld Catholicism in England for years before he was born. It was Challoner's mission, as Bishop Petre had prophesized, to be "as a shining and burning light in the Church, a leader beyond all cavil": the *Garden of the Soul* was to give new light and leadership, but down an already well-trodden path.

To a modern enquirer, believing, it may be, and possibly with justice, that increase in external devotions tends to development in spirituality, the impression given by the exercises in the *Garden of the Soul* is one of excessive length and aridity—they include, for instance, Communion at eight stated times a year and preparatory meditations suited to the seven preceding days. For good or ill, and certainly for comfort, we have got beyond that stage. But the point is that eighteenth century Catholics were in that stage. Oppressed, derided (it is not without significance that Sterne's *Dr. Slop* should have been a Catholic), and obscure, they could only cultivate a secret garden. Challoner's book was both inspiration and method in that undertaking, and like an iron tie hidden in crumbling masonry, this vein of solid "Garden-of-the-Soul" piety upheld the shaken edifice of English Catholicism.

But this matter has yet farther implication. The *Garden of the Soul* illustrates that piety; and from that piety, a reflected light is thrown upon Challoner himself, who nurtured and directed it, showing clearly why he should have appealed with equal force to two such opposite characters as the strong willed and energetic Dr. Witham and the meek and diffident Bishop Petre. Under that light the figure of Challoner becomes more clear; takes on a strange familiarity, like the sight of an Englishman in an alien place. Irresistibly the mind is carried back to another priest, the brother of a Plowman, of whom it was written that though his parish lay far-spread and its houses scattered, he never failed:

> In sickness nor in mischief to visit
> The farthest in his parish, rich and poor.

That

> "Benign he was and wonder diligent,
> And in adversity full patient";
> One who knew, and lived up to his knowledge, that
> "We ought a priest example for to give
> By his purity how that his sheep should live";

One who

> Waited after no pomp and reverence,
> Nor made him a spicéd conscience,
> But Christ's lore, and his Apostles twelve,
> He taught, but first he followed it himself.

Suddenly, moved from the crabbed misery of his epoch, Challoner is seen passing freely but unchanged in a brighter colored day; one whom Chaucer, most English of the English, would have recognized and loved as another such that April morning in the Tabard Inn at Southwark.

Of Challoner's life after being raised to the episcopate, no useful purpose would be served by going into details. And for the very reason that it was filled with details. Its history is the history of Catholicism in England for forty years. The man would tend to be lost in consideration of the work until, after many pages, it would seem almost incredible that any one man could have been responsible for so prodigious an output and dispersion. And when a man's work seems almost incredible, the man himself is in danger of fading into the shadowy gathering of things true but to us unrealizable.

But Challoner should not be allowed thus to elude our minds. He was real enough. He was a quiet, fair Englishman, about five feet ten inches tall, with a wrinkled forehead, and bright eyes, and a rather long, straight nose, and a singularly sensitive mouth. He commonly wore an inconspicuous brown suit, and he lived in cheap lodgings with a Mrs. Hanne, in Holborn.

Equally, there is another danger. Concentration on Challoner himself apart from the crowded activities of his life, causes him somehow to dwindle into a vague legendary figure moving dimly in an unreal eighteenth century. It tends to make him give a similar impression to that of certain saints of the early Church, whose "lives," to those unskilled in the history of their epochs, mean almost nothing, seem, as it were, but labels attached to whorls of sanctity spinning in a void.

The difficulty lies in the fact that when Bishop Petre achieved a coadjutor he obtained for the English Catholics one bishop, but the services of three men. There was an exceptionally able administrator of an unwieldy diocese throughout a period of grave difficulty. There was a learned student and theologian whose pen adorned every subject which it touched, and touched every subject in which it could further the cause of the Church. There was a saint, whose holiness was hidden behind almost impenetrable veils of reticence.

In order to get any just idea, then, of Challoner, it is necessary to consider him in these three aspects.

The magnitude of Challoner's episcopal work can best be realized through consideration of some of the difficulties, additional to those normal in any diocese, which he had to contend. In the first place, there were the penal laws. It is commonly supposed, since martyrdom ceased in England after 1681, that the penal laws were a dead letter and that Catholics suffered no more than exclusion from public life. This is false. Though the laws were not enforced in their full rigor, they were there, and they were enforceable. For instance, as late as 1767, a London priest named John Baptist Maloney was sentenced to perpetual imprisonment[2]; and all the time there was the steady, grinding exaction of the double land tax. "Shall I sit down satisfied,"

2. After four years, this was commuted to banishment for life.

Mr. Joseph Berington wrote in 1780, "because the good humor of a magistrate chooses to indulge me, while there are laws of which any miscreant has daily power to enforce the execution? My ease, my property and my life are at the disposal of every villain, and I am to be pleased because he is not at this time disposed to deprive me of them. Tomorrow his humor may vary, and I shall then be obliged to hide my head in some dark corner or to fly from this land of boasted liberty? It is surely better not to be than to live in a state of such anxious and dreadful uncertainty."

Apart, then, from more tangible sufferings, the Catholics of England were passing through a hundred years of dread. It is not surprising that some of Challoner's flock should have fallen away. There was this enormous social pressure ceaselessly upon them, and there was no hope of alleviation. This lack of hope was a grave difficulty in itself. It was impossible for Challoner to encourage his dwindling flock by talk of better times. Writing to Henry Roper, tenth Lord Teynham, in 1742, he could do little more than urge him "(whom divine providence seems to have designed for the chief support of religion in Kent) to follow with the constancy of a Christian nobleman the happy and glorious path of virtue and religion, in spite of all opposition of the world, the flesh, and the devil," to recommend daily meditations and various strengthening devotions, and to commend that energetic nobleman for avoiding idleness, "the mother of all vice," by employing himself on his farm. At that time there were less than three hundred Catholics in Kent, and eighty of them were in Lord Teynham's congregation. And, later, even the Ropers were to succumb to the pressure upon them.

This matter of the penal laws, then, was more than an affair of pains and penalties: it was a pervading atmosphere in which all Challoner's work had to be carried on. Even without them, the lot of the Catholics would have been hard; for the eighteenth century was an age of skepticism, and merely by taking religion seriously Catholics would have cut themselves off from the normal life of their time. With them, they were not only a race apart: they were in the position of a failing outpost in a hostile country.

Another grave difficulty in the way of Challoner's successful rule lay in the nature of the vicariate, almost the whole burden of which fell upon him on his appointment as coadjutor. The jurisdiction extended over London, with its twenty thousand Catholics, chiefly of the poorer sort, and the ten counties of Kent, Sussex, Hampshire, Berkshire, Surrey, Essex, Hertfordshire, Buckinghamshire, Bedfordshire, and Middlesex, over which were scattered between four and five thousand more. In addition, there was an ill-defined and troublesome sway over North America and the West Indies. At the present time it is normal to find a Catholic church in every place of importance and occasional country chapels. In the eighteenth century the situation was reversed. Catholic life in towns had almost ceased (Winchester, Reading, and Havant were notable exceptions), and in the country it was concentrated almost entirely in places where Catholic landlords maintained chaplains. These were necessarily scattered, with the result that Challoner's first visitation as coadjutor took over a year when combined with the ordinary work of the vicariate, and reads like a combination of a list of country houses and an itinerary in a "highways and byways" series. But this practice of private chaplaincies, essential as it was to the survival of English Catholicism, led to further difficulties. In the first place, if any family of position became extinct or conformed, the chaplaincy ceased, and the congregation was deprived not only of its priest, but of the support which the position of the family had given it. In the second, the fact that the chaplain was the paid servant of his employer while at the same time under obedience to the Vicar Apostolic was an obvious source of discord, a position which was still further complicated in the many cases where the clergy were members of religious orders and so under obedience to their own superiors. Where, in fact, in the inevitable disputed cases, did the final authority lie? The matter was allowed to drag on, a fruitful source of scandal and dissension, until 1753; and even then one of the clauses in the decree of settlement was impossible for the regulars to carry out, and Challoner himself had to apply for its repeated suspension.

In addition to these general matters of policy there was a succession of particular problems to be faced, such as an embittered difference with the English Jesuits over their expulsion by the French Government, in 1762, from their college at St. Omers, and its being handed over to the English secular clergy. The details of the dispute are of little moment now; both parties seem to have been victims of circumstances, and to have acted in good faith. But the matter is notable, in that Challoner found his actions the object of the disapproval of many among his own clergy. "It behooves therefore a bishop to be blameless," St. Paul wrote to the Bishop of Ephesus. On this occasion alone was Challoner's conduct held worthy of blame, and then only for showing perhaps excessive diffidence in holding possession even temporarily of property wrongly taken from others.

Apart from dealing successfully with these and other particular troubles, and with the more normal affairs of the vicariate—which included laborious visitations and secret preaching in public-houses in the slums—Challoner somehow found time for an astonishing literary output. Between his consecration and death, he produced over thirty books and pamphlets, not including new editions of his own works, which ranged from a translation of the Vulgate to the earliest form of the present penny catechism. It is noteworthy that the first of these should have been his *Memoirs of Missionary Priests, as well Secular as Regular and of other Catholics of both sexes, that have suffered death in England on Religious Accounts, from the Year of Our Lord 1577 to 1684.*

The most surprising thing about these *Memoirs* is that they should have been written by Challoner. He was already a leader in the last stand of Catholicism in England, and bearing the stress of missionary labors and coadjutorship. Of all people, it would seem that he could have least leisure or inclination for historical research. His action was comparable to that of a general who, while leading his forces with distinguished ability during the dark early days of the Boer War, should have managed to compile the first adequate account of that in the Crimea. He was making one page of history and writing another.

His purpose in doing so is plain; he could hold out no hopes to the English Catholics, but he could offer them the support of the memory of their predecessors. But there is more in the matter even than that. The *Memoirs* are in no way mere hortatory exercises. Even had there been no Catholics left in England, one feels that they would still have been written, and without the alteration of a word. "We pretend not to make panegyrics of any of these brave men"; he wrote, "but merely to deliver short memoirs of what we found most remarkable in their lives and particularly in their deaths." Behind the book, as behind his efforts for the restoration of English saints to the liturgy, there lies a quiet national piety: these men were English; they had died nobly; it was right that they should be commemorated.

The labor of doing so was immense. Practically nothing was in print, save some lists of their names and a few brief accounts of individuals. The rest was in the archives of the English colleges and congregations on the Continent. Away at Douay, the learned and laborious Alban Butler transcribed necessary papers; and out of the mass of material which accumulated, there grew in Challoner's poor London lodgings more than four hundred memoirs which modern research, with the immensely superior means at its disposal, has hardly been able to convict of error. They were written in the way which is perhaps the best for recording such things. It "is the way," as the Reverend Claude Williamson has written of some earlier annals, "of telling it just as it happened, quite simply and straightforwardly, and rather sadly, without pause or protest or debate; just as if you had been there, only it was long ago, and things sometimes looked dim to you, and yet they never could fade away." They have taken on the dignity of original documents; they are the foundation on which any future study of the martyrs must be based.

With the publication, in 1754, of his *Meditations for Every Day in the Year*, it becomes possible to make a closer approach to Challoner himself.

In the unsatisfactory occupation of assigning racial characteristics, there is one which may reasonably be claimed as particularly English: an unobtrusive capacity for seizing upon the practical aspects of a situation, for seeing things as they really are. It is a quality which is not exclusive of enthusiasm, or romance, or even of the idea of glory: it is, rather, a capacity for seeing the core of which such things are but adjuncts, and acting upon that knowledge.

Challoner possessed this quality in a peculiar degree. He had two definite tasks before him: to carry on Church government in England in face of the many difficulties in his way and to strengthen his fellow-Catholics that they might survive those difficulties. All his actions were directed towards those ends, and the means he used were always the simplest and most direct. "The great truths of the Christian religion," he wrote in the Preface, "are here briefly proposed in their own plain native colors." The last sentence might be taken as symbolic of all Challoner's activities: he was a plain man, working for plain men, and he did so in the plainest possible way.

The method may be gauged from the supreme common sense of his second "consideration" for 5th November: "that sanctity does not so much depend upon doing extraordinary actions, as upon doing our ordinary actions extraordinarily well."

Its adequacy, and so the natural similarity between the writer and those for whom he wrote, is seen in its success and its survival. Men still remember how in their youth, in English households as yet untouched by imported devotional trends, the Bible and Challoner's *Lives* or *Meditations* were established as family reading for Sunday afternoons.

But yet, as in its forerunner, *Think Well On't*, there is more in the *Meditations* than simple common sense for English people. In places, the curtain of national reticence is almost drawn aside, giving a more intimate glimpse—though no more than a glimpse—of the man within. There is that astonishing outburst, for instance, in the first "consideration" for 1st August, coming in the midst of a sober catalogue of the losses endured in hell: "Ah! unhappy wretches that cannot love!"

The phrase strikes with clarifying force on the accounts of Challoner's mode of living which have come down to us: his regularity; his delight in the Divine Office; his incredible industry; his ardor in meditation and prayer; his practical, ceaseless, and self-sacrificing charity; his inability, for tears, to read aloud from the life of St. Vincent de Paul.

Love was the only thing that mattered. "That indifference to the objects of sense," Milner wrote, "and to everything that engages the attention of the world, which seemed to approach to a degree of apathy in this saint-like old man, gave place to the quickest attention and to the warmest feelings of youth, whenever the interests of God were concerned or the salvation of a soul was at stake." Throughout his life he had "kept his soul at home," secure in that love. Prayer had long ceased to be an activity which he undertook when free from ordinary affairs. It had become a state from which he turned when duty summoned him. But since the performance of these duties was founded in this all-embracing charity, they too became a part of prayer. Their multiplicity only serves to illustrate the paradox that the more time a man allows for prayer, the more he has for other things. It is as though a man should cast his time upon the waters and receive at once a hundredfold.

It was upon this man, frail with age, that, in June 1780, there fell the full fury of the Gordon Riots; when, by the cowardice of the magistracy, London was delivered into the hands of the English Protestant mob. Of the details of that national ignominy there is no need to speak. They were the answer of the vile to the first, pitifully small alleviation granted to the Catholics of England. Away in Finchley, where he had been taken for refuge to the house of a Mr. Mawhood,

Challoner knelt in prayer. They came to tell him that this refuge was about to be attacked, that he must move again. But something very like the gift of prophecy had come upon him, though he disclaimed it; and he refused, saying he was confident that no harm would come upon the house. Near at hand, on Hampstead Heath, the pursuing mob had gathered. In London, the chapels where he had offered Mass, the hidden rooms where he had preached, the houses of his friends, had been destroyed, and the town itself was in the grip of fire. Once before he had spoken prophecy, when foreseeing future apostasies and the coming of "the second spring," saying: "There will be a new people." That prophecy also was fulfilled.

By the courage of King George III, the situation eventually was saved, and Challoner was able to return to Holborn. The last storm had passed. On the feast of St. Michael, he entered upon his ninetieth year. Just over three months of tranquility remained to him before the end. Twice only in that time is he known to have exercised his ministry. On the 5th of October he added one more to the ten thousand confirmations of his forty years episcopate. Christmas passed. On the 30th of December, he heard the confessions of Mr. and Mrs. Mawhood. On the 10th of January 1781, at the end of dinner, taken as usual with his priests, his last illness came upon him. He had time to say its name—"'Tis the palsy"; to give a slip of paper to his chaplain (but what was written thereon is not recorded); and, murmuring "Charity," to point to his pocket, wherein was some money which that morning had been given him for the poor. It was his last word. Shortly after midnight, on the morning of Friday, the 12th of January, he died. As by common consent, the Catholics of England gave to him the title of Venerable, which, technically, is due only when the cause of canonization has been introduced. So, in olden times, saints were added to the Church.

In his tenure, there had been placed, as it were, an assailed and dwindling fortress. He had held it, steadfastly, meekly, with incredible labor and exquisite courtesy, until the end"; doing always, with the superhuman energy that goes with selflessness, the task that lay before him: "giving knowledge of salvation to his people, unto the remission of their sins...enlightening them that sit in darkness and in the shadow of death; directing their feet into the way of peace"; guarding the broken remnant of Catholic England until the hour before the dawn of the day when Englishmen, "being delivered from the hand of their enemies, might serve Him without fear."

JOHN HENRY NEWMAN (1801–1890)

by M. C. D'ARCY, S.J.

THE OXFORD MOVEMENT CONJURES UP FOR MANY THE vision of vestments, rites and all the paraphernalia of Catholic ceremonies. To the founders of it, nevertheless, it stood first and foremost for a new life of holiness. Keble, Pusey and Newman were all three men of scrupulous conscience and pricked with a longing for perfection. The sluggish condition of the Established Church, with its comfortable clergy, its hunting parsons, its liberal dons and ecclesiastics, filled them with horror. United at the beginning in their desire for reform, each in after years went his own way, Keble remained the gentle and earnest country parson; Pusey went on to practice many of the habits of an early Christian, stiffened and starched, however, by the customs of a life led as a canon of Christ Church. Newman alone of the three wandered away to find perfection outside the Establishment. All of them, again, were children of their age, and in the case of Newman this must constantly be borne in mind, if we are to succeed in understanding him. His age and circumstances mark out his type of holiness, surrounding it with limitations which at times almost hide his virtues and making him characteristically English and Victorian English.

It will be well to begin with these limitations, as, unless they are seen in their right perspective, they will distort our judgment. They are due mainly to the attitude of the class to which he belonged by birth and education. The beginning of the Oxford Movement coincided with social conditions in England which were a national disgrace. Nevertheless, neither then nor afterwards did he seem to show the concern we expect with the plight of his fellow countrymen, to have been sensitive to their complaints, hurt with their hurt. It would not be difficult to show a connection between the young Tories fired by Disraeli and the many Anglo-Catholics who have given their lives to the poor, but Newman belonged to neither company. The author of *Sybil* and *Coningsby* was not an Oxford man; only an outsider. "I could not vote for Disraeli; that would be against the grain." Be it said, however, to his great honor, that he risked his life shortly after his conversion, ministering to the sick during an outbreak of cholera. There was nothing wanting in the will; it was the influence of his class and of his friends which served to blind him and confirm his prejudices against external changes in society. The political creed of his hero Wellington sufficed him all his life, whereas men of the world like Manning and others of the Tractarians were, through experience, won over to the policy of social reform.

In truth, the external business of life never stirred the deepest passions of Newman. Of course, as a man of great sensitiveness and fastidious tastes, brought up in the atmosphere of a university like Oxford, where certain forms of behavior were strictly enforced, he was momentarily unhappy in the presence of rough manners, coarse banter and over-familiarity; but his irritation was only skin-deep. His mind naturally and supernaturally travelled to the world of ideas, to spiritual issues; and he had more certainty of "the angel faces which I have loved long since" and of invisible forces than of the murmur of the external world. Only a shy man, apt to retire within himself and slow to accommodate his ideals to the give and take of society, could write of his youth: "Indeed, this is how I look on myself; very much (as the illustration goes) as a pane of glass, which transmits heat, being cold itself. I have a vivid perception of the consequences of certain admitted principles, have a considerable capacity of drawing them out, have the refinement to admire them, and a rhetorical or histrionic power to represent them; and having no great (i.e., no vivid) love of the world, whether riches, honors or anything else, and some firmness and natural dignity of character, take the profession of them upon me, as I might sing a tune which I like—loving the truth but not possessing it, for I believe myself at heart to be nearly 'hollow,' i.e., with little love, little self-denial. I believe I have some faith, that is all."

At Edgbaston in later years, it cost him a great effort to go to social functions, to travel up to London and be lionized by "swells." The shabby figure of the old man leaning on a style at Oxford or carrying his bag through London streets, contrasts with the picture, let us say, of Manning ruling the Vatican Council. Newman was happy with his community, and endears himself by being almost fussy at home. Fr. Edward Bellasis tells the amusing and characteristic anecdote of a baize bag. "He once lent me an old green baize fiddle-bag, worth, say, sixpence. Later on it could not be found, and whenever there was a question of lending aught else, you were met with, 'I think I once lent you a green baize bag.'"

He could be a little shocked by and certainly out of tune with the staunch but strong-stomached English clergy in the great seminaries and colleges. On a visit to Oscott on St. Cecilia's feast, he tells how he was regaled with cakes and remarkably stiff punch—"I was obliged to dilute it to twice or thrice its quantity with water"—and music. This was hardly the man to appreciate Irish hospitality with its mixture of generosity and sensitiveness. He did not welcome too rapid advances from strangers; he misunderstood sometimes softness and kindliness for servility and dissimulation; especially from those who opposed him on some policy or principle; and for this reason he could never appreciate Wiseman or make headway with the Irish bishops. Even with the English Catholics he was inclined to be on his guard with the suspicions inherited from a narrow Protestantism. "I was not going to let the bishop off on this evasion"; and poor Ullathorne would find himself talking to an icicle.

In all these ways, he showed himself a creature of his time and place—English as a Scot or Irishman thinks of an Englishman. He belongs to a different type from that made known to us by Chaucer and Shakespeare and Dickens. Newman's father had been a banker and brewer; his home had been bourgeois and puritanical, and the children of this class were soon, with the help of Arnold, to create the public school and speak with one cultivated accent. Newman himself was at an undistinguished school at Ealing, and home influences predominated until by a happy accident he went up to Oxford instead of Cambridge. How young in mind he was at this period of his life, how callow in his tastes, we can see from the pages of *Loss and Gain*. He indulged in hero worship, learned for the first time of the famous historical and religious disputes and joined in them with enthusiasm. No wonder he thought years afterwards that he had no originality, that "he was merely developing" the ideas of other people, such as Keble. In truth this was not so, for the culture of Oxford, clerical and full of shortcomings as it was, served to point the genius of Newman and to make of him the highest representative of that new type of Englishman which is now so familiar to us from our reading of the Victorian literature.

We are inclined, perhaps, at present to depreciate unduly the types which were so much admired by our grandparents. The religious layfolk, if not hypocritical, are at least a little too assured of the approval of the Almighty, and the clergy breathe the somewhat stuffy air of comfortable deaneries or Oxford colleges; they took for granted what was privilege, and spoke without meaning offense of "Italian missions" and uneducated foreigners. Newman, as has been said, had absorbed this spirit in his most impressionable years; his comments on foreign ways in his letters are urbanely tolerant or slightly supercilious, and he was always inclined to be scandalized by stories of Italian intrigue and tergiversation. It is much easier for us now to see the weaknesses of such a point of view than to appreciate the positive qualities which went with it, and it is always free to us to prefer, if we like, the English Catholic squires with their tenacious grasp of principle and their open-air contentment. Nevertheless, we do not only Newman but many of his generation, wrong if we make no attempt to correct or modify this superficial criticism. Everything considered, it is astonishing how little Newman allowed himself to be swayed by these prejudices, and the measure of his detachment and his sacrifice can be gauged when we think of him surrendering all that he prized so highly to join a foreign creed. That he had the strength to do so is due partly to the very same causes we have been criticizing. If his upbringing was narrow, it taught him at least to hold conscience sacred and to be sensitive to evil in a way unguessed by many who now talk of art and morals. That conscience, already in the sermons preached from St. Mary's pulpit reaching to a prophetical insight, served to keep his mind pure and direct in the midst of the liberal studies of Oxford, the while with his natural genius he absorbed what was best in that university into his earliest ideals and grew to become the living portrait of the humane scholar made living in the pages of the *Idea of a University*.

Oxford, then as now, has its enemies, and many of their criticisms are not without force. It does encourage Browning's grammarians, an attenuated gentility, a smoothness of perfection which suggests Winchester and New College and not the Mermaid Tavern, and its besetting sin is to encourage a tolerant aloofness like that of the Athenians at the Areopagus. But it also has secrets in its keeping, and these it bequeathed to Newman. The undergraduate of Trinity, the don of Oriel, has cast the slough of his boyhood and is getting ready to leap from the shadows of Oxford into the sun of truth. Each phase of his life taught him something permanent. The virtues and flaws in his temperament are best realized by a glance at the reflection of them in his brothers and sisters. His youngest brother was a ne'er-do-well, "the closest representative of an ancient cynic philosopher this nineteenth century can afford"; Francis, the other brother, was an agnostic, vegetarian and anti-vaccinationist, as well as a scholar of high rank; while "the Miss Newmans are very learned persons, deeply read in ecclesiastical history, and in all the old divines, both High Church and Puritanical. Nevertheless, they are very agreeable and unaffected." Do the composite traits of such a family give us John Henry Newman? Surely, Yes and No. Yes, in the portrait sketch of him of 1840 from St. Mary's, and in later life as in a palimpsest. No, because as a celebrity at Oxford he is already distinct in his genius and in his holiness. The undergraduates hushed their talk as he passed them in the street; young and old flocked to St. Mary's to listen to a starlight voice telling them authentic news of another reality than that of sense. Matthew Arnold called him a "spiritual apparition," and another spoke of his "intense stillness when in repose." All through his later days, something in his personality inspired awe, and among his close friends a reverential affection. The defects we notice and tend against our will to emphasize were to those who knew him insignificant compared with the virtue which went out from him. The best witnesses to this are the members of his own community. No one is a hero to his valet, and they lived with him in daily converse, watching him in all the trivial round of the day. There is no escaping their evidence that he remained to them always a being of a superior order, a prophet with a following. And if this be so, then neither the letters nor the history of his opinions can do him justice.

To supply what is wanting to his portrait we must, I think, turn from the natural plane and look to the divine providence. Fr. Lockhart, preaching after his death, said that "he rooted in the hearts and minds of the young men a personal conviction of the living God." Who that had experience "of contact with him" could forget Newman's majestic countenances—"the meekness, the humility, the purity of a virgin 'heart in work and will,' as the poet says, a purity that was expressed in his eyes, his kindness, the sweetness of his voice, his winning smile, his caressing way, which had in it nothing of softness, but which you felt was a communication to you of strength from a strong soul—a thing to be felt in order to be realized." Here is what set Newman apart, the gift which he had from early years of an inward, almost Augustinian, awareness of the reality of God. He rested "in the thought of two and two only absolute and luminously self-evident beings—myself and my Creator." Augustine sought for only two things, the knowledge of his God and of himself, and he found God within as the light of his mind and the prompter of his conscience. A similar experience seemed to have been vouchsafed to Newman. It preserved him from skepticism, disciplined his sensitive and almost feminine temperament, and fashioned his life to obedience to a living truth. If stung by the vulgar intrusions of others on his private griefs, he could cry out: "Why will you not let me die in peace? Wounded brutes creep into some hole to die in and no one grudges it them. Let me alone; I shall not trouble you long," he meant by this: "What people here can do for me and what they cannot, carries off my mind to Him who 'has fed me all my life long until this day,' whom I find protecting me most wonderfully under such new circumstances, just as He has ever before, and who can give me that sympathy which men cannot give."

This sense of God, which he often expressed in the word "conscience," had as its concomitant a profound belief in God's providential dispositions and particularly in his own regard. It is curious how often leaders of mankind, military and political as well as spiritual, have felt overshadowed by some destiny or directed by some daimon. Success might be said to account for it, but only partially, and in Newman's case success had to wait until the very end of his life. Yet he was not mistaken. When taken very ill in Sicily in 1833, his Neapolitan servant heard him cry out: "I shall not die, for I have not sinned against light. I have a work to do in England." Time and again we hear the echo of this cry in his hopes and disappointments as a Catholic, and as the years went on this sense of a high vocation trained him to patience and brought him a measure of sanctity which left an ineffaceable impression upon his contemporaries.

What God wished of him and intended that he should be, was made practical by the gift of conversion to the Catholic faith. Viewed even on the natural plane, this change did much to round off his character. The life of an Anglican clergyman one hundred years ago, with all its virtues, came too near to that of a hot-house plant to be healthy for a man. The members of it were protected and privileged, they formed a small society or class which cultivated a superior tone and taste, and it was necessarily cut off from the major interests of Europe and religious humanity. Newman never quite shook off the mannerisms and stiff demeanor of the Anglican clergyman; but his sermons bear witness to a new peace, and his wit becomes lively and human. He laughed now over the prim behavior of the characters in *Loss and Gain*, and it is told how on his conversion he took down the volumes of his loved Fathers from the shelves and said: "You are mine now; you are mine now." Quietly he entered into the great Catholic tradition, and felt and thought with its saints, and chose a happy, blithe spirit, his dear St. Philip, as his patron.

For years he had sought holiness. At Littlemore, he and his friends had practiced prayer and self-denial. Their cells were tiny; their order of the day austere. They rose at five-thirty, said office and prayed, communicated at eleven, and only after that broke their fast. In Lent they took nothing till five, and then only salt fish. As a Catholic, Newman relaxed only at the bidding of authority, and it is often forgotten with what patience he surrendered himself to lowly labors, to preaching to a few poor people, and to comparative neglect. Few can bear to be uprooted in middle age, to forsake friends and start afresh finding new ones. Dazzled by his fame as a writer and perturbed perhaps by the complaints which escape in his letters, we need to remind ourselves of the sacrifices he made, the cloud of misunderstanding raised by his so-called desertion, the constant cross his nature imposed upon him, his devotion to duty, his scrupulous honesty, his hidden life of prayer. Let one incident recall this latter. At the time of the Achilli trial, when he thought that Wiseman had gravely defaulted and that he was in danger of disgrace and prison, he "remained day and night, almost without interruption, before the Tabernacle."

On one occasion, not long after his conversion, Newman wrote: "I have ever made consistency the mark of a saint.... On looking closer, they perhaps had some one failing, wanted a certain elevation of mind, or were peevish or petulant, or had something about them which an *advocatus diaboli* would discover." Judged by these, his own standards, Newman was not technically a saint. He had a poor opinion of himself, and it is true that he was not always consistent nor, shall we say, of one mind. Though the saint has his struggles we are made conscious of an inner calm which is almost merry. The Curé d'Ars, a contemporary of Newman, suffered from supreme desolation, and nevertheless that desolation is ever in defeat like the dragon under the foot of Michael. There is a touch of winter in Newman; we feel the wind and rain of adversity; but if he misses the spring and constant sunshine of complete holiness, he may without fancifulness be compared with the rainbow which shines through and over the storm. The colors which constitute his life are plain to see, and they have the beauty of the sign set in the sky by God. If his political and social creed was antiquated, he was quick to perceive the dangers of intellectual liberalism; if Oxford dominated his mind too much, at least it kept him English in outlook when so many of the scholars in the country were succumbing without criticism to German methods and German culture. One, too, who showed himself in all his writings, and especially in the *Grammar of Assent*, such a master of the interior workings of the mind and will and soul was bound to be sensitive to the degree of weakness. Even his habit of grumbling is an English trait which is not so unattractive and certainly less serious than it appears. He knew well the difficulties he had to contend against. He says a little cynically, no doubt thinking of himself, that "No one seems to look for any great devotion or fervor in controversialists...it being taken for granted, rightly or wrongly, that such men are too intellectual to be spiritual." This might seem a mere echo of the complaint of Thomas à Kempis of the freezing quality of thought, but whereas the medieval theologian, like Aquinas or Bonaventure, and even the Renaissance scholar Thomas More, had the means to overcome it, the tradition of unity in head and heart had been for so long lost by the time of Newman that he felt acutely the division.

Thomas More and Newman are both typical Englishmen of their age, and if the comparison favors More, that is due partly to the fact that he stood so near to the genuine tradition of Christendom and breathed its spirit of hope and gaiety into the secular learning newly arrived. Newman gathers up in his person the ideas of an England that had been slowly Protestantized, and his greatness consists in this that he stood, nevertheless, and still stands forth as essentially Catholic. The spirits of Bunyan, of Hooker and Laud, of the Cambridge Platonists and Bishop Butler flit across his pages and speak in his voice; middle-class sentiment makes him truly Victorian, and he speaks with the accent of Oxford. Yet "God, who, with trickling increment, veins violets and tall trees, makes more and more," made use of his heritage and environment to fashion still another image of Christ, and we who follow after him delight to trace in God's handiwork the marks of a great Englishman and saintly Catholic.

~M. C. D'Arcy, S.J.